# BARRON'S
# GRE®
# MATH WORKBOOK

## 3RD EDITION

**Blair Madore, Ph.D.**
Associate Professor of Mathematics
State University of New York (SUNY) at Potsdam

**David Freeling**
Founder and Director, Insight Tutoring

BARRON'S

## About the Authors

Blair Madore is a native of Newfoundland who earned a BMATH from the University of Waterloo and an MSc and Ph.D. from the University of Toronto. He has been happily residing and teaching college math for the past fifteen years in Potsdam, New York. This is his first book for Barron's.

David Freeling is the founder and director of Insight Tutoring (of San Francisco) and has helped thousands of children and adults improve their basic math and English skills. He has taught classes for the GRE, SAT, and SSAT exams. Mr. Freeling is the author of *Barron's 6 GRE Practice Tests* and *Barron's GRE Math Workbook*, as well as the self-published *First Fun SAT Book*. He offers a free online library of test-prep videos at *www.NoeValleyTutor.com*. Mr. Freeling received a B.A. in mathematics from Columbia University and completed one year of graduate studies in math at Columbia.

## Acknowledgments

Many thanks to my wife, Margaret, and SUNY Potsdam for their support while working on this project. Special thanks to Harold Ellingsen, Joel Foisy, and Andrew Brouwer for their review of the math in this book.

*All inquiries should be addressed to:*
Barron's Educational Series, Inc.
250 Wireless Boulevard
Hauppauge, NY 11788
**www.barronseduc.com**

Library of Congress Catalog Card No.: 2015945375

ISBN: 978-1-4380-0632-1

PRINTED IN THE UNITED STATES OF AMERICA

9 8 7 6 5 4 3

10%
POST-CONSUMER
WASTE
Paper contains a minimum
of 10% post-consumer
waste (PCW). Paper used
in this book was derived
from certified, sustainable
forestlands.

# CONTENTS

# To the Student

Dear Student,

You're at a very exciting point in your life! You've completed, or will soon complete, your undergraduate degree and you're now planning to enter the most demanding, stimulating, and rewarding of educational experiences—graduate school.

Although you're probably not looking forward to taking yet another test, your GRE score is one of the several tools your future school will use to determine your admission or, even more importantly, the funding you may receive while attending graduate school. A small investment of time preparing for this exam could pay off very well.

We encourage you to take the GRE seriously and allocate time each week to prepare for the exam. A few hours of study spent each week is much more effective than cramming 20 hours just before you take the test. If you need motivation or extra help, look for a GRE prep course in your area. Many people find it easier to study when they have a teacher to consult and a group of other students to work with.

Every student's situation is different. You may be a physics whiz who needs to polish her math skills so you can score the 165 your dream graduate school expects. You may be a psychology major who hasn't formally studied math since high school and needs to improve his math skills so you can score the 155 your dream graduate school requires. To avoid disappointment and set clear expectations for yourself, it is suggested that you contact the graduate schools you intend to apply to and ask them what score is needed for admission (or even what score would earn you a top scholarship).

This workbook is designed to help you review the math typically tested on the GRE. Since virtually all high school math could potentially be covered on the exam, this book cannot attempt to be a complete replacement for your high school texts. Don't worry; even if you feel uncertain of your math skills, it is likely that you will recall most rudimentary ideas when reminded of them. Thus, this book reminds you of the basics and focuses on the topics that appear most frequently on the exam.

Good luck and happy studying!

# Guide to Using This Book

In Chapter 1, you will be introduced to the format of the quantitative reasoning section of the GRE. Here you will find information on the structure of the exam, explanations and examples of each of the question types, information on scoring, and tips for use of the onscreen calculator. Chapter 2 goes on to present strategies for approaching the different types of questions you will be faced with on the exam. Both chapters include GRE-style practice problems and solutions for you to test your newfound skills.

Chapters 3 through 6 include review of all the math skills needed to excel on the GRE quantitative reasoning test. Each section within these chapters concludes with Basic problems and GRE problems for you to complete. The Basic problems test the knowledge you gained from the section. In some cases, these problems are not very likely to appear as an actual problem on the GRE. The GRE problems are more challenging and are similar to problems that actually appear on the GRE. The GRE problems test more than just the skills you developed in the section. Detailed solutions for all problems are at the end of each chapter.

Chapter 7 contains two quantitative reasoning sample tests along with solutions for all problems. By taking these tests and evaluating the answers, you will be able to pinpoint areas that you may still need to brush up on.

The Appendix includes a list of suggested math facts to memorize. These include items such as common fractions and their decimal equivalents, common irrational number square roots and their decimal equivalents, inequalities, and key algebraic expressions.

# CHOOSE THE STUDY PLAN THAT IS RIGHT FOR YOU

Whether you are pretty confident in your math skills, or feel a little shaky with your knowledge of math, it is important to develop a study plan that makes the most out of your study time and fits your individual needs.

If you are confident in your math skills,

✔ Read Chapters 1 and 2, concentrating on the problem-solving strategies. These strategies can help improve your speed and help you with problems that you don't immediately know how to solve.

✔ Read Chapters 3 through 6, concentrating on the TIPS appearing throughout the chapters and the more challenging examples. Work through all of the GRE problems, returning to the chapter for more information as needed.

✔ Review the Appendix and memorize the facts presented there, if you don't know them already.

✔ Take the sample tests in Chapter 7 and review the solutions for each of the problems. Note the topics that caused you trouble, and review those sections of the book as needed.

If you are less certain of your math skills,

✔ Read Chapter 1 to familiarize yourself with the style of the test.

✔ Read Chapters 3 through 6, concentrating on the basic skills and examples. Work through all the Basic problems, returning to the chapter for more information as needed.

✔ Read Chapter 2 and concentrate on the problem-solving strategies. These strategies can help improve your speed and help you with problems that you don't immediately know how to solve.

✔ Reread Chapters 3 through 6, concentrating on the TIPS appearing throughout the chapters and the more challenging examples. Work through all of the GRE problems.

✔ Review the Appendix and memorize the facts presented there, if you don't know them already.

✔ Take the sample tests in Chapter 7 and review the solutions for each of the problems. Note the topics that caused you trouble, and review those sections of the book as needed.

# The GRE Quantitative Reasoning Exam

**1**

The GRE general test includes sections called Verbal Reasoning, Quantitative Reasoning, and Analytical Writing. This book focuses on the quantitative sections where your mathematical abilities are tested.

For more general information about taking the GRE, consult *www.ets.org* or your local testing center. Here you will find information on registering for the test and test dates.

The quantitative reasoning section of the GRE tests your knowledge of arithmetic, elementary algebra, some geometry, and very elementary probability and statistics. This is material that you studied in elementary, middle, and high school. It does not cover any calculus or advanced mathematics. It mainly tests your ability to reason logically.

Even though the material covered is pre-college, the test expects you to demonstrate the sophisticated reasoning skills of a (soon-to-be) college graduate. Math and science majors should not underestimate this test—there is challenge here for everyone. Students who have not studied mathematics in a number of years should not overestimate this test—with practice, a good score is possible for every reasonably good thinker.

## EXAM STRUCTURE

Most likely, you will be taking the computer-based GRE, which allows you to answer the questions within each section in any order and move around freely, changing your answers at any time. You will be able to "mark" questions that you know you will want to come back to later, and a calculator icon at the top of the screen will enable you to access a simple calculator during the quantitative reasoning sections. When taking the test, you will face two scored quantitative sections, each 35 minutes long and containing about 20 questions. Your exam may also contain a third, "experimental" quantitative section, used by the test makers to try out new questions. Because you never know which section, if any, is the experimental one, you will need to apply yourself equally to every section of the exam.

If you are taking the paper-based test, offered in parts of the world where computers are not readily available, you will now be able to enter your answers directly in the test booklet, rather than on a separate answer sheet. You will also be provided with an ETS calculator to use during the exam. You will not be permitted to use your own.

## QUESTION TYPES

There are four types of questions on the GRE quantitative reasoning test: Multiple-choice, quantitative comparison, multiple-answer, and numeric entry.

## Multiple-Choice Questions

*Multiple-choice questions* are familiar to most people. A question and five answer choices are given, and you must choose the *best* answer. For convenient reference we will refer to these choices as A, B, C, D, and E in this book, although on the actual exam, you will select your answer by clicking the oval next to the answer choice.

---

**EXAMPLE 1**

You are given two circles with radii $r$ and $R$, respectively. The second circle has twice the area of the first. What is the relationship between the radii?

(A) $2r = R$

(B) $r = 2R$

(C) $r^2 = 2R^2$

(D) $2r^2 = R^2$

(E) $r = \sqrt{2}R$

**Solution:** The area of the first is $\pi r^2$ and the area of the second is $\pi R^2$. Since the area of the second is twice the first, $\pi R^2 = 2\pi r^2$. We cancel $\pi$ from each side and see that $R^2 = 2r^2$. Choose **D**. If we take the square root of both sides, we see that $R = \sqrt{2}r$ is an alternate solution, but not one of the choices.

---

We say you should choose the *best* answer because it is not uncommon to work a problem and determine an answer that is not exactly equal to any of the given answers. This can happen when you make a mistake and you're wrong. This can also happen when you're right but some rounding in the calculation can lead your answer and the given answer to not match exactly. If your answer is close to a given answer choice but not exactly the same, it's probably the right answer. If your answer lies halfway between two given answer choices, it's time to go back and check things over (unless you're in a time rush, when you'd guess one of those two choices).

---

**EXAMPLE 2**

Which number is closest to $\sqrt{3} \times \sqrt{13} \times \sqrt{5}$?

(A) 12

(B) 13

(C) 14

(D) 15

(E) 16

**Solution:** Typing this on the calculator shows a number between 13 and 14, but look carefully at the digits to the right of the decimal: 13.96 is much closer to 14 than to 13. Choose **C**. One important note: It is easier and faster to enter this on the calculator by first typing $3 \times 13 \times 5 = 195$, and then pressing the square-root button just once. This shortcut is valid because $\sqrt{ab} = \sqrt{a} \cdot \sqrt{b}$, for all positive numbers, $a$ and $b$.

---

## Multiple-Answer Questions

*Multiple-answer questions* require you to select all answers that are correct, which could be as few as one choice or as many as all of the choices. **No credit is given unless you pick every correct answer and no others**. On these problems, look for square answer boxes instead of the usual oval-shaped bubbles that appear with "regular" multiple-choice questions. Remember, you must click *all* boxes that include correct answers.

---

**EXAMPLE 3**

Ann's salary is more than 75 percent of Bob's salary but less than 80 percent of Claire's salary. If Bob's salary is $35 per hour and Claire's is $40 per hour, which of the following could be Ann's salary, per hour?

Indicate *all* that apply.

- [A] $25
- [B] $26
- [C] $27
- [D] $30
- [E] $32
- [F] $35

**Solution:** Seventy-five percent of $35 equals .75 × 35 = $26.25, while 80 percent of 40 equals .8 × 40 = $32. This means that Ann earned between $26.25 and $32 per hour. Choose **C** and **D**. Note that choice E, 32, is not less than 32.

---

## Quantitative Comparison Questions

*Quantitative comparison questions* are usually found only on the GRE (or some other standardized tests). For that reason, it is most important to familiarize yourself with this type of question and any strategies that are appropriate for them. You are given two quantities, one in Quantity A and one in Quantity B. You must determine the relationship between the quantities. You will be given four possible answers to choose from:

- (A) Quantity A is greater.
- (B) Quantity B is greater.
- (C) The two quantities are equal.
- (D) It is impossible to determine which quantity is greater.

**TIP**

In this book from this point forward, these four answer choices will be referred to as A, B, C, and D, respectively.

---

**EXAMPLE 4**

| Quantity A | Quantity B |
|:---:|:---:|
| $\left(3+\dfrac{1}{5}\right)\left(3-\dfrac{1}{5}\right)$ | $\left(3+\dfrac{1}{4}\right)\left(3-\dfrac{1}{4}\right)$ |

**Solution:** You could just calculate both quantities as fractions and compare but this is tedious at best. If you remember your rule for difference of squares (see Chapter 4), then Quantity A is $3^2 - \left(\dfrac{1}{5}\right)^2 = 9 - \dfrac{1}{25}$ while Quantity B is $3^2 - \left(\dfrac{1}{4}\right)^2 = 9 - \dfrac{1}{16}$. Since, $\dfrac{1}{25} < \dfrac{1}{16}$, $9 - \dfrac{1}{25} > 9 - \dfrac{1}{16}$. Choose **A**, since Quantity A is larger than Quantity B. Notice that here knowing your math is much faster than trying to type all these fractions on the simple GRE calculator that you are given.

---

| Quantity A | Quantity B |
|---|---|
| $(3 + x)(3 - x)$ | $(x + 3)(x - 3)$ |

**Solution:** Using difference of squares (see Chapter 4) to expand, we discover that Quantity A is $9 - x^2$ while Quantity B is $x^2 - 9$. Which is larger? It will depend on the value of $x$. When $x = 0$, Quantity A is 9, and Quantity B is –9. When $x = 4$, Quantity A is –7, and Quantity B is 7. So sometimes Quantity A is larger and sometimes Quantity B is larger. Choose **D**, it cannot be determined (without knowing more about $x$).

## Numeric Entry Questions

*Numeric entry questions* ask you to give a decimal or fraction as the answer to a question. If it is a fraction, you will be asked to enter the numerator and denominator separately. This type of question tests your ability to work directly to an answer.

The town council charges each residence for services including $2 each week for trash pickup, $10 a month for water hookup plus $0.002 per gallon of water used, and $25 each fall for leaf removal. Bills are calculated annually but paid in quarterly installments. Kareem's family used 125,000 gallons of water last year. What did they pay each quarter?

$ [ ]

**Solution:** They paid

| | |
|---|---|
| 52 weeks × $2/week | = $104 for trash |
| 12 months × $10/month | = $120 for water hookup |
| 125,000 gallons × $0.002/gallon | = $250 for water used |
| | $25 for leaf collection |
| Total | $499 |

So each quarter they paid $499/4 = $124.75.

In a school with 240 boys and 210 girls, there are 8 right-handed students for every 1 left-handed student. How many students at the school are left-handed?

[ ]

**Solution:** First note that there are 240 + 210 = 450 total students at the school. There are 8 "righties" for every 1 "lefty" for every 8 + 1 = 9 students. Therefore, lefties make up $\frac{1}{9}$ of all students. $\frac{1}{9} \times 450 = \frac{450}{9} = 50$.

## TOPICS AND SCORING

The quantitative test covers many kinds of quantitative reasoning. This includes working with integers, fractions, rates of change, proportions, measurement, decimals, radicals, exponents, GCDs, LCMs, primes, factoring, polynomials, solving equations and inequalities, functions, percentages, averages, charts and graphs, probability, counting, triangles, quadrilaterals, circles, Pythagorean Theorem, perimeter, area, surface area, and volume. Most questions cover more than one topic. In any given GRE test, almost every one of these topics will be covered. None of them appear very frequently so all topics need attention. Yes, it is important to know the basics of each topic, but the test wants you to show you can reason—not just recite a mathematical fact or formula. Above all else, developing and improving your reasoning skill is very important.

GRE quantitative and verbal scores range from 130 to 170. Your score depends primarily on the number of questions you answer correctly. There is no penalty for guessing, so be sure to answer every question. A question left unanswered counts the same as a wrong answer.

A rough estimate of your quantitative score can be obtained by averaging the number of incorrect answers per section, multiplying this by 2, and then deducting the result from 170. For example, if you get an average of 5 wrong per 20-question section, your score is roughly $170 - (5 \times 2) = 160$, while scoring only 1 wrong out of 20 would translate to roughly $170 - (1 \times 2) = 168$, a very high score. This assumes that the other questions are all correct.

However, a number of complex factors, mainly based on the level of difficulty of each question, will influence your final score.

ETS has recently added a new scoring feature called *ScoreSelect* to the computer-based exam. *ScoreSelect* allows you to decide which of your GRE scores you want to send to your designated institutions. When viewing your score at the testing center **ON** test day, you will be given the following two options:

1. *ScoreSelect **Most Recent**—*Send your score from the current administration to up to four institutions for free.
2. *ScoreSelect **All**—*Send your scores from all administrations within the past five years to up to four institutions for free.

If you are sending your score reports **AFTER** test day, you will be given the following three options

1. *ScoreSelect **Most Recent**—*Send your score from the current administration to up to four institutions for free.
2. *ScoreSelect **All**—*Send your scores from all administrations within the past five years to up to four institutions for free.
3. *ScoreSelect **Any**—*Send your scores from one OR more test administrations in the past five years to up to four institutions for free.

You will be able retake the GRE once every 30 days, but no more than five times within any 12-month period.

For the most up-to-date information on the *ScoreSelect* option and retesting policy visit *www.ets.org/gre*.

## CALCULATOR USE

You can access the calculator at any time by clicking the calculator icon at the top of the screen. Be aware that only five basic operations are featured on the machine: $+, -, \times, \div, \sqrt{\ }$. As soon as

**TIP**

Since every question has equal weight and you can answer questions in any order, do the easiest ones first. What is easy for you may not be easy for other students. Still most students find the data analysis questions challenging. You would be wise to leave them until last.

you open the calculator, move it to a part of the screen where it will not cover any part of the problem. Notice that the Transfer button is active only on *numeric entry questions*, where you can use it to transfer your last calculator answer directly to the problem's answer box.

The GRE calculator will save you from having to do tedious computations in your head or longhand, but sometimes it is just as important to know when not to crunch numbers on the calculator. It is often best to reason through a problem before making any computations.

---

**EXAMPLE 8**

Jose earns $12 on every day of the year.
Raul earns $367 in every month of the year.

| Quantity A | Quantity B |
|---|---|
| Jose's earnings in one full year beginning January 1. | Raul's earnings in one full year beginning January 1. |

**Solution:** There are 365 days in a year, so Quantity A is 365 × 12 (or at most 366 × 12 in a leap year). There are 12 months in a year, so Quantity B is 367 × 12. Don't waste time typing these values blindly on the calculator. It should be obvious that 367 × 12 > 365 × 12. Choose **B**.

---

Below you will find several useful numerical methods. Because of the calculator feature, mastering these is not absolutely essential. However, because these math situations come up frequently on the exam, it is well worth studying the following math tips, which will both save you time and improve your quantitative skills.

- **Reason. Don't calculate.** Part of the reason you can sometimes do better without a calculator is that many situations do not actually require one. Multiple-choice questions like "In which year was the percentage of blank highest?" or "Which has the largest area?" may not require you to calculate anything. Try to determine answers with comparisons and not calculation. Many quantitative comparison questions can be approached this way.

---

**EXAMPLE 9**

Which of the five following figures has the largest shaded area?

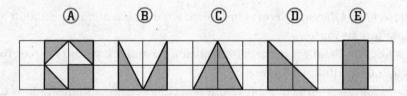

Ⓐ    Ⓑ    Ⓒ    Ⓓ    Ⓔ

**Solution:** You do not need to calculate the area of any of these figures to solve the problem. If we divide C with a vertical line you'll see it is made of two shapes congruent to B. If you flip one of the triangles vertically, those two triangles could be combined to form the rectangle in E. Hence B, C, and E all have the same area. If you think of D as a square and two small triangles, you can rotate and move the bottom left small triangle beside the top one to make a 2 × 1 rectangle. So D and E have the same area. Finally, A is comprised of one small square and three small triangles, while D has one square and two small triangles. A has more area than D. So B, C, D, and E have the same area while A has more. Choose **A**.

---

- **Memorize some basic facts that help make calculations quicker and easier.** We presume you know your times tables. It is also helpful to know the perfect squares like $12^2 = 144$, $13^2 = 169, \ldots, 20^2 = 400$ (or even more). The most common fractions that appear are $\frac{1}{2}$, $\frac{1}{3}$, and $\frac{2}{3}$. It is helpful to know that $\frac{2}{3} - \frac{1}{2} = \frac{1}{6}$ and other related facts like $\frac{1}{2} + \frac{1}{6} = \frac{2}{3}$, $\frac{1}{2} - \frac{1}{3} = \frac{1}{6}$, and $\frac{1}{2} + \frac{1}{3} = \frac{5}{6}$.

  The appendix gives a list of facts to memorize.

- **Use the distributive property.** Instead of multiplying $42 \times 30$, we can use the distributive property to break this into pieces you can multiply in your head.
  $$42 \times 30 = (40 + 2) \times 30 = 40 \times 30 + 2 \times 30 = 1{,}200 + 60 = 1{,}260$$
  This also works well with subtraction.
  $$38 \times 25 = (40 - 2) \times 25 = (40 \times 25) - (2 \times 25) = 1{,}000 - 50 = 950$$

- **Find the difference of squares.** You may know this as a rule of algebra, $A^2 - B^2 = (A - B)(A + B)$, but it can be useful for some calculations. To find $77^2 - 23^2$, instead of calculating each square, we find $(77 - 23)(77 + 23)$. The first factor is easy to subtract $77 - 23 = 54$, and the second factor is easy to add $77 + 23 = 100$. Their product $54 \times 100 = 5{,}400$ is also easy. This whole computation could even be done in your head and quickly!

- **Cancel before you calculate.** Always try to cancel factors before you calculate. This reduces the size of the numbers you have to work with. To simplify $\frac{3}{7} \times \frac{10}{33} \times \frac{14}{26}$, we factor the terms first and then use cancellation $\frac{\cancel{3}}{\cancel{7}} \times \frac{\cancel{2} \times 5}{\cancel{3} \times 11} \times \frac{2 \times \cancel{7}}{\cancel{2} \times 13}$.

  Now it is easy to see the answer is $\frac{5 \times 2}{13 \times 11}$, which equals $\frac{10}{143}$. The toughest part of this problem was multiplying 13 by 11, which is not so tough if you do $13 \times 10 + 13 \times 1 = 130 + 13 = 143$.

- **Estimate, don't calculate.** Which is larger $137 \times 2{,}185$ or $89 \times 5{,}856$? It would be time consuming to calculate these even with the on-screen calculator, but a rough estimate will give us the answer. We approximate $137 \times 2{,}185$ as $100 \times 2{,}000$, which equals 200,000. We approximate $89 \times 5{,}856$ as $90 \times 5{,}000$, which equals 450,000. Even allowing for some serious error in our approximation, we can be certain the second product is larger than the first.

## PROBLEMS

Remember, for quantitative comparison questions choose:

(A) If Quantity A is greater.

(B) If Quantity B is greater.

(C) If the two quantities are equal.

(D) If it is impossible to determine which quantity is greater.

1.  | Quantity A | Quantity B |
    |---|---|
    | $20^2 - 10^2$ | $11^2 + 13^2$ |

2.  | Quantity A | Quantity B |
    |---|---|
    | $x^2 - y^3$ | $x^2 + y^3$ |

3.  | Quantity A | Quantity B |
    |---|---|
    | $(9x + 1)(9x - 1)$ | $81x^2$ |

4.  $$p > q > 0$$

    | Quantity A | Quantity B |
    |---|---|
    | $52p \times 48q$ | $51p \times 49q$ |

5.  | Quantity A | Quantity B |
    |---|---|
    | $\dfrac{20 \times 18 \times 16}{9 \times 8 \times 7}$ | $\dfrac{12 \times 10 \times 8}{4 \times 3 \times 2}$ |

6.  $$x \neq 5$$

    | Quantity A | Quantity B |
    |---|---|
    | $\dfrac{1}{x-5}$ | $x + 5$ |

7.  | Quantity A | Quantity B |
    |---|---|
    | $5^{-5}(9 \times 7 \times 5 \times 3 \times 1)$ | $6^{-5}(10 \times 8 \times 6 \times 4 \times 2)$ |

8. Which of the following values is closest to $\sqrt[3]{40}$?

   (A) 2    (B) 3    (C) 3.5    (D) 4    (E) 11

9. Cole Corporation earned $3.6 million in profits in 2011. It pays 10% taxes on the first million, 15% on the second million, and 18% on any further profits. Approximately how much tax does it owe (in thousands of dollars)?

   (A) 360    (B) 400    (C) 500    (D) 600    (E) 700

10. In 2010 Cole Corporation paid $220,000 in tax on $1.4 million in profits. What was its *average* tax rate, to the nearest percent?

   (A) 10%    (B) 14%    (C) 16%    (D) 18%    (E) 20%

11. Sammi has 36 marbles. Some are red, some are blue, and some are both red and blue. Twenty have red on them and 30 have blue on them. What fraction of her marbles are both red and blue?

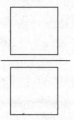

12. What is $\frac{1}{3}$ of 2% of $\frac{4}{5}$ of 9? Express your answer as a decimal.

## SOLUTIONS

1. **(A)** Do not make the classic mistake of thinking that $20^2 - 10^2 = 10^2$. Using difference of squares you can see that $20^2 - 10^2 = (20 - 10)(20 + 10) = 10 \times 30 = 300$. If you know your perfect squares, then you know that $11^2 = 121$ and $13^2 = 169$. Adding, 121 plus 169 equals 290. That is less than 300.

2. **(D)** Because both sides have $x^2$, and $x^2$ is always nonnegative, it has no impact on the question. We focus on $y^3$. Isn't $y^3$ always larger than $-y^3$? No. When $y = -1$, $y^3 = -1$ and $-y^3 = -(-1) = 1$. When $y = 1$, $y^3 = 1$ and $-y^3 = -1$. So sometimes the first is larger and sometimes the second is larger. It depends on the value of $y$.

3. **(B)** Quantity A fits the $(A + B)(A - B)$ difference of squares pattern and therefore equals $(9x)^2 - 1^2 = 81x^2 - 1$. No matter what $x$ is, $81x^2 - 1$ must be less than $81x^2$. Subtracting 1, or any positive number, from a quantity always produces a smaller quantity.

4. **(B)** First determine the quantities $52 \times 48$ and $51 \times 49$. Notice that $52 \times 48 = (50 + 2)(50 - 2) = 2,500 - 4 = 2,496$, while $51 \times 49 = (50 + 1)(50 - 1) = 2,500 - 1 = 2,499$. You can also compute these values on the calculator. Quantity A is then $2,496pq$, while Quantity B is $2,499pq$. Quantity B looks bigger, but is it *always* greater than A? Notice that the given information, $p > q > 0$, implies that $p$ and $q$ are positive, so their product, $pq$, is positive. A larger number times any positive quantity is always greater than a smaller number the same quantity.

5. **(B)** Cancellation helps a lot here. In Quantity A, 9 divides into 18 twice and 8 divides into 16 twice leaving $\dfrac{20 \times \cancel{18}^{2} \times \cancel{16}^{2}}{\cancel{9} \times \cancel{8} \times 7} = \dfrac{20 \times 2 \times 2}{7} = \dfrac{80}{7}$. In Quantity B, $3 \times 4$ cancels with 12 and 2 divides into 8 four times leaving $\dfrac{\cancel{12} \times 10 \times \cancel{8}^{4}}{\cancel{4 \times 3} \times \cancel{2}} = 4 \times 10 = 40$. Notice that $40 = \dfrac{80}{2}$, which is larger than $\dfrac{80}{7}$.

6. **(D)** If you only consider positive integers $x + 5$ will always be larger than $\dfrac{1}{(x - 5)}$. For instance $(10) + 5 = 15$, which is larger than $\dfrac{1}{(10 - 5)} = \dfrac{1}{5}$. But, when $x$ is a number very

close to 5, like $x = 5.01$, then $\dfrac{1}{(x-5)} = \dfrac{1}{(5.01-5)} = \dfrac{1}{(0.01)} = 100$. At the same time, $x + 5 = 5.01 + 5 = 10.01$. Hence, it depends on the value of $x$.

7. **(B)** First we cancelled as many factors as possible and then multiplied out.

$5^{-5}(9 \times 7 \times 5 \times 3 \times 1) = \dfrac{9 \times 7 \times \cancel{5} \times 3 \times 1}{5 \times 5 \times \cancel{5} \times 5 \times 5} = \dfrac{63 \times 3}{25 \times 25} = \dfrac{189}{625}$. We knew our perfect squares

$(25^2 = 625)$, and we used distribution to find $63 \times 3 = (60 + 3) \times 3 = 60 \times 3 + 3 \times 3 = 180 + 9$.

Then a very rough approximation shows that $\dfrac{189}{625} \cong \dfrac{200}{600} = \dfrac{1}{3}$. In Quantity B,

$6^{-5}(10 \times 8 \times 6 \times 4 \times 2) = \dfrac{10 \times \cancel{8} \times \cancel{6} \times 4 \times \cancel{2}}{\cancel{6} \times \cancel{6}_3 \times \cancel{6}_3 \times \cancel{6}_3 \times \cancel{6}_3} = \dfrac{40}{3^4} = \dfrac{40}{81}$, which is approximately $\dfrac{1}{2}$.

8. **(C)** To approximate $\sqrt[3]{40}$, we note that $3^3 = 27$ and $4^3 = 64$. Since 40 is much closer to 27 than 64, we know $\sqrt[3]{40}$ is closer to 3 than 4. Is it closer to 3 or 3.5? We check 3.5 as a possible answer by multiplication. On your calculator type $3.5 \times 3.5 \times 3.5 \approx 43$. Since 40 is much closer to 43 than 27, we expect $\sqrt[3]{40}$ to be closer to 3.5 than 3.

9. **(C)** Ten percent on the first million is 100,000. Fifteen percent on the second million is 150,000. Eighteen percent on the next million is 180,000. Eighteen percent on the next half million would be half of 180,000 or 90,000. That makes a total of at least 100K + 150K + 180K + 90K = 520K. The actual tax will only be slightly larger than this.

10. **(C)** We need to find a percentage $\dfrac{\$220,000}{\$1,400,000} \times 100\%$. Use cancellation to simplify

$\dfrac{\$220,\cancel{000}}{\$1,4\cancel{00},\cancel{000}} \times 100\% = \dfrac{220}{14}\%$. Type $220 \div 14$ on the calculator to obtain 15.7%, which rounds to 16%.

11. $\left(\dfrac{\mathbf{7}}{\mathbf{18}}\right)$ Since Sammi has 36 marbles and 20 of them have red, $16\ (= 36 - 20)$ have just blue on them. If 16 have just blue on them but 30 have blue on them then $14\ (= 30 - 16)$ must have red and blue on them. As a fraction, $\dfrac{14}{36} = \dfrac{7}{18}$ of her marbles are both red and blue. You can enter $\boxed{\dfrac{7}{18}}$, $\boxed{\dfrac{14}{36}}$, or any equivalent fraction. The numeric entry questions do not require fractions to be in lowest form.

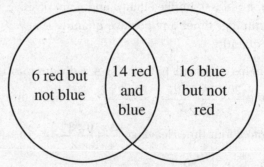

12. **(.048)** Remembering that *of* means multiplication, $\dfrac{1}{3}$ of 2% of $\dfrac{4}{5}$ of 9 =

$\dfrac{1}{\cancel{3}} \times \dfrac{2}{\cancel{100}_{25}} \times \dfrac{\cancel{4}}{5} \times \cancel{9}^{3} = \dfrac{2 \times 3}{25 \times 5} = \dfrac{6}{125}$. Type $6 \div 125$, which equals 0.048. You should enter $\boxed{0.048}$ or $\boxed{.048}$. Either will be accepted.

# Strategies and Problem Solving

**2**

## TEST-TAKING STRATEGIES

Strategies for answering individual questions are addressed throughout the book. In addition to typical test-taking strategies (get a good night's rest, monitor your time, etc.), there are specific general strategies for the GRE quantitative reasoning test.

*In the paper-based test*, you have the option to return to questions, so it is a good idea to start by quickly answering all questions that you know how to do. Of course, you should watch the clock and ensure you have sufficient time to attempt every problem. Do not spend too much time on any one question (no matter how fascinating it is) as all questions count equally. Return to the unanswered questions, and use your best strategies to eliminate wrong answers, and then, if necessary, guess. Record an answer for every question—even if you have to guess. There is no penalty for guessing!

On the computer-based test, you can jump to any question in a section at any time, but it is not wise to jump too much. Take the questions in the order that they come, marking ones that you will want to go back to later by clicking the Mark button. It is usually best to make one pass through the entire section before reviewing any questions. It is hard to score well if you don't finish the test. If there are several questions at the end of each section that you never reach, you probably spent too long working on the harder problems and may have missed an opportunity to get a few easier ones right. Use the onscreen clock to try to keep a pace of about 1.5 minutes per question. This will leave you about 5 minutes at the end to review any problems. But don't let the clock distract you too much; a good place to check in on time is after question 6. If you have used less than 10 minutes, you are right on pace to complete the test *and* should have a few minutes to review at the end.

If you are making progress on a problem and close to solving it, it is usually worth investing a little more time to nail the right answer.

Sometimes, to keep on pace, you will have to guess and move on. Try to avoid wild random guessing. When you're behind, resist the urge to "just pick C and go on" to catch up. It will likely not help you. Always take a few seconds to read a question and eliminate wrong answers before guessing.

> **TIP**
>
> If you complete all the questions, be sure to review your answers! When I took the GRE general written exam, I completed my quantitative sections with plenty of time to spare, so I put my head down and rested. I had to take the exam at 7 A.M. on a Sunday morning, so I was tired! In the end, I received 790 because I got two fairly easy questions wrong. If I had been better rested and checked over my answers, I might have gotten that perfect 800 and a better scholarship in graduate school.
>
> —Blair Madore

# PROBLEM SOLVING

George Polya was famous for being an excellent problem solver. He is even more famous for teaching many other people to become excellent problem solvers. Practicing for the GRE will make you a better problem solver—especially if you try some of Polya's ideas.

Polya emphasizes four steps to problem solving:

P1. Understand the problem
P2. Make a plan for solving the problem
P3. Carry out the plan
P4. Look back

**TIP**

Do not make the mistake of thinking you *have* to use Polya's four steps and the strategies presented in this chapter to solve GRE problems. When you already know how to solve a problem—just go ahead and do it. The material in this chapter is meant to help you know what to do when you *don't* immediately know how to solve a problem.

You don't have to follow these four steps with every problem you solve, but if you're not sure how to solve a problem, these steps will help.

We illustrate the meaning of the steps with the following example.

## EXAMPLE 1

If $H$ hot dogs cost $D$ dollars and $S$ sodas cost $C$ cents, how much will it cost to feed $K$ kids 2 hot dogs and one soda each?

**Solution:**

| Step | Meaning | Example |
|------|---------|---------|
| P1. Understand the problem | Read the problem one or two times. Sometimes you might have to plug in a number for a variable and do a few computations to understand what it really means. Or sometimes you might have to draw a diagram to help understand the relationships involved. | After reading the problem twice, I'm still uncertain so I decided to put numbers into the question. "If 5 hot dogs cost 10 dollars and two sodas cost 150 cents how much will it cost to feed 7 kids." OK—now I get it. |

| Step | Meaning | Example |
|------|---------|---------|
| P2. Make a plan | If you already know how to solve this problem, your plan is just solve it. Otherwise, your plan might be to employ a specific strategy that we talk about in this chapter—or maybe an idea of your own. | Find the price for each hot dog and each soda. Use numbers first instead of letters to understand what to do. |
| P3. Carry out the plan | Follow the steps needed to complete your plan. Usually this means solving the problem—though sometimes you'll get stuck. Then you can return to Step 2. | If 5 hot dogs cost 10 dollars then each hot dog costs $2 = \dfrac{\$10}{5}$. So if $H$ hot dogs cost $D$ dollars then each hot dog costs $\dfrac{D}{H}$ dollars. Similarly, each soda costs $\dfrac{C}{S}$ cents. To convert to dollars we divide by 100. So each soda costs $\dfrac{C}{100S}$. Each kid gets 2 hot dogs and one soda so that would cost $\dfrac{2D}{H}$ plus $\dfrac{C}{100S}$. And we have $K$ kids so that is $K\left(\dfrac{2D}{H} + \dfrac{C}{100S}\right)$ or $\dfrac{2DK}{H} + \dfrac{KC}{100S}$ dollars. |
| P4. Look back | Check your answer. This can also mean to look for patterns that would enable you to solve other (similar) problems. | One way to check would be to plug numbers into our final answer $K = 7$, $H = 5$, $D = 10$, $S = 2$, $C = 150$. $\dfrac{2DK}{H} + \dfrac{KC}{100S} = 2 \times 10 \times \dfrac{7}{5} + 7 \times \dfrac{150}{(100 \times 2)} = 28 + 5.25 = \$33.25$. At \$2 per hot dog and 75 cents per drink that makes sense (since $4.75 \times 7 = 33.25$)! |

**EXAMPLE 2**

If there are 37 people at a party, and everyone greets everyone else with a handshake, how many handshakes take place?

(A) $37^2$

(B) $36 \times 37$

(C) $18 \times 37$

(D) $19 \times 37$

(E) $36^2$

**Solution:** Step 1—After reading the problem several times, you understand that you must count the total number of handshakes at the party.

Step 2—Having no idea how to proceed, you decide to try the strategy of solving an easier problem. For a small party, you could actually count handshakes.

Step 3—What if there were only 4 people at the party? Call them *K, L, M,* and *N.* First *K* shakes hands with *L,* then *K* shakes hands with *M,* and then *K* shakes hands with *N.* Then *L* shakes hands with *M,* and *L* shakes hands with *N. L* doesn't need to shake hands with *K,* because *K* already shook her hand! *M* shakes hands with *N. N* has already shaken hands with everyone else. That makes a total of 3 + 2 + 1 = 6 handshakes.

What if there were five people at the party? Call them *K, L, M, N,* and *O. K* would do 4 shakes, *L* would do 3, *M* would do 2, and *N,* 1. *O* would have already shaken everyone's hand. That would be 4 + 3 + 2 + 1 = 10 handshakes.

Now you can see that at a party of 37 people there would be 36 + 35 + ⋯ + 2 + 1 handshakes. How much is that? You may recall that the sum of the first *n* numbers is $\frac{1}{2}n(n+1)$. So $1 + 2 + \cdots + 35 + 36 = \frac{1}{2}(36 \times 37) = 18 \times 37$.

Step 4—You notice that from the point of view of each person they shook 36 other hands. Why isn't the answer $37 \times 36$? If we did that each handshake would be counted twice, once for each person shaking. So another approach is $(37 \times 36) \div 2$, which leads to the same answer. Choose **C.**

## GENERAL STRATEGIES

There are many strategies developed throughout this book. The most important strategy to remember is—if you already know how to solve it, then just do it! Strategies are what you use when you aren't sure how to solve the problem. We outline four strategies that work for many different problems.

STRATEGY

### Use a Diagram

Many questions can be solved more easily using a diagram. If one is not given, then draw one! A diagram allows you to see relationships you might not notice just by reading the problem.

**TIP**

**Draw a diagram while rereading the problem.**

**EXAMPLE 3**

If *A* is the point (1,0) and *B* is the point (2,2), what is the area of the circle that has *AB* as its radius?

(A) $\pi$

(B) $\sqrt{3}\pi$

(C) $2\pi$

(D) $\sqrt{5}\pi$

(E) $5\pi$

**Solution:** While reading the question for the second time, draw a diagram with points *A* and *B* labeled on it. *AB* is the radius of the circle but what is the center of the circle? It doesn't matter, since the circle will have the same area no matter which of the two points is the center, so let's choose *A*. Sketch the circle.

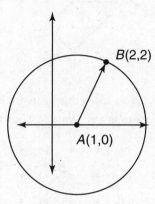

You should now realize the key to this question is determining the length of *AB*—the radius. Use the given points to find the lengths of the legs of the triangle, and use the Pythagorean theorem.

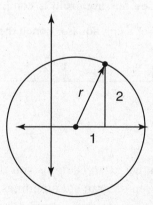

Then $r^2 = 2^2 + 1^2 = 5$. We need the area of the circle $A = \pi r^2$, so $A = \pi \times 5$. The area is $5\pi$ square units. Choose **E**. Notice we did not bother to find *r*. We did not need to know *r* if we knew $r^2$.

**TIP**

Add to a given diagram.

Diagrams are often given, but embellishing the diagram may be necessary to express other information given in the question or information needed to solve the problem.

EXAMPLE 4

Find the area of trapezoid *ABCD*.

(A) 2
(B) 2.5
(C) 3
(D) 3.5
(E) 6

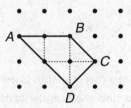

**Solution:** One of the easiest ways to solve this problem is to divide the trapezoid into shapes that have easy to calculate areas. We add lines to do this.

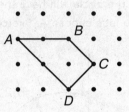

You should now be able to see our trapezoid is composed of one unit square and four right triangles, each half of a unit square. Hence the area of *ABCD* is $1 + 4 \times \dfrac{1}{2} = 3$ square units. Choose **C**.

**TIP**

Trust a diagram drawn to scale and estimate, when you can.

The instructions for the quantitative exam cautions you that diagrams are not necessarily drawn to scale. Can you trust given diagrams? Sometimes you cannot. A triangle with two equal sides could appear with three acute angles, but it is possible for such a triangle to have an obtuse angle. You should be careful not to assume all angles in a triangle are exactly as drawn.

 OR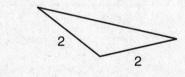

**EXAMPLE 5**

A triangle has two sides 5 cm long

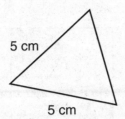

5 cm

5 cm

| Quantity A | Quantity B |
|------------|------------|
| Perimeter of the triangle | 16 cm |

**Incorrect Answer:** If we trust that the triangle looks like what is drawn, then the third side must be close to 5 cm in length. According to the triangle inequality relationship (see the alternate solution), there's no way it could be more than 5 cm. So the perimeter is less than 5 cm + 5 cm + 5 cm = 15 cm. Choose **B**.

**Solution:** The angle between the two 5-cm long sides could be any angle between 0° and 180°.

5 cm

5 cm

5 cm

5 cm

If the angle is near 0° then the third side is near 0 cm in length so the perimeter is a little more than 10 cm. If the angle is near 180° the third side is nearly 10 cm long. Then the perimeter is nearly 20 cm. Choose **D**. The perimeter could be more or less than 16 cm.

**Alternate Solution:** The triangle inequality relationship tells us that a triangle with lengths $a$, $b$, and $c$ exists if and only if the sum of any two sides is more than the third. If $a = 5$ and $b = 5$, this means we need $5 + 5 > c$, $5 + c > 5$, and $c + 5 > 5$. The second two inequalities guarantee that $c > 0$ while the first guarantees that $c < 10$. So for any $c$ between 0 and 10, a triangle with side lengths 5, 5, and $c$ exists. Hence any perimeter between 10 and 20 is possible. Choose **D**.

Sometimes you can trust a diagram to be accurate. If the question states it is a square (equal sides and four right angles), then it is one.

EXAMPLE 6

This is a unit square with circular arcs that are centered at opposite corners of the square.

Quantity A
The area of the shaded region

Quantity B
$\frac{1}{3}$

**Solution:** It is fair to trust this diagram—it is a square and the circular arcs could not be drawn another way. The square is divided into three pieces and the shaded piece is clearly larger than each of the other pieces. Hence, the shaded area is more than $\frac{1}{3}$ the area of the square and $\frac{1}{3}$ of $1^2$ is $\frac{1}{3}$. Choose **A**.

**TIP**

Subtract to find shaded areas.

Most GRE tests ask you to find the area of figures. They are usually nonstandard shapes—you can't just apply a formula like you might with a triangle or rectangle. A good tip is to decompose figures and find areas by subtracting (or adding) the areas of standard figures. We illustrate with two different solutions for Example 6.

ALTERNATE SOLUTION TO EXAMPLE 6

Label the regions in the square ①, ②, and ③.

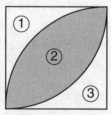

Then notice that the area of region ③ is equal to the area of the square minus a quarter circle.

  =    −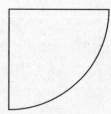

Hence region ③ has area $1^2 - \frac{1}{4}\pi 1^2 = 1 - \frac{\pi}{4}$. But region ① is congruent to and thus equal in area to region ③. Hence, the shaded region is equal to a square minus two times region ③.

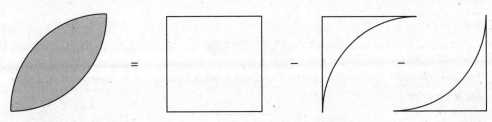

That is, $1^2 - \left(1 - \frac{\pi}{4}\right) - \left(1 - \frac{\pi}{4}\right) = \frac{\pi}{2} - 1$ or approximately 0.57 square units in area. Clearly that is much more than $\frac{1}{3}$.

**ANOTHER SOLUTION TO EXAMPLE 6**

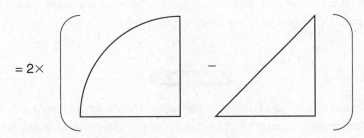

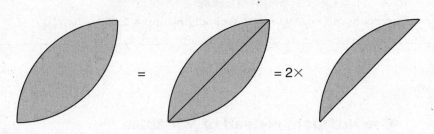

Hence, the shaded area is $2 \times \left(\frac{1}{4}\pi 1^2 - \frac{1}{2} \times 1 \times 1\right) = \frac{\pi}{2} - 1$.

## Pay Attention to Units

You may encounter several different units of measure in the same question. Be careful to convert appropriately.

---

**EXAMPLE 7**

If an ant can walk 7 inches per minute and the road is 28 feet wide, how many seconds will it take for the ant to cross?

**Incorrect Solution:** It is very tempting to divide 28 by 7 and get 4. That would be wrong. The road is measured in feet and the ant's rate of speed is in inches per minute. And your answer must be reported in seconds, not minutes!

**Solution:** 28 feet × (12 inches/foot) = 28 × 12 inches. Notice we didn't multiply this out. Some things are going to cancel before we get the final answer saving us a lot of computation. $28 \times 12 \text{ inches} \times \dfrac{1 \text{ minute}}{7 \text{ inches}} = 4 \times 12 \text{ minutes} = 48 \text{ minutes}$. And to convert to seconds, 48 minutes × (60 seconds/minute) = **2,880**.

---

## Use Numbers Instead of Variables

Some questions appear difficult because they have many different variables in them. It can be easier to understand these problems when you replace each variable with a number, and reread the question. Often you can then proceed to solve the problem, even with variables.

---

**EXAMPLE 8**

A math professor has $x + 2$ students in her class. They each answer $x - 2$ problems on an assignment. If a quarter of their problems are solved incorrectly, what is the total number of incorrectly solved problems the professor must grade?

(A) $\dfrac{x}{2}$

(B) $\dfrac{x^2 - 2}{4}$

(C) $x^2 - 4$

(D) $\dfrac{x^2}{4} - 1$

(E) $\dfrac{x^2}{4}$

---

**Solution:** We replace $x$ with 18 and try to solve the problem. We chose 18 because $18 + 2$ and $18 - 2$ are easy numbers to work with. There are $18 + 2 = 20$ students in class. Each answers $18 - 2 = 16$ problems. A quarter of their problems are answered incorrectly, so $\frac{1}{4} \times 16 = 4$ problems are incorrect for each student. Thus the professor grades 4 incorrect problems for each student or $20 \times 4 = 80$ incorrect problems in total.

Now we follow the same steps with the variables in place. There are $x + 2$ students in class. Each answers $x - 2$, a quarter of which, $\frac{1}{4} \times (x - 2)$, are incorrect. Thus the professor grades $(x + 2) \times \frac{1}{4} \times (x - 2)$ incorrect problems, in total. Now we simplify the algebra $(x + 2) \times \frac{1}{4} \times (x - 2) = \frac{(x+2)(x-2)}{4} = \frac{x^2 - 4}{4} = \frac{x^2}{4} - \frac{4}{4} = \frac{x^2}{4} - 1$. Choose **D**.

What numbers are best to choose for your variables? We try to choose numbers that are easy to compute with like 10, 20, or 100. You can also use simple numbers like 0 or 1 though they may not make sense for all problems.

## STRATEGIES FOR MULTIPLE-CHOICE QUESTIONS

We will describe three helpful strategies that apply specifically to multiple-choice questions.

STRATEGY

### Test Answers Starting with C

---

**EXAMPLE 9**

Kirk starts a new business making fly fishing rods. It costs, in dollars, $1{,}500 + 65x$ to make $x$ rods. Kirk can sell this lot of $x$ rods to a retailer for $125x$ dollars. The retailer insists on receiving the fishing rods in multiples of 10. What is the least number of rods Kirk can manufacture, without losing money?

(A) 10
(B) 20
(C) 30
(D) 50
(E) 100

**Solution:** Rather than trying to solve the problem, we use the answers to check and see if they are valid solutions. We start with C and then work left or right to find the correct answer. If Kirk makes 30 rods it will cost $1{,}500 + 65(30) = 1{,}500 + 1{,}950 = 3{,}450$ dollars. He will receive $\$125(30) = \$3{,}750$ for a net profit of $\$300$. So he will not lose money making 30 (or more) rods, but he could still potentially manufacture 20 rods and still be profitable. Let's check B. Then 20 rods cost $1{,}500 + 65(20) = 1{,}500 + 1{,}300 = 2{,}800$ dollars to make. He will receive only $\$125(20) = \$2{,}500$ and lose money. Choose **C**.

# Use Numbers Instead of Variables

---

**ALTERNATE SOLUTION TO EXAMPLE 8**

After solving the problem with $x = 18$, we know the answer is 80. Plug $x = 18$ into each of the answers and see which ones equal 80.

(A) $\dfrac{x}{2} = \dfrac{18}{2} = 9$

(B) $\dfrac{x^2 - 2}{4} = \dfrac{18^2 - 2}{4} = \dfrac{324 - 2}{4} = \dfrac{322}{4} = 80.5$

(C) $x^2 - 4 = 18^2 - 4 = 324 - 4 = 320$

(D) $\dfrac{x^2}{4} - 1 = \dfrac{18^2}{4} - 1 = \dfrac{324}{4} - 1 = 81 - 1 = 80$

(E) $\dfrac{x^2}{4} = \dfrac{18^2}{4} = \dfrac{324}{4} = 81$

Clearly the answer is **D**.

---

In the alternate solution we tested E even after we found the correct solution D. Why? Depending on the numbers you choose for variables, you may get more than one solution that gives the correct answer. If this happens, try other values for your variables.

---

**EXAMPLE 10**

Marty is having lunch with $n$ of his friends. A sandwich uses two slices of bread, and they usually eat $m$ sandwiches each. If there are $s$ slices of bread in a loaf, how many loaves of bread should Marty buy?

(A) $\dfrac{2nm}{s}$

(B) $\dfrac{2nm}{s} + \dfrac{2m}{s}$

(C) $\dfrac{(2n + 1)m}{s}$

(D) $\dfrac{2ns}{m}$

(E) $\dfrac{2(n + 1)s}{m}$

**Solution:** We try $n = 2$, $m = 2$, $s = 2$. Although this does not make a lot of sense, the algebra should be easy! There are three people at lunch, and they each eat 2 sandwiches. That is 6 sandwiches, so we need 12 slices of bread. If there are 2 slices in each loaf that means 6 loaves are needed. Now we substitute into the given solutions and look for 6.

---

Ⓐ $\frac{2nm}{s} = 2 \times 2 \times \frac{2}{2} = 4$

Ⓑ $\frac{2nm}{s} + \frac{2m}{s} = 2 \times 2 \times \frac{2}{2} + 2 \times \frac{2}{2} = 4 + 2 = 6$

Ⓒ $\frac{(2n+1)m}{s} = (2(2)+1) \times \frac{2}{2} = 5$

Ⓓ $\frac{2ns}{m} = 2 \times 2 \times \frac{2}{2} = 4$

Ⓔ $\frac{2(n+1)s}{m} = 2(2+1) \times \frac{2}{2} = 6$

So which is the correct answer—B or E? We don't know. We'll try again with $n = 3$, $m = 4$, and $s = 8$. So we have 4 people in total eating 4 sandwiches each. Marty needs $4 \times 4 \times 2 = 32$ pieces of bread and at 8 slices per loaf that is $\frac{32}{8} = 4$ loaves. Now we try our numbers but only in the answers for B and E (we already know A, C, and D are incorrect).

(B) $\frac{2nm}{s} + \frac{2m}{s} = \frac{2(3)(4)}{(8)} + \frac{2(4)}{8} = \frac{24}{8} + \frac{8}{8} = 3 + 1 = 4$.

(E) $\frac{2(n+1)s}{m} = \frac{2(3+1)(8)}{(4)} = 16$.

Choose **B**.

STRATEGY

## 3 Eliminate Choices, Then Guess

### EXAMPLE 11

If $1 < xy < 2$, which of the following could be true?

Ⓐ $x > 0$ and $y < 0$

Ⓑ $x < -1$ and $y < -2$

Ⓒ $x < -1$ and $0 < y < 2$

Ⓓ $0 < x < 1$ and $1 < y < 2$

Ⓔ $\frac{1}{2} < x < 1$ and $4 < y$

**Partial Solution:** You know that the product of a positive and negative number is negative. That means that A and C can be eliminated. You thought that you could multiply inequalities, part by part. In B that would mean that $xy < (-1)(-2) = 2$. But this doesn't seem right; if $x = -3$ and $y = -3$, then $x < -1$ and $y < -2$, but $xy = 9$, which is not less than 2. You are confused but your gut says B is not correct. Not wanting to waste any more time you guess between D and E. Choose **E**.

**Actual Solution:** The product of two negatives is always positive so in B, $x < -1$ and $y < -2$ implies that $xy > (-1)(-2) = 2$. So you were correct—B is not the answer. With positive numbers, you can multiply inequalities so $x < 1$ and $y < 2$ implies $xy < 1 \times 2 = 2$. And $x > 0$ and $y > 1$ implies that $xy > 0 \times 1 = 0$. So D might be the answer. In E, we are again dealing with only positive numbers so $\frac{1}{2} < x$ and $4 < y$ means $4 \times \frac{1}{2} < xy$ or $2 < xy$. This shows E is not the answer. Choose **D**. In fact if you take $x = 0.9$ and $y = 1.9$, we get $xy = 0.9 \times 1.9 = 1.71$.

You may think partial solutions in which answers are eliminated are not very satisfying. Nobody likes to leave a question without knowing the answer. But time is limited and guessing wisely can be an important part of earning a good score. Statistics support this, guessing randomly you have only a 20% chance of getting a problem correct. If you eliminate three incorrect solutions first, you now have a 50% chance of being correct!

## STRATEGIES FOR DATA INTERPRETATION QUESTIONS

**TIP**

Study your charts first for about 10 seconds before reading any questions.

Most people begin by reading the question and then looking at the data charts. If you do so, your mind is consumed by the question, and you may not notice all the important details in the chart. Some charts are complicated or have subtle details. You should always start by reviewing the chart and then reading the question.

EXAMPLES 12 AND 13 REFER TO THE FOLLOWING CHARTS.

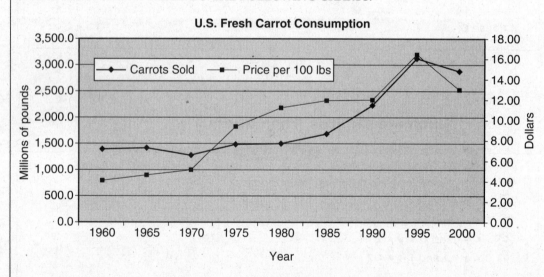

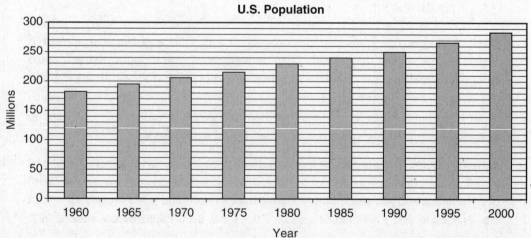

If you look carefully at these charts you should notice:

- The carrots sold are measured in millions of pounds.
- The price is measured in dollars but the unit of weight is not mentioned. We have to look in the legend to see it is dollars per hundred pounds.
- Data is given for each five years—the lines in between just join the data points. They do not represent what may have happened then.

## Estimate, Don't Calculate

Calculating exact values can be tedious or even difficult. Try to avoid tricky calculations by estimating.

---

**EXAMPLE 12**

The average consumption peaked at 11 pounds annually per person in what year?

(A) 1965

(B) 1975

(C) 1985

(D) 1995

(E) 2000

**Solution:** To calculate this precisely for each year we must divide the pounds sold by the population. Reading from the charts we see that in millions of pounds per million people we have approximately $\frac{1,400}{190}$ for 1965, $\frac{1,500}{220}$ for 1975, $\frac{1,700}{240}$ for 1985, $\frac{3,200}{268}$ for 1995, and $\frac{2,900}{280}$ for 2000. In 1965, 1975, and 1985, the numerator is less than 10 times the denominator so they are not the answer. For the year 2000, $\frac{2,900}{280}$ is approximately 10 and in 1995, $\frac{3,200}{268}$ is considerably more than 10 (as 3,200 > 2,680).

Choose **D**.

---

## Try to Visualize Rather Than Calculate

In Example 12 you didn't need to know the actual average consumption for each year; just knowing the approximate value and how it compared to the other was sufficient. Sometimes these comparisons can be done just by looking at relative sizes on graphs.

EXAMPLE 13

The net value of the fresh carrot sales increased most in what period?

(A) 1960–1965

(B) 1970–1975

(C) 1980–1985

(D) 1990–1995

(E) 1995–2000

**Solution:** To actually calculate the increase in value, we would have to calculate a net value (price multiplied by weight sold) for each year and subtract. It is much easier to look at where things change and by how much. Common sense tells us that net value changes the most when the price or the weight (or both) increase considerably. By observation we can see that the price increased the most in 1970–1975 or 1990–1995. But in 1990–1995 the weight sold increased more than in 1970–1975. Choose **D**.

## STRATEGIES FOR QUANTITATIVE COMPARISON QUESTIONS

Probably the most unusual part of the exam for you will be the quantitative comparison questions. Thus it's very important to become accustomed to them through practice and to learn some strategies for answering them.

STRATEGY

### Do the Same Thing to Each Quantity

You can treat the two quantities as if they are two sides of an equality (or inequality). If you do the same thing to each side, you will preserve the equality (inequality). The resulting quantities may be easier to compare. Of course you must use only operations that would not change the inequality! It is safe to add (subtract) the same value to (from) both quantities, multiply (divide) both quantities by a positive number, and take the square root of both quantities if both are nonnegative. It may not be safe to square both sides. If you multiply (divide) both sides by a negative, it reverses the inequality sign.

EXAMPLE 14

$$x > 12$$

| Quantity A | Quantity B |
|------------|------------|
| $2x + 5$   | $3x - 7$   |

**Solution:** You can assume the centered statement, $x > 12$, is a fact. At first glance you may think that $3x$ is bigger than $2x$ so B would be larger. But subtracting 7 from B may erase that advantage, especially as 5 is added to A. You can proceed as follows:

| | | |
|---|---|---|
| Add 7 | $2x + 12$ | $3x$ |
| Subtract $2x$ | 12 | $x$ |

Since $x > 12$, choose **B**.

EXAMPLE 15

| Quantity A | Quantity B |
|------------|------------|
| $2x + 5$ | $3x - 7$ |

**Solution:** If we are given no condition on $x$, we can still solve this problem, but the answer may change.

| | | |
|---|---|---|
| Add 7 | $2x + 12$ | $3x$ |
| Subtract $2x$ | 12 | $x$ |

Since we do not know what $x$ is, it may be greater than, less than, or equal to 12. Choose **D**.

STRATEGY

## 2 Compare, Don't Calculate

Many times you can compare quantities without doing calculations. This is especially useful when given two numeric quantities.

EXAMPLE 16

| Quantity A | Quantity B |
|------------|------------|
| $(0.07)^2 (0.07)^4$ | $(0.07)^7$ |

**Solution:** It would be quite tedious to calculate all these powers of decimals. First we should notice that in Quantity A we can keep the base and add the exponents to get $(0.07)^6$. Now how does this compare with $(0.07)^7$? Most people expect $(0.07)^7$ to be larger, but that is not the case. You may recall that for numbers between 0 and 1, raising it to a higher power decreases the value. Another way to look at this is that $(0.07)^7 = (0.07)(0.07)^6 = 7\%$ of $(0.07)^6$. Clearly 7% of a positive number is less than the number.

**Alternate Solution:** First divide both quantities by $(0.07)^2$. That leaves

$(0.07)^4$         $(0.07)^5$

Then divide both quantities by $(0.07)^4$ to leave

1         $(0.07)$

Clearly $1 > 0.07$. Choose **A**.

## Replace Variables with Numbers

This is one of the most important techniques for quantitative comparison questions. It is easy to do this and even if it doesn't give you an immediate answer—it will often stimulate the right idea to lead you to an answer.

What values should you try? This can depend on the question, but here are some good suggestions.

- Try a positive and a negative number.
- Try zero.
- Try a number between 0 and 1 and a number greater than one.
- Try a very small number (like 0.001) and a very large number like 1,000.
- Try a prime number and a composite number.

---

**EXAMPLE 17**

*a* and *c* are nonzero.

| Quantity A | Quantity B |
|------------|------------|
| $\dfrac{a+c}{c}$ | $1 + (c \div a)^{-1}$ |

**Solution:** Try $a = c = 1$. Then Quantity A is $\dfrac{2}{1} = 2$ and Quantity B is $1 + (1 \div 1)^{-1} = 1 + (1)^{-1}$

$= 1 + 1 = 2$. They have the same value! We try some other values, $a = 10$ and

$c = \dfrac{1}{2}$. Then Quantity A is $\dfrac{10.5}{0.5} = 21$. Quantity B is $1 + \left(\dfrac{1}{2} \div 10\right)^{-1} = 1 + \left(\dfrac{1}{2} \times \dfrac{1}{10}\right)^{-1}$

$= 1 + \left(\dfrac{1}{20}\right)^{-1} = 1 + 20 = 21$. Again they are equal! Now you should suspect they might

always be equal. We try simplifying Quantity B. $1 + (c \div a)^{-1} = 1 + \left(\dfrac{c}{a}\right)^{-1} = 1 + \dfrac{a}{c} = \dfrac{c}{c} + \dfrac{a}{c}$

$\dfrac{c+a}{c}$, which is equal to Quantity A. Choose **C**.

---

Trying values will convince you that one quantity is larger than the other or that the quantities are equal. But it cannot prove that fact. Trying values can prove that the answer is D—it cannot be determined. If for one value of the variables, A is larger than B and for another value B is larger than or equal to A, then the answer cannot be determined. This is the best technique to determine if the answer is D.

---

**EXAMPLE 18**

$$r > s$$

| Quantity A | Quantity B |
|:---:|:---:|
| $\dfrac{r-s}{r^2-s^2}$ | $r+s$ |

**Solution:** You may notice that the left-hand side can be factored, and then some cancellation will occur =: $\dfrac{r-s}{r^2-s^2} = \dfrac{\cancel{r-s}}{\cancel{(r-s)}(r+s)} = \dfrac{1}{r+s}$. So now we have to compare $\dfrac{1}{r+s}$ with $r+s$. If we try $r=5$ and $s=4$, we get $\dfrac{1}{9} < 9$. But if we try $r=\dfrac{1}{2}$ and $s=\dfrac{1}{4}$, we get $\dfrac{1}{\frac{1}{2}+\frac{1}{4}} = \dfrac{1}{\frac{3}{4}} = \dfrac{4}{3}$ in Quantity A and $\dfrac{1}{2}+\dfrac{1}{4}=\dfrac{3}{4}$ in Quantity B. Since Quantity B is larger in the first case and smaller in the second, we conclude the answer is **D**.

---

STRATEGY

## Choose a Good Number for the Whole

Some problems refer to an unnamed quantity, for example, "37% of a number" or "$\dfrac{1}{5}$ of the class." In these problems it can often be useful to work with a specific value. One hundred is a common choice but 60 can be a better choice when you have to divide because it is divisible by 2, 3, 4, 5, 6, 10, 15, 20, and 30. Choosing a number that works best will make solving the problem much easier.

---

**EXAMPLE 19**

$$x > 0$$

| Quantity A | Quantity B |
|:---:|:---:|
| $\dfrac{1}{3}$ of $x$ plus 20% of half of $x$ | $\dfrac{2}{5}$ of $x$ plus 10% of half of $x$ |

**Solution 1:** Assume $x = 100$. One-third of 100 is $33\dfrac{1}{3}$. Half of 100 is 50, and 20% of 50 is 10 (2 out of 10 for each of five tens). Thus Quantity A is $33\dfrac{1}{3}+10 = 43\dfrac{1}{3}$. Two-fifths of 100 is 40. Ten percent of 50 (half of 100) is 5. So Quantity B is 45. Choose **B**.

**Solution 2:** Assume $x = 60$. One-third of 60 is 20. Half of 60 is 30, and 20% of 30 is 6 (2 out of 10 for each of three tens). Thus Quantity A is $20 + 6 = 26$. Two-fifths of 60 is 24. Ten percent of 30 (half of 60) is 3. So Quantity B is $24 + 3 = 27$. Choose **B**.

---

Neither solution is easy, but we like avoiding the fractions in the second solution.

## Guess

As in multiple-choice questions, sometimes you have no choice but to guess. Even in this case, be sure to eliminate impossible choices before guessing. Here are some tips to improve your guessing:

- Never answer E for a quantitative comparison question. Even though it may be on your answer sheet (on the paper version) it is not a choice for quantitative comparison questions. Don't waste your guess!
- If the quantities have only numbers, don't choose D. Given two numbers, they are either equal or one of them is larger. Even if you can't tell what the answer is, it is determinable by someone.
- If the question involves just switching order in a computation guess C. Many such questions are designed to test if you know when you can and can't switch order. As such it's probably a fifty-fifty chance that C is correct.

---

**EXAMPLE 20**

| Quantity A | Quantity B |
|:---:|:---:|
| $2^{(3^4)}$ | $(2^3)^4$ |

**Solution 1:** Both quantities are numbers so do not choose D. This question is really about determining the right order for evaluating exponents. As such, if you don't know what to do, it would be a reasonable guess that it may not make any difference and choose C. You would be wrong, but it's a reasonable guess. $3^4 = 3 \times 3 \times 3 \times 3 = 81$ so Quantity A is $2^{81}$. Since $2^3 = 2 \times 2 \times 2 = 8$ Quantity B is $8^4$. Instinct tells me that 81 factors of 2 will be larger than four factors of 8. Choose **A**.

**Solution 2:** In Quantity A, $2^{(3^4)} = 2^{81}$, since $3^4 = 81$. In Quantity B, $(2^3)^4 = 2^{3 \times 4} = 2^{12}$. Since $2^{81} > 2^{12}$, choose **A**.

---

**EXAMPLE 21**

| Quantity A | Quantity B |
|:---:|:---:|
| 2% of 3% of 4 | 4% of 3% of 2 |

**Solution:** Both quantities are numbers so do not choose D. This question uses the same values in different orders. As such, if you don't know what to do, it would be a reasonable guess that it may not make any difference and choose C. In this case you would be right. In fact 2% of 3% of $4 = \dfrac{2}{100} \times \dfrac{3}{100} \times 4 = \dfrac{(2 \times 3 \times 4)}{100^2}$. Also 4% of 3% of $2 = \dfrac{4}{100} \times \dfrac{3}{100} \times 2 = \dfrac{(4 \times 3 \times 2)}{100^2}$. Choose **C**.

---

# STRATEGIES FOR NUMERIC ENTRY QUESTIONS

The recently developed numeric entry questions are a very fair type of problem, in that you are free to enter virtually any number as your answer, making it very hard to guess or outsmart the test. Just click the answer box and type your answer, which may be a whole number such as 2,500, or a decimal such as 1.125. If the answer is meant to be a fraction, the answer grid will take on a new appearance, with two answer boxes separated by a division bar. Type one number as the numerator of your fraction and one as the denominator. In this case, enter integer values. Never try to enter a decimal within the "fraction answer boxes."

These questions really test whether you know your math, because it's difficult to guess or narrow down when the answer could be almost anything. One key: Make sure you don't waste precious time on a problem that you know is too hard for you. Sometimes you will just have to guess and move on.

On occasion, you may be able to make a ballpark estimate of the answer and generate some hypothetical answer choices, which can then be tested for the right answer.

---

**EXAMPLE 22**

If $3^x + 3^x + 3^x = 3^5$, what is the value of $x$?

**Incorrect solution:** $x + x + x = 5$, so $3x = 5$, and $x = \dfrac{5}{3} \approx 1.67$. When adding algebraic terms, you cannot simply add the exponents.

**Solution 1:** Do you see why $x$ must be less than 5? Otherwise, the left side would be greater than the right. Because $x$ could be any real number, there are an infinite number of possible answers. But if we are lucky, $x$ may be a whole number, in which case we can infer $x = 0, 1, 2, 3,$ or $4$ and adopt a "testing answers" approach. Start with $x = 2$, the middle value of these. Then $3^x = 3^2 = 9$, and the left side is $9 + 9 + 9 = 27$. For the right side, multiply out $3 \times 3 \times 3 \times 3 \times 3$ on the calculator to obtain 243. Since 27 is much less than 243, test $x = 4$ next. $3^4 = 81$, and $81 + 81 + 81$ does equal 243, so choose **4**.

**Solution 2:** The term $3^x$ is added to itself 3 times, so the left side equals $3 \times 3^x$. When multiplying expressions with the same base, add the exponents: $3^1 \times 3^x = 3^{1+x}$. Then $3^{1+x} = 3^5$. The two sides now have a base equal to 3 and will be equal if and only if the exponents are equal. Therefore $1 + x = 5$, and $x = $ **4**.

## Don't Simplify Fractions

You should take careful note that you do not need to simplify fractions. This can save you valuable time.

---

**EXAMPLE 23**

To find the sale price of a bottle of liquor, the owner starts with the wholesale price and then adds 50%. He then reduces the price by 30% for a sale. Finally he adds 10% for taxes. The sale price is what fraction of the wholesale price?

Give your answer as a fraction:

**Solution:** Assume the wholesale price is $10. To add 50% multiply by $\frac{3}{2}$, to reduce by 30% multiply by $\frac{7}{10}$, and to add 10% multiply by $\frac{11}{10}$. That means the sale price is $\$10 \times \frac{3}{2} \times \frac{7}{10} \times \frac{11}{10}$. As a fraction of the wholesale price that is $\left(\$10 \times \frac{3}{2} \times \frac{7}{10} \times \frac{11}{10}\right) \div \$10 = \frac{3 \times 7 \times 11}{2 \times 10 \times 10}$. That is $\frac{231}{200}$. Don't try to reduce the fraction to lowest terms. Just enter $\frac{231}{200}$.

---

## STRATEGIES FOR MULTIPLE-ANSWER QUESTIONS

Most of the same strategies from the "regular" multiple-choice questions apply here. But remember the answer may be many answer choices or just one.

---

**EXAMPLE 24**

If $\frac{x}{4}$, $\frac{x}{5}$, and $\frac{x}{6}$ are all positive integers, which of the following could be $x$?

Indicate *all* that apply.

- (A) 15
- (B) 20
- (C) 30
- (D) 60
- (E) 120

**Solution:** For the three quotients to be integers means that the division performed leaves no remainder or decimal part. Test A: 15 ÷ 4 is not an integer. Test B: 20 divided by either 4 or 5 is an integer, but 20 ÷ 6 is not an integer. Test C: 30 is divisible by 5 and 6, but not by 4. Eliminate A, B, and C. Test D on the calculator if you have to: 60 ÷ 4 = 15, 60 ÷ 5 = 12, 60 ÷ 6 = 10. Because 15, 12, and 10 are all integers, D is correct. Since 120 is a multiple of 60, it will also be divisible by 4, 5, and 6, so E is correct. Choose **D** and **E**.

---

# PROBLEMS

1.

| Quantity A | Quantity B |
|---|---|
| $\frac{1}{3}$ of the price after a 40% discount. | $\frac{1}{4}$ of the price after a 25% discount. |

2.

$$x > 1$$

| Quantity A | Quantity B |
|---|---|
| $3x^2 + 47$ | $5x^3 - 56$ |

3.

$$x + 3 < 0$$

| Quantity A | Quantity B |
|---|---|
| $(x - 3)^2$ | $(x + 2)^2$ |

4.

$$x > 1$$

| Quantity A | Quantity B |
|---|---|
| $\dfrac{x}{x-1}$ | $\dfrac{x}{x+1}$ |

5.

| Quantity A | Quantity B |
|---|---|
| $p^2 - q^2$ | $(p - q)^2$ |

6.

$$x > y > 0$$

| Quantity A | Quantity B |
|---|---|
| $(x - y)^2$ | $x^2 - y^2$ |

7. If $2^7 5^n \geq 10{,}000{,}000$, which of the following could be the value of $n$?

   Indicate *all* that apply.

   - [A] 2
   - [B] 5
   - [C] 6
   - [D] 7
   - [E] 10
   - [F] $2^7$

8. The average test score for the 24 students in class A is 88. The average test score for the $n$ students in class B is 76. If the average test score for the two classes considered together is at least 82, which of the following could be $n$?

   Indicate *all* that apply.

   - [A] 1
   - [B] 10
   - [C] 20
   - [D] 28
   - [E] 88

9. On November 7, $\frac{1}{7}$ of the school is absent due to a virus. Of those present, $\frac{3}{4}$ remain in school while the rest go on a field trip. Only $\frac{2}{3}$ of those in school eat the lunch special. What fraction of the total school population did not eat the lunch special that day?

Give your answer as a fraction: $\dfrac{\phantom{XXX}}{\phantom{XXX}}$

PROBLEMS 10 AND 11 ARE CONCERNED WITH THE FOLLOWING TWO CHARTS:

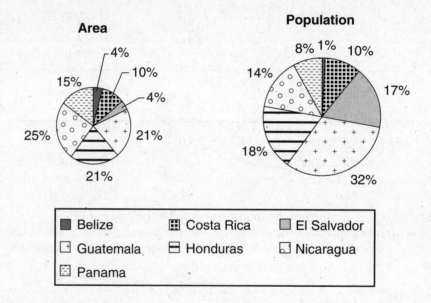

10. Which country has the highest population density (average population per square mile)?

Ⓐ Guatemala
Ⓑ Nicaragua
Ⓒ El Salvador
Ⓓ Belize
Ⓔ Honduras

11. Approximately 70% of Central Americans identify their ethnicity as Mestizo. The Mestizo would have to be at least what portion of the population of Guatemala?

Ⓐ 70%
Ⓑ 45%
Ⓒ 6%
Ⓓ 2%
Ⓔ 1%

PROBLEM 12 IS BASED ON THE CHARTS ABOUT CARROT CONSUMPTION ON PAGE 24.

12. Which carrot consumption would cost the most?

  (A) 100 lb in 1960
  (B) 50 lb in 1975
  (C) 50 lb in 1980
  (D) 25 lb in 1990
  (E) 20 lb in 1995

13. A bus was full (48 people) when leaving the subway station. At the first stop, $\frac{1}{3}$ of the people on the bus left. Four got on. At the second stop, $\frac{1}{4}$ of the people on the bus left and 8 got on. At the third stop no one left but 1 got on. What fraction of the bus is empty?

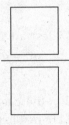

14. If $-1 < xy < 1$, which of the following is *not* possibly true?

  (A) $x < 0$ and $y < 0$
  (B) $x < -1$ and $y < -2$
  (C) $-1 < x < 0$ and $y > 2$
  (D) $0 < x < 1$ and $1 < y < 2$
  (E) $0 < x < \frac{1}{2}$ and $4 < y$

## SOLUTIONS

1. **(A)** Assume the price is $100. After a 40% discount ($40 off), the price is $60. One-third of $60 is $20. After a 25% discount ($25 off), the price is $75. One quarter of $75 is less than $20 since $20 is one quarter of $80.

2. **(D)** Try $x = 2$. Then $3x^2 + 47 = 3(2^2) + 47 = 59$, while $5x^3 - 56 = 5(2^3) - 56 = -16$. When $x = 2$, A is larger. Now try a much larger value for $x$ that is easy to compute with, say $x = 10$. Then $3x^2 + 47 = 3(10^2) + 47 = 347$ while $5x^3 - 56 = 5(10^3) - 56 = 5,000 - 56$. This time B is larger.

3. **(A)** As $x + 3 < 0$, subtracting 6 from both sides we see that $x - 3 < -6$. As $x + 3 < 0$, subtracting one from both sides we see that $x + 2 < -1$. Take the square root of both quantities but be careful to take the positive, not the negative root. Make the answers positive by taking the opposite of $x - 3$ and $x + 2$.

$\sqrt{(x-3)^2}$      $\sqrt{(x+2)^2}$
$-(x - 3)$         $-(x + 2)$
$-x + 3$           $-x - 2$

Cancel $x$ on both sides.

3         $-2$

Alternatively, as $x - 3 < x + 2 < -1$, when we square all parts, the inequality is reversed, as each of the parts is negative.
So $(x - 3)^2 > (x + 2)^2 > 1$.

4. **(A)** Multiply both quantities by $(x - 1)(x + 1)$ to clear the denominators. Since $x > 1$ we are multiplying by a positive value and not changing the relationship between Quantity A and Quantity B.

$$\frac{x(x+1)(x-1)}{x-1} \qquad \frac{x(x+1)(x-1)}{x+1}$$

Simplify.                  $x^2 + x$                  $x^2 - x$
Subtract $x^2$.            $x$                        $-x$
As $x > 1$ clearly $x > -x$.

**Alternate solution:** Since $0 < x - 1 < x + 1$, dividing $x$ by a smaller value, $(x - 1)$, gives a larger result.

5. **(D)** Many people (incorrectly) think these are equal. When $p = 0$ and $q$ is not zero, A is $-q^2$, a negative number, while B is $(0 - q)^2 = q^2$, a positive number. When $p = q$, both quantities are zero.

6. **(B)** This is the same as question 5, but there are further restrictions on the variable, so our answer for question 5 is not valid here. First we factor both quantities.

$(x - y)(x - y) \qquad (x - y)(x + y)$
Since $x > y$, $(x - y)$ is positive. Divide both quantities by $(x - y)$.

$(x - y) \qquad\qquad (x + y)$
Subtract $x$ from each quantity.

$-y \qquad\qquad y$
Since $y > 0$, we know $y > -y$.

7. **(D, E, F)** The number 10,000,000 in scientific notation is $1 \times 10^7$. In general, a number written as 1 followed by $x$ zeroes equals $10^x$. Here, $10{,}000{,}000 = 10^7 = (2 \times 5)^7 = 2^7 5^7$, meaning that if $n = 7$, the two sides are equal and that if $n \geq 7$, then $2^7 5^n \geq 10{,}000{,}000$. Choose the answers that are at least 7, namely D, E, and F.

8. **(A, B, C)** Notice that the combined class average is at a minimum of 82, which happens to be the number exactly halfway between the two class averages of 76 and 88. This observation can be made by noting that $82 - 76 = 6 = 88 - 82$, or that 82 is the average of the other numbers: $\frac{76 + 88}{2} = 82$. Because the combined class average is closer to class A's average than to class B's average (or at least as close), class A must have at least as many students as class B. This situation is often called a "weighted average," because the greater number of students in class A pulls or weighs the combined average toward the class A average. Therefore, $n$, the number of students in class B, must be less than or equal to 24. Choose $n$ so that $n \leq 24$.

9. It is much easier to calculate the fraction that did eat the lunch special; $\frac{6}{7}$ were in school. Of those, $\frac{3}{4}$ stayed. Of those, $\frac{2}{3}$ ate the special. So $\frac{6}{7} \times \frac{3}{4} \times \frac{2}{3}$ ate the special. We cancel 2 and 6 in the numerator with 3 and 4 in the denominator to see that $\frac{3}{7}$ of the school population ate the special that day. That means $\frac{4}{7}$ did not eat the special. Give your answer as a fraction: $\boxed{\dfrac{4}{7}}$

Alternatively, we did not have to reduce the fraction; we could have just multiplied across to get $\frac{6}{7} \times \frac{3}{4} \times \frac{2}{3} = \frac{36}{84}$. Then $\frac{48}{84}$ would have also been an acceptable answer.

10. **(C)** Population density is given by population per unit area. If the total area of Central America is $R$ and the population of Central America is $P$, we could calculate the population density for Belize as $\frac{0.01P}{0.04R}$. As we only need to compare, it suffices to just look at the ratio of the percentage of the population to the percentage of the area. This can even be eyeballed rather than calculated. El Salvador and Guatemala are the only countries that have a greater percentage of the population than area. For Guatemala it is $\frac{32}{21}$, and for El Salvador, $\frac{17}{4}$. El Salvador has the greatest population density.

11. **(C)** Assume there are 100 people in Central America. Where do the 70 Mestizo live? Even if everyone outside Guatemala is Mestizo that would be only 68 Mestizos. So at least 2 must live in Guatemala. Thus the minimum percentage of Guatemala that is Mestizo is $\frac{2}{32} \times 100\%$, which is approximately 6%.

12. **(C)** First we notice that the price per 100 lb in 1975 is more than double the price per 100 lb in 1960. So B > A. Also, the price in 1980 is more than the price in 1975 so C > B. The price in 1990 is similar to the price in 1980 but consuming less carrots means D < C. That leaves E or C as the answer. Now we need to calculate: 100 lb in 1995 is about $16 so 20 lb is about $\frac{\$16}{5}$ or $3.20; 100 lb in 1980 is at least $11, so 50 lb would be $5.50.

13. Start with 48 people. $\frac{1}{3}$ of 48, or 16, leave and then 4 got on. Now there are 36 people on the bus. $\frac{1}{4}$ of 36, or 9, leave. Thus 27 are on the bus, 8 more get on, and then one more gets on. That makes 27 + 8 + 1 = 36 people on the bus. So 48 − 36 = 12 seats are empty. $\frac{12}{48}$ of the bus is empty. This is $\frac{1}{4}$ but you do not need to reduce the fraction. Give your answer as a fraction: $\boxed{\dfrac{12}{48}}$

14. **(B)** We do not see an ideal strategy for this type of question. It can be time consuming but we recommend checking each answer to see if it is possible. Consider A, $x < 0$ and $y < 0$. If $x < 0$ and $y < 0$, then $xy > 0$. But could $xy$ be less than 1? Not if you stick to integers, but if we use rational numbers like $x = -0.1$ and $y = -0.1$, then $xy = (-0.1)(-0.1) = 0.01$. So A could be true. Consider B, $x < -1$ and $y < -2$. Then $xy$ is positive and greater than $(-1)(-2) = 2$. This is not possible. Choose B. Since only one answer is correct, we do not need to check C, D, and E.

# Numbers

The GRE uses the word *numbers* to mean real numbers—all numbers that you can find on the number line.

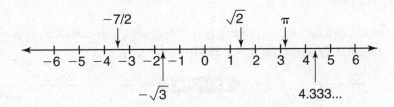

These include the integers (like –2, 0, and 137), rational numbers (like $\frac{5}{8}$, $\frac{-7}{13}$, or $\frac{2}{5}$), and irrational numbers (like $\sqrt{2}$ or $\pi$).

Numbers

$\frac{3}{4}$   $\frac{2}{-11}$   $\frac{-1}{5}$

Rational Numbers

$\sqrt{2}$   $\pi$

Irrational Numbers

–132   – 5   $\frac{33}{7}$   $e$   $\sqrt{7}$

1

Integers

–2   0

3   $-56\frac{1}{8}$   $1 - \pi$

78

## NUMBERS

## Operations

There are two basic operations for numbers, addition (+) and multiplication (×). The numbers being added are called *addends*, and the result is called the *sum*. The numbers multiplied are called *factors*, and the result is called the *product*.

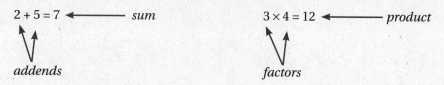

$2 + 5 = 7$ ⟵ sum          $3 \times 4 = 12$ ⟵ product

addends          factors

The opposite (inverse) of addition is subtraction (−), and the opposite of multiplication is division (÷). In a subtraction problem the result is called the *difference*. In a division problem the first number is called the *dividend*, the second is called the *divisor*, and the result is called the *quotient*.

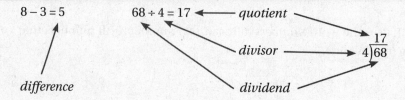

$8 − 3 = 5$          $68 ÷ 4 = 17$ ⟵ quotient

difference          divisor

dividend

You can always add, subtract, or multiply two numbers. You can always divide a number by a nonzero number, but you can never divide by zero.

---

**EXAMPLE 1**

There are two positive integers whose difference is 2 and quotient is $\frac{4}{3}$

| Quantity A | Quantity B |
|:---:|:---:|
| Sum of the numbers | Product of the numbers |

**Solution:** As their quotient is $\frac{4}{3}$, the numbers must be multiples of 4 and 3 since

$$\frac{4}{3} = \frac{8}{6} = \frac{12}{9} = \frac{16}{12} = \cdots$$

Because the difference between the numbers is 2 they must be 8 and 6. $8 + 6 = 14$, and $8 \times 6 = 48$. Choose **B**.

**Alternate solution:** We use algebra (see Solving Systems of Linear Equations on page 111). Let $x$ and $y$ be the two numbers. We have $x − y = 2$ and $\frac{x}{y} = \frac{4}{3}$. If we multiply both sides by $y$ in the second equation, we get $x = \frac{4}{3}y$. Substitute into the first equation and solve for $y$.

$$\frac{4}{3}y − y = 2$$
$$\left(\frac{4}{3} − 1\right)y = 2$$
$$\frac{1}{3}y = 2$$
$$y = 6$$

Substitute $y = 6$ into the first equation $x − (6) = 2$, and then solve to find $x = 8$. So their sum is $6 + 8 = 14$, and their product is $6 \times 8 = 48$. Choose **B**.

---

## Basic Properties

Our number system has many properties.

- Both addition and multiplication are *commutative*; that means you get the same result no matter what order you perform the operation: $7 + 9 = 9 + 7$ and $5 \times 11 = 11 \times 5$.

- Subtraction and division are not commutative; as you can see, since $4 - 3 \neq 3 - 4$ and $8 \div 4 \neq 4 \div 8$.

- Every number $a$ has an *opposite* (or additive inverse), which is $-a$ and $a + (-a) = 0 = (-a) + a$. The opposite of 3 is $-3$ and the opposite of $-3$ is $-(-3) = 3$. Subtracting a number is the same as adding its opposite, $8 - 5 = 8 + (-5) = 3$.

- Every nonzero number $a$ has a *reciprocal* (or multiplicative inverse) which is $\dfrac{1}{a}$ and $a \times \dfrac{1}{a} = 1 = \dfrac{1}{a} \times a$. The reciprocal of 5 is $\dfrac{1}{5}$ and the reciprocal of $\dfrac{2}{3}$ is $\dfrac{1}{\frac{2}{3}} = \dfrac{1 \times 3}{\frac{2}{3} \times 3} = \dfrac{3}{2}$.

  The reciprocal of $\dfrac{a}{b}$ is $\dfrac{b}{a}$. Dividing by a number is the same as multiplying by its reciprocal: $20 \div 5 = 20 \times \dfrac{1}{5} = \dfrac{20}{5} = 4$.

- Multiplication *distributes* over addition: $5 \times (6 + 7) = (5 \times 6) + (5 \times 7)$. Also $(5 + 6) \times 7 = (5 \times 7) + (6 \times 7)$.

- Multiply any number, $a$, by the number 1, and the product is that number: $a \times 1 = 1 \times a = a$. The number 1 is called the *multiplicative identity*.

- Add zero to any number, $a$, and the sum is that number: $a + 0 = 0 + a = a$. Zero is called the *additive identity*.

- Multiply any number by zero, and the product is zero. For example, $5 \times 0 = 0$, $\pi \times 0 = 0$, and even $0 \times 0 = 0$.

- If the product of two or more numbers is zero, one of them must be zero. If $a \times b = 0$ then $a = 0$ or $b = 0$.

---

**EXAMPLE 2**

| Quantity A | Quantity B |
|---|---|
| $\dfrac{5 \times (2 + 11)}{\frac{34}{7} + \frac{1}{9}} \times \dfrac{\frac{1}{9} + \frac{34}{7}}{(5 \times 2) + (5 \times 11)}$ | $1$ |

**Solution:** There is no need to do any long and difficult computation to solve this problem. The numerator of the first fraction equals the denominator of the second fraction because of the distributive property. The denominator of the first fraction equals the numerator of the second fraction because of the commutative property. Thus, the second fraction is the reciprocal of the first. The product of a number and its reciprocal is always 1. So the answer is **C**, they are equal.

EXAMPLE 3

| Quantity A | Quantity B |
|---|---|
| 34 × 71 ÷ 32 × 0 × 113 | 34 + 71 − 32 + 0 + 113 |

**Solution:** Do not try to compute the results here. Quantity A has zero as a factor. Anything multiplied by zero will be zero. So Quantity A is zero. Without computing, it is still clear that Quantity B is greater than zero, as only 32 is subtracted and the other values clearly add up to more than 32. Hence the answer is **B**.

EXAMPLE 4

*a* is a nonzero number

| Quantity A | Quantity B |
|---|---|
| The product of the opposite of *a* and the reciprocal of *a*. | The product of *a* and the reciprocal of *a*. |

**Solution:** A good strategy for this problem is to use a number for *a*, say 4. The opposite of 4 is −4 and the reciprocal of 4 is $\frac{1}{4}$. So Quantity A is $-4 \times \frac{1}{4} = -1$. In fact for any number *a*, Quantity A is $-a \times \frac{1}{a} = \frac{-a}{a} = -1$. Quantity B is 1, since the product of any number and its reciprocal is 1. So Quantity **B** is larger.

## Absolute Value

The absolute value of a number is its distance from zero on the number line. For example $|3| = 3$ and $|-7| = 7$.

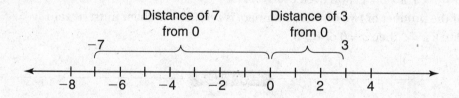

Of course the absolute value of zero is zero. If a number is positive, its absolute value is itself. If a number is negative, its absolute value is the number without the negative sign $|-7| = 7$. It is also the opposite of the negative number. For instance, $|-7| = -(-7) = 7$. This approach to absolute value can be very useful when dealing with expressions.

EXAMPLE 5

| Quantity A | Quantity B |
|---|---|
| $|3 - \pi|$ | $\pi - 3$ |

**Solution 1:** Recall that $\pi$ is approximately 3.14 ($\pi \approx 3.14$). $3 - \pi$ is negative, as 3 is less than $\pi$. Hence, the absolute value of $3 - \pi$ is its opposite: $-(3 - \pi) = -3 - (-\pi) = -3 + \pi$. Clearly this is equal to $\pi - 3$ so the answer is **C**.

**Solution 2:** Recall that $\pi$ is approximately 3.14. So $|3 - \pi| \approx |-.14| = .14$. Quantity B, $\pi - 3 \approx 3.14 - 3 = .14$. Choose **C**.

**EXAMPLE 6**

| Quantity A | Quantity B |
|---|---|
| $\left\|\dfrac{\pi - 4}{5^2 - 3^2}\right\|$ | $\left\|\dfrac{4 - \pi}{5^2 - 3^2}\right\|$ |

**Solution:** There is no need to do any computations here. Notice that the only difference is the numerators and $-(\pi - 4) = 4 - \pi$. So the numbers inside the absolute value signs are opposites of each other (opposite of $\dfrac{a}{b}$ is $-\dfrac{a}{b}$). Thus the answer is **C**.

## Order of Operations: PEMDAS

When performing multiple operations there is a standard order in which they must be applied. In most cases parentheses make this clear, but when there is uncertainty follow these guidelines.

<u>P</u>arentheses—First do any operations in parentheses (. . .), using PEMDAS if necessary.

<u>E</u>xponents—Second, evaluate all powers $a^b$. If need be, evaluate the exponent before calculating the power.

<u>M</u>ultiplication and <u>D</u>ivision—Next multiply and divide in order from left to right. Multiplication and division have equal priority so do not do all multiplications and then all divisions.

<u>A</u>ddition and <u>S</u>ubtraction—Finally add and subtract in order from left to right. Addition and subtraction have equal priority so do not do all additions and then all subtractions.

The order of operations can easily be remembered using the mnemonic "<u>P</u>lease <u>E</u>xcuse <u>My</u> <u>D</u>ear <u>A</u>unt <u>S</u>ally" or just PEMDAS. Here are some examples of PEMDAS being used:

| | | | | |
|---|---|---|---|---|
| $(9 - 6) \div 3$ | [*Parentheses*] | | $9 - 6 \div 3$ | [*Divide*] |
| $= 3 \div 3$ | [*Divide*] | | $= 9 - 2$ | [*Subtract*] |
| $= 1$ | | | $= 7$ | |

In the first example, parentheses force subtraction to take place before division.

| | | | | |
|---|---|---|---|---|
| $6 \div 3 \times 2 \div 4$ | [*Divide*] | | $6 \div (3 \times 2) \div 4$ | [*Parentheses*] |
| $= 2 \times 2 \div 4$ | [*Multiply*] | | $= 6 \div 6 \div 4$ | [*Divide (L to R)*] |
| $= 4 \div 4$ | [*Divide*] | | $= 1 \div 4$ | [*Divide*] |
| $= 1$ | | | $= \dfrac{1}{4}$ | |

Remember to proceed from left to right with multiplication and division doing whichever comes first. When multiplication is done before the division (the right example) again the result is very different.

$$(5 \times 2 - 3)^2 - 9 \quad [\textit{Parentheses Multiply}]$$
$$= (10 - 3)^2 - 9 \quad [\textit{Parentheses Subtract}]$$
$$= (7)^2 - 9 \quad [\textit{Exponents}]$$
$$= 49 - 9 \quad [\textit{Subtract}]$$
$$= 40$$

This example shows that PEMDAS applies inside the parentheses as well.

$$4^{5-3}$$
$$= 4^{(5-3)} \quad [\textit{Parentheses}]$$
$$= 4^2 \quad\quad [\textit{Exponent}]$$
$$= 16$$

Finally we see that sometimes complicated expressions appear in the exponent. We should always evaluate the exponent $(5 - 3)$ before calculating the power $(4^2)$. You might say that implicitly all exponents are parenthesized.

---

### EXAMPLE 7

What is the difference between $(6 \times (2^3 + 24)) \div 3$ and $6 \times 2^3 + 24 \div 3$?

(A) 8

(B) 24

(C) 40

(D) 56

(E) 64

**Solution:** Well let's calculate. We start with the exponent inside the innermost parentheses $(6 \times (2^3 + 24)) \div 3$ [exponent] $= (6 \times (8 + 24)) \div 3$ [add] $= (6 \times 32) \div 3$ [multiply] $= 192 \div 3$ [divide] $= 64$. In the second expression, $6 \times 2^3 + 24 \div 3$ [exponents] $= 6 \times 8 + 24 \div 3$ [multiply] $= 48 + 24 \div 3$ [divide] $= 48 + 8$ [add] $= 56$. The answers are 64 and 56, which has a difference of 8. The answer is **A**.

---

### EXAMPLE 8

$(100 - 2)^2 - 4 =$

(A) 964

(B) 9,600

(C) 9,604

(D) 9,996

(E) 9,992

**Solution:** Apply PEMDAS, and calculate $(100 - 2)^2 - 4 = 98^2 - 4 = 9,604 - 4 = 9,600$. Choose **B**.

---

## PROBLEMS (Solutions on page 87)
## Basic Problems

1. When the positive integer $n$ is divided by 9, the quotient is 8 and the remainder is 7. What is the value of $n$?

2. Which of the following is equal to the reciprocal of $\frac{2}{5}$?

Indicate *all* that apply.

A $\dfrac{\frac{1}{5}}{2}$

B 2.5

C $5 \div 2$

3.

| Quantity A | Quantity B |
|---|---|
| $a$ | opposite of $a$ |

4.

$$abc = 0, \text{ and } b > 1$$

| Quantity A | Quantity B |
|---|---|
| $a$ | $c$ |

5.

| Quantity A | Quantity B |
|---|---|
| $\left| \dfrac{3,456 - 2,345}{34 \times 24 \div 14} \right|$ | $-1$ |

6.

| Quantity A | Quantity B |
|---|---|
| $2 + 8 \div 4 \times 3$ | $((2 + 8) \div 4) \times 3$ |

## GRE Problems

7.

$$0 < a < b < c < 10$$

| Quantity A | Quantity B |
|---|---|
| $c \div a$ | $b$ |

8.

$$1 < x \le y < 2$$

| Quantity A | Quantity B |
|---|---|
| $x + y$ | $xy$ |

9.

There are two positive integers, $a$ and $b$, whose sum is 11 and product is 30

| Quantity A | Quantity B |
|---|---|
| $a - b$ | $\dfrac{a}{b}$ |

10.

$a$ is a nonzero number

| Quantity A | Quantity B |
|---|---|
| The quotient of the opposite of $a$ and the reciprocal of $a$ | The quotient of $a$ and the reciprocal of $a$ |

11.

$a$ is an integer, and $|a| \le 2$

| Quantity A | Quantity B |
|---|---|
| $(a + 2)(a + 1)a(a - 1)(a - 2)$ | $4$ |

12.

$a \ne b$, and $|b - a| = a - b$

| Quantity A | Quantity B |
|---|---|
| $a$ | $b$ |

# INTEGERS

The integers consist of zero and all positive and negative whole numbers.

$$\text{Integers} = \{\ldots, -3, -2, -1, 0, 1, 2, 3, \ldots\}$$

All integers are rational numbers but not all rational numbers are integers. For instance, $5 = \frac{10}{2}$ but $\frac{1}{2}$ cannot be expressed as an integer since it is not a whole number.

The *positive integers* are $\{1, 2, 3, 4, \ldots\}$, and the *negative integers* are $\{\ldots, -4, -3, -2, -1\}$. Neither set includes zero. Zero is neither positive nor negative.

---

**EXAMPLE 1**

How many integer solutions are there to the equation $(x - 2)(2x - 1)(x + 3) = 0$?

(A) 0

(B) 1

(C) 2

(D) 3

(E) None of the above

**Solution:** A product can only be zero if one of the multiplicands is zero. So at least one of $(x - 2)$, $(2x - 1)$, and $(x + 3)$ must equal zero. We solve each

$$\begin{array}{ccc}
x - 2 = 0 & 2x - 1 = 0 & x + 3 = 0 \\
x = 2 & 2x = 1 & x = -3 \\
& x = \dfrac{1}{2} &
\end{array}$$

We conclude that there are three solutions: $x = -3$, $x = 2$, and $x = \frac{1}{2}$. But $\frac{1}{2}$ is not an integer so the answer is **C**.

---

All integers are (real) numbers, but not all numbers are integers. In fact a common mistake is to overlook answers that are not integers.

---

**EXAMPLE 2**

Which of the following numbers satisfies the inequality $x^2 > 89.89$?

Indicate *all* that apply.

[A] 20

[B] 9.89

[C] 8.99

[D] −8.88

[E] −9.99

[F] −99

**Solution:** Because $x^2 > 89.89$, it is tempting to take the square root of each side to obtain $x > 9.48$. Then you would mark A and B. Those choices do work, but don't forget that a negative squared is positive. This means that choices E and F work too, because in absolute value they are also greater than $\sqrt{89.89}$. For example, $(-9.99)^2 \approx 100$. Choose **A, B, E,** and **F.**

---

You can add, subtract, or multiply integers, and the result is always an integer. Dividing integers may result in a noninteger fraction $(6 \div 10 = \frac{3}{5})$, may result in an integer $(6 \div 3 = 2)$, or may be impossible $(6 \div 0$ is undefined).

---

**EXAMPLE 3**

Find all positive integers $n$ so that $n^2 = |n|$.

(A) $n = -1, 1$
(B) $n = -2, -1, 1, 2$
(C) $n = -1, 0, 1$
(D) $n = 1$
(E) None of the above

**Solution:** We are only looking for positive $n$ so we can substitute $n^2$ for $|n|$. Thus we need to solve for $n$ in the equation $n^2 = n$.

$$n^2 - n = 0 \text{ [bring everything to one side]}$$
$$n(n - 1) = 0 \text{ [factor]}$$
$$n = 0 \text{ or } n - 1 = 0$$
$$n = 0 \text{ or } n = 1.$$

Zero is not a positive integer but 1 is. The answer is **D**.

---

**TIP**

If $n$ is odd, the sum of $n$ consecutive numbers is $n$ times the middle number.

## Consecutive Integers

A sequence of integers that increase (or decrease) by one are called consecutive integers. 3, 4, 5, 6, 7 are consecutive integers but 3, 4, 7, 5, 6 are not. Also, −2, −3, −4, −5 are consecutive integers but 8, 6, 4, 2 are not.

---

**EXAMPLE 4**

The sum of three consecutive integers is 21. What is the smallest of the three integers?

**Solution:** A conventional way to solve this problem is to use algebra. If the smallest of the three numbers is $x$, then the three consecutive integers are $x$, $x + 1$, and $x + 2$. Their sum is 21 so $x + (x + 1) + (x + 2) = 21$, We can solve for $x$.

$$x + (x + 1) + (x + 2) = 21$$
$$3x + 3 = 21$$
$$3x = 18$$
$$x = 6.$$

Hence, the smallest of the consecutive integers is 6 so the answer is **6**.

---

**EXAMPLE 5**

| Quantity A | Quantity B |
|---|---|
| Sum of integers from 1 to 13 | Sum of integers from 15 to 19 |

**Solution:** Since there are 13 consecutive numbers from 1 to 13 and 7 is the middle number, the sum $1 + 2 + \cdots + 13 = 13 \times 7 = 91$. Similarly, $15 + 16 + 17 + 18 + 19 = 5 \times 17 = 85$. Choose **A**.

## PROBLEMS (Solutions on page 88)

## Basic Problems

IN QUESTIONS 1–3, $x$ AND $y$ ARE NEGATIVE INTEGERS.

| | Quantity A | Quantity B |
|---|---|---|
| 1. | $x - y$ | $x + y$ |

| | Quantity A | Quantity B |
|---|---|---|
| 2. | $xy$ | $x + y$ |

| | Quantity A | Quantity B |
|---|---|---|
| 3. | $xy$ | $x - y$ |

IN QUESTIONS 4 AND 5, $a$, $b$, AND $c$, IN THAT ORDER, ARE CONSECUTIVE INCREASING INTEGERS.

| | Quantity A | Quantity B |
|---|---|---|
| 4. | $a - b$ | $b - c$ |

| | Quantity A | Quantity B |
|---|---|---|
| 5. | $a - b$ | $c - b$ |

6. $n$ is an integer such that $n^2 \le n$

| Quantity A | Quantity B |
|---|---|
| $n$ | 1 |

7. $n$ is an integer such that $n^2 \ge 5$

| Quantity A | Quantity B |
|---|---|
| $n$ | 2 |

| | Quantity A | Quantity B |
|---|---|---|
| 8. | Product of consecutive integers from −5 to 5 | Product of consecutive integers from −5 to 10 |

9. The sum of nine consecutive even integers is zero. What is the greatest of these integers?

10. If $P$ is the product of five consecutive positive integers, what is the remainder when $P$ is divided by 5?

$$\boxed{\phantom{xxxxxxxxxx}}$$

11. If the sum of three consecutive integers is 39, what is their product?

$$\boxed{\phantom{xxxxxxxxxx}}$$

12. The product of three consecutive odd integers is 693. What is the sum of the integers?

$$\boxed{\phantom{xxxxxxxxxx}}$$

13. How many positive integers satisfy $x^2 \leq 9$?

(A) Infinitely many

(B) 0

(C) 1

(D) 2

(E) 3

14. If $x$ and $y$ are integers so that $-3 \leq x \leq 3$ and $-3 \leq y \leq 3$, what is the smallest integer that $x - y$ could be?

(A) $-5$

(B) $-3$

(C) $-2$

(D) 21

(E) None of the above

## GRE Problems

15. If $x$ and $y$ are integers such that $-9 \leq x \leq 7$, and $-8 \leq y \leq 10$, what is the greatest possible value of $xy$?

$$\boxed{\phantom{xxxxxxxxxx}}$$

16. For how many integers, $x$, is $x^2 + x + 1 \leq 2$?

(A) Infinitely many

(B) 0

(C) 1

(D) 2

(E) 3

17. For how many negative integers, $x$, is $x^3 \geq x^2$?

    (A) 0

    (B) 1

    (C) 2

    (D) 3

    (E) None of the above

18. The product of three consecutive integers is negative. What is the largest value one of those integers could have?

    (A) 1

    (B) 0

    (C) −1

    (D) −2

    (E) −3

19. The average of $n$ consecutive integers is one of those integers. Which of the following could be $n$?

    (A) 2

    (B) 3

    (C) 4

    (D) 8

    (E) 16

20. Let $S$ be the sum of five consecutive integers. Which of the following must be true?

    Indicate *all* that apply.

    A  $S$ is a multiple of 5.

    B  $S$ is greater than or equal to 15.

    C  $S$ is odd.

21. Let $S$ be the sum of five consecutive positive integers. Which of the following *cannot* be true?

    Indicate *all* that apply.

    A  $S$ is divisible by 5.

    B  $S$ is less than 10.

    C  $S$ is even.

22. If the sum of four consecutive integers is 46, what is the sum of the next three consecutive integers?

23. If $a$, $b$, and $c$ are consecutive positive integers, what must be true of the number $abc + 1$?

(A) It is a perfect square.
(B) It is prime.
(C) It is odd.
(D) It is a multiple of 5.
(E) It is greater than 12.

IN QUESTIONS 24 AND 25, $a$, $b$ ARE CONSECUTIVE DECREASING INTEGERS.

| 24. | Quantity A | Quantity B |
|---|---|---|
| | $a^2 - ab$ | $a$ |

| 25. | Quantity A | Quantity B |
|---|---|---|
| | $a^2$ | $a + ab$ |

| 26. | Quantity A | Quantity B |
|---|---|---|
| | Sum of consecutive integers from −5 to 5 | Sum of consecutive integers from −10 to 10 |

## NUMBER THEORY

If you divide one integer by another and there is no remainder, then we can write an equation like $24 \div 8 = 3$ or the equivalent relationship $24 = 8 \times 3$. This relationship will illustrate at least four definitions.

8 is a _divisor_ of 24 since $24 \div 8 = 3$ with no remainder (3 is also a divisor of 24).
24 is _divisible_ by 8 since $24 \div 8 = 3$ with no remainder (24 is also divisible by 3).
24 is a _multiple_ of 8 since $24 = 8 \times 3$ (24 is also a multiple of 3).
8 is a _factor_ of 24 since $24 = 8 \times 3$ (3 is also a factor of 24).

Note that zero is divisible by any nonzero number $n$, since $n$ divides evenly into zero, zero times. For instance, $0 \div 7 = 0$ so 0 is divisible by 7.

---

**EXAMPLE 1**

Which of the following is a multiple of 2 and a factor of 36?
(A) 8
(B) 9
(C) 10
(D) 12
(E) 16

**Solution:** Multiples of 2 include 2, 4, 6, 8, 10, 12, 14, and 16 so B is not the answer. The factors of 36 are 1, 36, 2, 18, 3, 12, 4, 9, and 6. So the solution is 12—**D**.

---

- **1 and the number itself are always factors.**

- **Factors usually come in pairs (24 = 8 × 3 and 24 = 2 × 12) but the number of factors is not always even.**

- **Only perfect squares have an odd number of positive factors. For instance, 36 has nine factors (1, 2, 3, 4, 6, 9, 12, 18, and 36) and 16 has five factors (1, 2, 4, 8, and 16).**

**EXAMPLE 2**

Which of the following has exactly three positive factors?

(A) 8

(B) 18

(C) 25

(D) 36

(E) 64

**Solution:** We know that only perfect squares have an odd number of positive factors. As 8 and 18 are not perfect squares, we will check 25, 36, and 64. The positive factors of 25 are 1, 25, and 5. So the answer is **C**. Just to double check we find the positive factors of 36 (1, 2, 3, 4, 6, 9, 12, 18, and 36) and see there are nine of them. Also, 64 has seven positive factors (1, 2, 4, 8, 16, 32, and 64).

## Divisibility Rules

Sometimes you may want to test if one number is divisible by another number. One easy way to do this is to divide the numbers on the calculator. If the result is a whole number with no decimal part, the first number is divisible by the second number. For example, 9,876 is not divisible by 9, because the result of $9,876 \div 9$ is $1,097.3333 \ldots$, not an integer.

There are also many classic rules for checking if an integer is divisible by a specific number, quickly, efficiently, and without having to open the calculator. For instance, most people know that a number that ends in 0 is a multiple of ten. We present rules for divisibility by 2, 3, 4, 5, 6, 8, and 9:

- A number is divisible by 2 when the ones digits is 0, 2, 4, 6, or 8.
- A number is divisible by 3 when the sum of its digits is divisible by 3.
- A number is divisible by 4 when the last two digits are divisible by 4.
- A number is divisible by 5 when the ones digits is 0 or 5.
- A number is divisible by 6 when it is divisible by 2 and 3.
- A number is divisible by 8 when the last three digits are divisible by 8.
- A number is divisible by 9 when the sum of its digits is divisible by 9.

**TIP**

While not applicable for all numbers, a number is divisible by 7 if it can be separated into groups of adjacent digits that are multiples of 7. For instance, 14,287 is divisible by 7 since 14, 28, and 7 are all multiples of 7. This idea works for any divisor, not just 7. You can see that 2,255 is divisible by 11 since 22 and 55 are multiples of 11.

Here is an example of how knowing these rules can be useful and much faster than crunching numbers on a calculator.

EXAMPLE 3

The number 254,688 is divisible by which of the following?

Indicate *all* that apply.

- **A** 2
- **B** 3
- **C** 4
- **D** 5
- **E** 6
- **F** 7
- **G** 8
- **H** 9

**Solution:** 254,688 is divisible by 2 since the last digit is 8 (even). 254,688 is divisible by 4 since 88, the last two digits, is divisible by 4. 254,688 is divisible by 8 since 688, the last three digits, is divisible by 8. 254,688 is divisible by 3 since 2 + 5 + 4 + 6 + 8 + 8 = 33, which is divisible by 3. 254,688 is divisible by 6 since it is divisible by 2 and 3. 254,688 is not divisible by 9 since 2 + 5 + 4 + 6 + 8 + 8 = 33, which is not divisible by 9. 254,688 is not divisible by 5 since it does not end in 0 or 5. 254,688 is an example of a number that is divisible by 7 even though the tip above does not help us determine that. The easiest way to check is to use the calculator to divide: 254,688 ÷ 7 = 36,384. So the correct answers are **A, B, C, E, F**, and **G**.

EXAMPLE 4

Which of the following is divisible by 3 but not 4?

- **A** 144
- **B** 84
- **C** 48
- **D** 40
- **E** 30

**Solution:** 144 = 12 × 12 and 12 = 3 × 4 so 144 is a multiple of 4 and A is not the answer. In fact any number divisible by 12 will be divisible by 3 and 4. As 84 = 7 × 12 and 48 = 4 × 12, neither is the answer. Since 40 is divisible by 4 (40 ÷ 4 = 10), it cannot be the answer. That leaves 30 which is divisible by 3, 30 = 3 × 10, and not divisible by 4, 30 ÷ 4 = 7 R2. The answer is **E**.

**EXAMPLE 5**

If $d$ represents a single digit from 0 to 9 and $3023783d93$ is divisible by 9, what is $d$?

(A) 0

(B) 2

(C) 5

(D) 7

(E) None of the above

**Solution:** To be divisible by 9 the sum of the digits must be divisible by 9. In this case the sum of the digits is $3 + 0 + 2 + 3 + 7 + 8 + 3 + d + 9 + 3 = 38 + d$. The first multiple of 9 after 38 is 45. So $38 + d = 45$ or $d = 7$. The answer is **D**.

## Odds and Evens

An integer that is divisible by 2 is called *even*. If an integer is not even it is called *odd*. There are many equivalent ways to determine if a number is even or odd.

$n$ is even

$\Leftrightarrow n$ is a multiple of two

$\Leftrightarrow n \div 2$ has remainder 0

$\Leftrightarrow n$ has ones digit 0, 2, 4, 6 or 8

$n$ is odd

$\Leftrightarrow n$ is one more than a multiple of two

$\Leftrightarrow n \div 2$ has remainder 1

$\Leftrightarrow n$ has ones digit 1, 3, 5, 7, or 9

Odd and even numbers have many nice properties. Some are illustrated in the table below.

| Property | Example |
|---|---|
| Sum of evens is even | $4 + 8 = 12$ |
| Sum of two odds is even | $7 + 11 = 18$ |
| Odd plus even is odd | $5 + 6 = 11$ |
| Product of odds is odd | $5 \times 7 = 35$ |
| Product of an even integer and any integer is even | $6 \times 4 = 24$ and $6 \times 5 = 30$ |

**EXAMPLE 6**

If *E* is even and *O* is odd, which of the following is even?

(A) $E + O$

(B) $5 \times 7 \times 9 \times E$

(C) $5 + 7 + 9 + E$

(D) $O \times (E + 1)$

(E) $O \times (E - 1)$

**Solution:** An even plus an odd is odd—A is not the answer. Anything ($5 \times 7 \times 9$) times an even is even. The answer is **B**. Let's check the other answers, too. In C, 5 + 7 is even since it's odd plus odd. 9 + *E* is odd since it's odd plus even. So even (5 + 7) plus odd (9 + *E*) is odd. C is not the answer. Since *E* is even, *E* + 1 is odd. An odd, *O*, times an odd, *E* + 1, is odd. D is not the answer. Since *E* is even, *E* − 1 is odd. An odd, *O*, times an odd, *E* − 1, is odd. E is not the answer.

## Prime Numbers

A positive integer is called *prime* if it has exactly two distinct positive factors.

| Number | Positive Factors | Primality |
|:------:|:----------------:|:---------:|
| 1 | 1 | Not prime |
| 2 | 1, 2 | Prime |
| 3 | 1, 3 | Prime |
| 4 | 1, 2, 4 | Not prime |
| 5 | 1, 5 | Prime |
| 6 | 1, 2, 3, 6 | Not prime |
| 7 | 1, 7 | Prime |
| 8 | 1, 2, 4, 8 | Not prime |

**Notes:**

- 1 is not a prime. It has only one positive factor—itself.
- A prime number can only be the product of two positive integers if they are one and itself. If it can be factored any other way as the product of positive integers then it is not a prime number. For instance, $24 = 4 \times 6$ so 24 is not a prime.
- 2 is the only even prime number.
- There are an infinite number of primes.
- You should recognize small primes like 2, 3, 5, 7, 11, 13, 17, 19, 23, 29, etc. Memorize them if you don't know them.

**TIP**

To check if a number is prime, you need only see if it is divisible by any primes from 2 up to the square root of the number. Consider 79. $\sqrt{79} \approx 8.9$ so we check if 79 is divisible by primes from 2 to 8.9, that would be 2, 3, 5, and 7. Now 79 ÷ 2 = 39 R1, 79 ÷ 3 = 26 R1, 79 ÷ 5 = 15 R4, and 79 ÷ 7 = 11 R2. In all four cases there is a remainder, so 79 is not divisible by any of the primes 2, 3, 5, and 7. Thus 79 is prime.

**EXAMPLE 7**

Which of the following numbers are prime?

Indicate *all* that apply.

- [A] 49
- [B] 51
- [C] 53
- [D] 55
- [E] 57
- [F] 59
- [G] 63

**Solution:** If you remember your times tables, you may recognize that 49 is $7 \times 7$ and 63 is $9 \times 7$. Then eliminate A and G; by definition, 49 and 63 are not prime because they have factors other than 1 and the number itself. D can be eliminated because a number ending in 5 or 0 is divisible by 5. We are left to consider 51, 53, 57, and 59. Notice that 51 and 57 are composite by the divisibility test for the number 3, because $5 + 1 = 6$ and $5 + 7 = 12$. Since 6 and 12 are divisible by 3, so are 51 and 57. The remaining numbers, 53 and 59, are both prime. Choose **C** and **F**.

**EXAMPLE 8**

Which of the following is prime?

(A) 25
(B) $7^2 - 5^2$
(C) 51
(D) 73
(E) $2 \times 3 \times 5 + 3$

**Solution:** $25 = 5 \times 5$ so A is not prime. Using difference of squares we see that $7^2 - 5^2 = (7 - 5) \times (7 + 5) = 2 \times 12$ so B is not prime. Using the commutative and distributive laws $2 \times 3 \times 5 + 3 = 30 + 3 = 33 = 3 \times 11$ so E is not prime. To check if 51 is prime we need only check for divisibility by primes up to $\sqrt{51}$, which is a little more than 7 (recall $7^2 = 49$). So we check primes 2, 3, 5, and 7. 51 is odd so it is not divisible by 2. $5 + 1 = 6$ which is divisible by 3, so 51 is divisible by 3 (in fact $51 = 3 \times 17$). So C is not prime. That leaves only 73 to be a prime. The answer is **D**.

EXAMPLE 9

If $p$ and $q$ are odd primes, which of the following could be a prime?

(A) $pq$

(B) $p^2 + p$

(C) $p + q$

(D) $p + q + 1$

(E) $2p + 4q$

**Solution:** For A we see that $pq$ is not a prime since $pq = p \times q$ (and neither $p$ nor $q$ is 1). For B we factor $p^2 + p = p (p + 1)$ so it is not a prime. For C, $p$ and $q$ are both odd so $p + q$ is even. And, since 1 is not prime, $p + q$ cannot be equal to 2, $p + q$ is at least 3 + 5, so it is not prime. D is one more than C so it is odd, maybe it could be a prime. For E we factor $2p + 4q = 2(p + 2q)$ and see that it is not prime. So **D** is the only possible answer. And if $p = 3$ and $q = 7$ then $p + q + 1 = 11$, which is prime.

Every positive integer can be written uniquely as a product of primes. For example, $30 = 2 \times 3 \times 5$, $45 = 3^2 \times 5$, and $100 = 2^2 \times 5^2$. To find the *prime factorization* of a number first find two factors, then find the factors of the factors. Repeat until all your factors are prime. This is commonly done with a *factor tree*, as seen below.

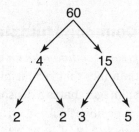

$$60 = 2 \times 2 \times 3 \times 5 = 2^2 \times 3 \times 5$$

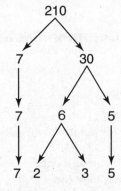

$$210 = 7 \times 2 \times 3 \times 5$$

The prime factorization is often easier to find than a list of all positive factors. Its structure can also identify a lot of information about the number quickly—for instance, the prime factors or the number of positive factors.

**EXAMPLE 10**

Which of the following has exactly three distinct *prime* factors?

(A) 20

(B) 30

(C) 49

(D) 91

(E) 320

**Solution:** We used factor trees (not shown) to find the prime factorization of each number.

$$20 = 2^2 \times 5$$
$$30 = 2 \times 3 \times 5$$
$$49 = 7^2$$
$$320 = 2^6 \times 5$$
$$420 = 2^2 \times 3 \times 5 \times 7$$

You can see that 20 has three prime factors (2, 2, and 5), but they are not all distinct. Also, 49 has three positive factors (1, 7, and 49), but they are not all prime. Clearly, 30 is the only given number with exactly three prime factors. The answer is **B**.

## Greatest Common Factor and Lowest Common Multiple

**TIP**

- $GCF(n,m) \leq n \leq m \leq LCM(n,m)$.
- $n \times m \div GCF(n,m) = LCM(n,m)$. This relationship can be very useful for determining one from the other.
- Another way to determine GCF is to write out the numbers' prime factorizations fully (no exponents) and take what they have in common.
- Another way to determine LCM is to write out the numbers' prime factorizations fully (no exponents) and for each prime take how many $n$ has or how many $m$ has, whichever is larger.

The GCF($a,b$) is the *greatest common factor* of two integers, $a$ and $b$—the largest number that is a factor of both $a$ and $b$. It is also the largest integer that is a divisor of both $a$ and $b$. For example, 15 has positive factors 1, 3, 5, and 15, while 24 has positive factors 1, 2, 3, 4, 6, 8, 12, and 24 so the GCF(15, 24) = 3.

The LCM($a,b$) is the *lowest common multiple* of $a$ and $b$—the smallest positive number that is a multiple of $a$ and is a multiple of $b$. 15 has multiples 15, 30, 45, 60, 75, 90, 105, 120, 135, etc., while 24 has multiples 24, 48, 72, 96, 120, 144, etc., so LCM(15, 24) = 120.

EXAMPLE 11

Find the GCF(36,60).

(A) 1

(B) 4

(C) 6

(D) 12

(E) 60

**Solution:** The positive factors of 36 are 1, 2, 3, 4, 6, 9, 12, 18, and 36. The positive factors of 60 are 1, 2, 3, 4, 5, 6, 10, 12, 15, 20, 30, and 60. Clearly the largest factor they have in common is 12 so the GCF(36,60) = 12. The answer is **D**.

EXAMPLE 12

If $a = 2^3 \times 3^2 \times 5$ and $b = 3^3 \times 5 \times 7$, find GCF($a,b$) + LCM($a,b$).

(A) 45

(B) 360

(C) $2^3 \times 3^5 \times 5^2 \times 7$

(D) 7,560

(E) 7,605

**Solution:** There is no nice formula for the sum of the GCF and LCM. This question is simply making you compute both of them. Since the prime factorization is already given to us, we'll use the techniques given in the tips above. First we'll find the GCF.

$$a = 2 \times 2 \times 2 \times \underline{3 \times 3 \times 5}$$
$$b = 3 \times \underline{3 \times 3 \times 5} \times 7$$

The common factors are 3, 3, and 5 so the GCF($a,b$) = $3^2 \times 5$ = 45. Now we find the LCM.

$$a = 2 \times 2 \times 2 \times 3 \times 3 \times 5$$
$$b = 3 \times 3 \times 3 \times 5 \times 7$$

Hence, LCM($a,b$) = $2 \times 2 \times 2 \times 3 \times 3 \times 3 \times 5 \times 7 = 2^3 \times 3^3 \times 5 \times 7 = 7,560$. Here we take three factors of 2 because $a$ has three and $b$ has none, we take three factors of 3 because $b$ has three and $a$ only two, we take one factor of 5 as both have one, and we take one factor of 7 as $b$ has one and $a$ has none.

Another way to compute the LCM, after finding the GCF, would be to take ($a \times b$) ÷ 45, as in the first tip above. The sum GCF($a,b$) + LCM($a,b$) is 45 + 7,560 = 7,605. The answer is **E**.

## PROBLEMS (Solutions on page 91)
## Basic Problems

1. 

| Quantity A | Quantity B |
|---|---|
| Smallest positive factor of 24 | Largest factor of 8 |

2. 

| Quantity A | Quantity B |
|---|---|
| Smallest prime factor of 91 | Largest prime factor of 63 |

3. 

| Quantity A | Quantity B |
|---|---|
| Number of even one-digit positive integers | Number of odd one-digit positive integers |

IN QUESTIONS 4 AND 5, *a* AND *b* ARE POSITIVE INTEGERS.

4. 

| Quantity A | Quantity B |
|---|---|
| $ab \div \text{GCF}(a,b)$ | $\text{LCM}(a,b)$ |

5. 

| Quantity A | Quantity B |
|---|---|
| $\text{LCM}(a,b) \times \text{GCF}(a,b)$ | $a \times b$ |

6. 

| Quantity A | Quantity B |
|---|---|
| An even prime number | 3 |

7. 

| Quantity A | Quantity B |
|---|---|
| An odd prime | 3 |

8. *N* is prime

| Quantity A | Quantity B |
|---|---|
| Product of positive factors of $N$ | $N$ |

9. The prime factorization of 72 is

(A) $2 \times 7$

(B) $2 \times 6^2$

(C) $2^3 \times 9$

(D) $8 \times 9$

(E) $2^3 \times 3^2$

10. *D* is a single digit so that $937,D24$ is divisible by 2, 3, 4, 8, and 9. What is *D*?

(A) 0

(B) 1

(C) 2

(D) 3

(E) Greater than 3

11. If $x$ is even and $y$ is odd, which of the following must be odd?

(A) $xy$

(B) $8x$

(C) $\dfrac{x}{2}$

(D) $x - y$

(E) $\dfrac{(y+1)}{2}$

## GRE Problems

IN QUESTIONS 12 AND 13, $x$ IS A POSITIVE INTEGER.

12.
| Quantity A | Quantity B |
|---|---|
| Twice the number of positive divisors of $x$ | Number of positive divisors of $2x$ |

13.
| Quantity A | Quantity B |
|---|---|
| Number of distinct prime factors of $x$ | Number of distinct prime factors of $2x$ |

14.
| Quantity A | Quantity B |
|---|---|
| Number of even two digit positive integers | Number of odd two digit positive integers |

$a$ and $b$ are positive integers

15.
| Quantity A | Quantity B |
|---|---|
| GCF($a,ab$) | GCF($b,ba$) |

16.
| Quantity A | Quantity B |
|---|---|
| Smallest positive multiple of 7 and 3 that is even | Smallest positive multiple of 7 and 3 that is odd |

17.
| Quantity A | Quantity B |
|---|---|
| Smallest positive number divisible by both 5 and 7 | 70 |

18.
| Quantity A | Quantity B |
|---|---|
| Largest number that is a factor of both 30 and 90 | 15 |

19. $N$ is greater than 4 and not prime

| Quantity A | Quantity B |
|---|---|
| Product of positive factors of $N$ | $2N$ |

20. $N$ is positive and divisible by 2, 3, 4, and 8

| Quantity A | Quantity B |
|---|---|
| $N$ | 192 |

21. $N$ is greater than 1,000 and divisible by 8

| Quantity A | Quantity B |
|---|---|
| $N$ | 1,004 |

22. If the sum of the positive factors of $N$ is $N + 1$, then $N$ must be

(A) odd

(B) even

(C) a perfect square

(D) prime

(E) not prime

23. Which of the following has precisely three positive factors?

Indicate *all* that apply.

[A] 8

[B] 12

[C] 15

[D] 25

[E] 39

[F] 49

[G] $19^2$

24. $D$ is a single digit so that $728, D49$ is divisible by 3 and 7. What is $D$?

(A) 0

(B) 1

(C) 2

(D) 3

(E) Greater than 3

25. If $p$ is an odd prime, which of the following could be a prime?

(A) $p^2$

(B) $p + 2$

(C) $p + 3$

(D) $17 \times 23$

(E) $71 \times 72 \times 73 + 3$

26. If $a$ is a factor of $b$, and $b$ is a factor of $c$, which of the following must be true?

Indicate *all* that apply.

[A] $c$ is a multiple of $b$

[B] $c$ is a multiple of $a$

[C] $c$ is a multiple of $ab$

[D] $a$ is a factor of $b + c$

# FRACTIONS

By forming ratios (fractions) of integers, but never dividing by zero, we obtain the rational numbers.

$$\text{Rational numbers} = \left\{\frac{a}{b} : a, b \text{ are integers}, b \neq 0\right\}$$

Fractions occur naturally in everyday life and thus occur in many GRE questions. If you have 3 chocolate bars and you want to share evenly with 5 of your friends, how will you do it? One way is to divide each bar into 6 pieces and each person gets one piece from each bar. So each person gets 3 pieces of size $\frac{1}{6}$ each. That is $\frac{3}{6}$. Another way is to divide each bar in half. Now you have 6 equal size portions (each $\frac{1}{2}$ a bar) so each person takes one. In either case each person gets the same amount of chocolate. We see that $\frac{3}{6} = \frac{1}{2}$.

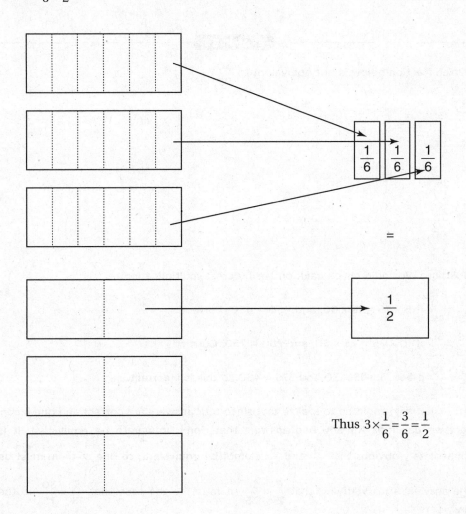

$$\text{Thus } 3 \times \frac{1}{6} = \frac{3}{6} = \frac{1}{2}$$

## Equivalent Fractions

Any given fraction can be expressed an infinite number of ways, for example $\frac{1}{2} = \frac{2}{4} = \frac{3}{6} = \frac{4}{8} = \ldots$ These are called *equivalent fractions* since they appear different but express the same value. One way to check if fractions are equivalent is to cross multiply.

$\frac{a}{b}$ is equivalent (equal) to $\frac{c}{d}$ if $a \times d = b \times c$. For example,

$\frac{6}{14}$ is equivalent to $\frac{3}{7}$ since $6 \times 7 = 14 \times 3$.

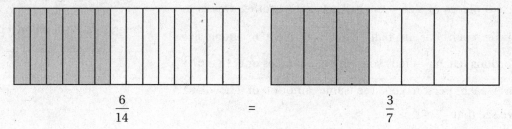

$$\frac{6}{14} \qquad = \qquad \frac{3}{7}$$

---

**EXAMPLE 1**

Which fraction below is not equivalent to $\frac{30}{75}$?

(A) $\frac{6}{15}$

(B) $\frac{10}{25}$

(C) $\frac{5}{15}$

(D) $\frac{2}{5}$

(E) $\frac{90}{225}$

**Solution:** We could check each one using cross multiplication.

$\frac{6}{15} = \frac{30}{75}$ if $6 \times 75 = 15 \times 30$, and $450 = 450$. Correct!

$\frac{10}{25} = \frac{30}{75}$ if $10 \times 75 = 25 \times 30$, and $750 = 750$. Correct!

$\frac{5}{15} = \frac{30}{75}$ if $5 \times 75 = 15 \times 30$ and $375 \neq 450$ so this is incorrect.

An easier way would be to realize that since four answers are correct and one incorrect we can look for any two answers that don't appear to be equivalent. It is immediately obvious that $\frac{6}{15}$ and $\frac{5}{15}$ cannot be equivalent, so one of them must be the answer. After verifying that $\frac{6}{15} = \frac{30}{75}$, it must be the case that $\frac{5}{15} \neq \frac{30}{75}$ so the answer is **C**.

For a given fractional value, there are many equivalent fractions. So which one should you use for an answer? The preferred answer is always the one *in lowest terms*. That is, the GCF of the numerator and denominator is 1. For example $\frac{12}{15}$ is not in lowest terms since the GCF(12,15) is not 1. But $\frac{12}{15}$ is equivalent to $\frac{4}{5}$ (check $12 \times 5 = 15 \times 4$) and GCF(4,5) is 1. So $\frac{4}{5}$ is in lowest terms.

The usual way to find lowest terms is to find common factors for the numerator and denominator and then use the Cancellation Law. *The Cancellation Law* says that if $b$ and $c$ are nonzero numbers, then $\frac{a \times b}{c \times b} = \frac{a}{c}$. We think of canceling the $b$'s, $\frac{a \times \not{b}}{c \times \not{b}}$ to be left with $\frac{a}{c}$. Using this law and sometimes several steps, we can reduce any fraction to lowest terms. For example, $\frac{75}{240} = \frac{\not{5} \times 15}{\not{5} \times 48} = \frac{15}{48} = \frac{\not{3} \times 5}{\not{3} \times 16} = \frac{5}{16}$.

Since GCF(5,16) = 1 this fraction is now in lowest terms.

---

**EXAMPLE 2**

Which fraction is not in lowest terms?

(A) $\frac{2}{3}$

(B) $\frac{4}{9}$

(C) $\frac{13}{39}$

(D) $\frac{10}{43}$

(E) $\frac{30}{49}$

**Solution:** For each fraction we look at the GCF (numerator, denominator). If it is 1, then the fraction is in lowest terms. It's easiest to check each individually.

GCF(2,3) = 1, not A.

GCF(4,9) = GCF(2 × 2, 3 × 3) = 1 so not B.

GCF(13,39) = GCF(13, 3 × 13) = 13. So $\frac{13}{39} = \frac{13}{3 \times 13} = \frac{1}{3}$. So $\frac{13}{39}$ is not in lowest terms.

The answer is **C**.

---

## Mixed Fractions

A mixed fraction (or mixed number) is an integer and a fraction added together but expressed without the plus sign. For example $3\frac{1}{3}$ (three and one-third), $5\frac{1}{2}$ (five and one-half), and $-3\frac{1}{4}$ (negative three and one-quarter) are all mixed fractions. Be careful, $3\frac{1}{4}$ means $3+\frac{1}{4}$, not $3 \times \frac{1}{4}$. Also, $-3\frac{1}{4} = -\left(3+\frac{1}{4}\right)$, not $-3+\frac{1}{4}$.

A fraction, $\frac{a}{b}$, can be expressed as a mixed fraction if $a > b$. For instance $\frac{3}{2} = \frac{1}{2} + \frac{1}{2} + \frac{1}{2} = 1 + \frac{1}{2} = 1\frac{1}{2}$. To convert from a fraction to a mixed fraction is easy—just divide $b$ into $a$. For example, as $7 \div 3 = 2$ R1, we know that $\frac{7}{3} = 2\frac{1}{3}$.

$$7 \div 3 = 2 \text{ R1}$$

$$\frac{7}{3} = 2\frac{1}{3}$$

A mixed fraction, $n\frac{p}{q}$, has an integer part $n$ and a fractional part $\frac{p}{q}$. To convert to a fraction, first multiply $n$ by $q$ and add $p$. The result is the numerator, while $q$ is still the denominator. For example $2\frac{1}{3} = \frac{(3 \times 2 + 1)}{3} = \frac{7}{3}$.

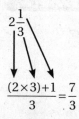

$$\frac{(2 \times 3) + 1}{3} = \frac{7}{3}$$

---

### EXAMPLE 3

Which of the following mixed fractions are equivalent to 12/5?

(A) $1\frac{2}{5}$

(B) $2\frac{1}{5}$

(C) $2\frac{2}{5}$

(D) $5\frac{1}{2}$

(E) $12\frac{1}{5}$

**Solution:** Let's convert each answer to a fraction.

$1\frac{2}{5} = \frac{(5 \times 1) + 2}{5} = \frac{7}{5}$, which is clearly not correct.

$2\frac{1}{5} = \frac{(5 \times 2) + 1}{5} = \frac{11}{5}$, which is not correct.

$2\frac{2}{5} = \frac{(5 \times 2) + 2}{5} = \frac{12}{5}$, which is correct!

Alternatively, we could have converted $\frac{12}{5}$ to a mixed fraction. $12 \div 5 = 2$ R2 so $\frac{12}{5} = 2\frac{2}{5}$. Either way, the answer is **C**.

# Operations on Fractions

It is easy *to add fractions* if they have the same denominator. For instance, two-fifths plus one-fifth equals three-fifths $\left(\dfrac{2}{5}+\dfrac{1}{5}=\dfrac{3}{5}\right)$ in the same way that two apples plus one apple equals three apples. More simply, when they have equal denominators, you add fractions by keeping the denominator and adding the numerators. $\dfrac{a}{b}+\dfrac{c}{b}=\dfrac{a+c}{b}$.

$$\frac{2}{5}+\frac{1}{5}=\frac{3}{5}$$

If they do not have equal denominators, you can use equivalent fractions to find a common denominator. Usually we use the lowest common multiple of the original denominators. For example, the LCM(2,5) = 10 so in the following problem we convert our original fractions to equivalent fractions with denominator 10.

$$\frac{1}{2}+\frac{3}{5}=\frac{?}{10}+\frac{?}{10}=\frac{5}{10}+\frac{6}{10}=\frac{5+6}{10}=\frac{11}{10}$$

$$\frac{1}{2}+\frac{3}{5}=\frac{11}{10}$$

**Diagram: Adding fractions**

*Subtraction* is very similar to addition. For example,

$$\frac{3}{5}-\frac{1}{2}=\frac{?}{10}-\frac{?}{10}=\frac{6}{10}-\frac{5}{10}=\frac{6-5}{10}=\frac{1}{10}.$$

*To multiply fractions*, simply multiply numerator by numerator and denominator by denominator to get the product. For example,

$$\frac{4}{7}\times\frac{2}{3}=\frac{4\times2}{7\times3}=\frac{8}{21}.$$

You can also see how this works pictorially. The product is the double shaded area in the diagram below.

$$\frac{4}{7}\times\frac{2}{3}=\frac{8}{21}$$

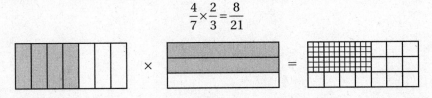

*To divide fractions* recall that for any numbers $x$ and $y$, $x \div y = x \times \dfrac{1}{y}$. When $x$ and $y$ are fractions, to divide we simply "invert and multiply." For example,

$$\frac{4}{3} \div \frac{2}{3} = \frac{4}{3} \times \frac{3}{2} = \frac{4^2 \times 3}{3 \times 2} = \frac{2}{1} = 2$$

This should seem appropriate since four apples (thirds) divided by two apples (thirds) equals two.

How can we *compare fractions*? Well, clearly $\dfrac{3}{5} < \dfrac{4}{5}$ (in the same way that three apples [fifths] is less than four apples [fifths]). How can we tell if $\dfrac{1}{2} > \dfrac{5}{10}$? The easiest way is to find a common denominator and then compare numerators. In this case LCM(2,5) = 10 so the denominator is 10. So $\dfrac{1}{2} = \dfrac{5}{10}$ and $\dfrac{2}{5} = \dfrac{4}{10}$. As $\dfrac{5}{10} > \dfrac{4}{10}$, we conclude that $\dfrac{1}{2} > \dfrac{2}{5}$.

---

### EXAMPLE 4

| Quantity A | Quantity B |
|---|---|
| $\dfrac{3}{10} \times \dfrac{5}{6} + \dfrac{1}{5}$ | $\dfrac{3}{10} \div \dfrac{5}{6} - \dfrac{1}{5}$ |

**Solution:** First we multiply $\dfrac{3}{10} \times \dfrac{5}{6} = \dfrac{3 \times 5}{2 \times 5 \times 2 \times 3} = \dfrac{1}{4}$. Now we add $\dfrac{1}{4} + \dfrac{1}{5}$. The LCM(4,5) = 20 so $\dfrac{1}{4} + \dfrac{1}{5} = \dfrac{5}{20} + \dfrac{4}{20} = \dfrac{9}{20}$.

Now to divide $\dfrac{3}{10} \div \dfrac{5}{6}$, we invert and multiply to get $\dfrac{3}{10} \times \dfrac{6}{5} = \dfrac{3 \times 2 \times 3}{2 \times 5 \times 5} = \dfrac{9}{25}$.

Now to compare $\dfrac{9}{20}$ and $\dfrac{9}{25}$ we could find a common denominator. The LCM(20,25) = 100 and $\dfrac{9}{20} = \dfrac{45}{100}$ and $\dfrac{9}{25} = \dfrac{36}{100}$. We see that $\dfrac{45}{100} > \dfrac{36}{100}$ and thus $\dfrac{9}{20} > \dfrac{9}{25}$.

Alternatively we might note that 9 divided into only 20 parts must be larger than 9 divided into a greater number (25) of parts. Even without subtracting $\dfrac{1}{5}$, which would make B even smaller, we already see that A is larger than B. The answer is **A**.

**EXAMPLE 5**

Which fraction is the largest?

(A) $\frac{11}{20}$  (B) $\frac{5}{6}$  (C) $\frac{5}{8}$  (D) $\frac{3}{7}$  (E) $\frac{2}{3}$

**Solution 1:** We'll use equivalent fractions and the first tip above to answer this question. First, we note that $\frac{5}{6} > \frac{5}{8}$ as the numerators are equal and 6 < 8. So C is not the answer. Then we note that $\frac{2}{3} = \frac{4}{6}$ and $\frac{4}{6} < \frac{5}{6}$ so E is not the answer. By the first tip $\frac{3}{7} < \frac{3}{6}$ and $\frac{3}{6} < \frac{5}{6}$ so D is not the answer. That leaves only A and B. We note that, $\frac{11}{20}$ is close to $\frac{10}{20}$, which equals $\frac{1}{2}$ and we know $\frac{5}{6} > \frac{3}{6} = \frac{1}{2}$. So we think B is the answer. Just to be absolutely certain, we can find a common denominator. As LCM(6,20) = 60 we find equivalent fractions $\frac{11}{20} = \frac{33}{60}$ and $\frac{5}{6} = \frac{50}{60}$. Clearly $\frac{50}{60} > \frac{33}{60}$ so $\frac{5}{6} > \frac{11}{20}$. The answer is **B**.

**Solution 2:** Many students would find it easier to type each fraction on the calculator, using the ÷ operation, in order to compare the decimal values of the answer choices. The calculator shows that $\frac{5}{6} \approx 0.833$, which is greater than any of the other choices. Choose **B**.

## Simplifying Complex Fractions

Sometimes you have to deal with *complex fractions*—fractions where the numerator and denominator are not just numbers but expressions or even other fractions. What is the best way to simplify these expressions? Consider for example, the fraction $\dfrac{\frac{1}{2} + \frac{4}{5}}{\frac{3}{10} - \frac{1}{4}}$.

First, we simplify it using PEMDAS—the numerator and denominator are treated like parentheses.

$$\frac{1}{2}+\frac{4}{5}=\frac{5}{10}+\frac{8}{10}=\frac{13}{10} \text{ and } \frac{3}{10}-\frac{1}{4}=\frac{6}{20}-\frac{5}{20}=\frac{1}{20}$$

$$\text{hence } \frac{\dfrac{1}{2}+\dfrac{4}{5}}{\dfrac{13}{10}-\dfrac{1}{4}}=\frac{\dfrac{13}{10}}{\dfrac{1}{20}}=\frac{13}{10}\times\frac{20}{1}=\frac{13\times2\times10}{10}=\frac{26}{1}=26$$

Second, we try an alternate technique called *clearing the denominators*. Multiplying both numerator and denominator by the same number does not change the value of the fraction, it simply makes an equivalent fraction. So we carefully choose a multiplier as the LCM of all denominators in the expression. LCM(2,5,4,10) is 20. This technique makes numbers larger but reduces the amount of work with fractions. First, we have $\dfrac{20}{20}\times\dfrac{\dfrac{1}{2}+\dfrac{4}{5}}{\dfrac{3}{10}-\dfrac{1}{4}}=\dfrac{20\times\dfrac{1}{2}+20\times\dfrac{4}{5}}{20\times\dfrac{3}{10}-20\times\dfrac{1}{4}}$.

Then we use cancellation to obtain $\dfrac{10+16}{6-5}$, which equals $\dfrac{26}{1}$ or 26.

---

**EXAMPLE 6**

| Quantity A | Quantity B |
|:---:|:---:|
| $\dfrac{\dfrac{3}{10}\times\dfrac{3}{10}\times\dfrac{3}{10}}{\dfrac{4}{5}+\dfrac{4}{5}}$ | $\dfrac{\dfrac{3}{10}+\dfrac{3}{10}+\dfrac{3}{10}}{\dfrac{4}{5}\div\dfrac{4}{5}}$ |

**Solution:** To simplify Quantity A, we'll multiply numerator and denominator by 1,000 (10 × 10 × 10).

$$\frac{\dfrac{3}{10}\times\dfrac{3}{10}\times\dfrac{3}{10}}{\dfrac{4}{5}+\dfrac{4}{5}}\times\frac{1,000}{1,000}=\frac{3\times3\times3}{200\times4+200\times4}=\frac{27}{1,600}$$

To simplify Quantity B we multiply numerator and denominator by 10

$$\frac{\dfrac{3}{10}+\dfrac{3}{10}+\dfrac{3}{10}}{\dfrac{4}{5}\div\dfrac{4}{5}}\times\frac{10}{10}=\frac{3+3+3}{\dfrac{\cancel{4}}{\cancel{5}}\times\dfrac{\cancel{5}}{\cancel{4}}\times10}=\frac{9}{10}$$

Clearly B is much larger than A.

## Solving Fraction Problems with Diagrams

A very valuable technique for solving fractions that is often overlooked is using a diagram. The diagram helps you keep track of the information in the problem and can help avoid difficult calculations—especially in multistep problems. Just be careful to remember what in your diagram represents 1 (the whole). It can change at each step.

**EXAMPLE 7**

At the first stop on Leroy Street, half the people get off the bus. At the second stop on Leroy Street, two-thirds as many people on the bus, get onto the bus. At the third stop on Leroy Street, three-fifths leave the bus. At the fourth stop, half get off, and there are 4 left. How many people were on the bus before arriving at Leroy Street?

(A) 0

(B) 1—the driver

(C) 4

(D) 20

(E) 24

**Solution:** We'll use a chart to see what happens at each stage.

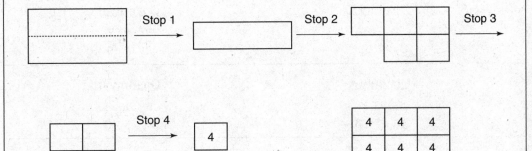

Four are left. This tells us that each small rectangle represents four people. Looking back at step one, we see that the bus can be divided into six small rectangles. Thus there were 6 × 4 = 24 people on the bus at the start. The answer is **E**.

To solve this problem using algebra we could let the number of people on the bus initially be $B$. Then after stop 1 we have $\frac{B}{2}$ people on the bus. At stop 2 we add $\frac{2}{3}$ of ($\frac{B}{2}$) so we have $\frac{B}{2}+\left(\frac{2}{3}\times\frac{B}{2}\right)$. At stop 4 we lose three-fifths (and thus retain $\frac{2}{5}$). So we have $\frac{2}{5}\left(\frac{B}{2}+\left(\frac{2}{3}\times\frac{B}{2}\right)\right)$. Finally at the last stop we lose half and the result is 4. $\frac{1}{2}\times\left(\frac{2}{5}\left(\frac{B}{2}+\left(\frac{2}{3}\times\frac{B}{2}\right)\right)\right)=4$. Then we solve for $B$.

A third approach would be to work backwards. Start with 4. Double it to get 8. Subtracting $\frac{3}{5}$ of a value is the same as taking $\frac{2}{5}$ of the value. So multiply by $\frac{5}{2}$ (the inverse of $\frac{2}{5}$) to get 20. Subtract $\frac{2}{5}$ of 20 to get 12. Double it to get 24. In some ways, this is the simplest approach, though it is very challenging to understand and determine the right fractions to use without a diagram.

## PROBLEMS (Solutions on page 93)

## Basic Problems

1.          Quantity A                           Quantity B

$$\frac{1}{1+\frac{1}{2}}$$                      $$\frac{2}{2+\frac{2}{1}}$$

---

2.          Quantity A                           Quantity B

Reciprocal of $2\frac{2}{3}$                     $$\frac{3}{7}$$

---

3.          Quantity A                           Quantity B

$$\frac{3}{5}\div\frac{5}{7}\div\frac{7}{9}$$    $$\frac{3}{5}\times\frac{5}{7}\times\frac{7}{9}$$

---

4.          Quantity A                           Quantity B

$$\frac{2}{10}+\frac{3}{7}+\frac{8}{6}$$         $$\frac{6}{14}+\frac{1}{5}+\frac{4}{3}$$

---

5.          Quantity A                           Quantity B

$$\frac{1}{2}-\frac{1}{3}+\frac{1}{4}$$          $$\frac{1}{3}-\frac{1}{4}+\frac{1}{5}$$

---

6.

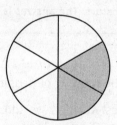     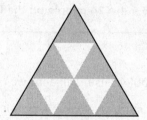

Quantity A                                       Quantity B

The fraction the white                           The fraction the shaded
part is of the whole                             part is of the whole

7. What fraction is smallest?

(A) $\frac{11}{20}$

(B) $\frac{5}{6}$

(C) $\frac{3}{8}$

(D) $\frac{2}{7}$

(E) $\frac{1}{3}$

8. Math class has 22 girls and 18 boys. What fraction of the class are girls?

(A) $\dfrac{22}{18}$

(B) $\dfrac{11}{9}$

(C) $\dfrac{11}{20}$

(D) $\dfrac{9}{20}$

(E) $\dfrac{9}{11}$

9. If $\dfrac{3}{8}$ of $x$ equals 6, what is $\dfrac{3}{4}$ of $x$?

## GRE Problems

10.

| Quantity A | Quantity B |
|---|---|
| $\dfrac{\dfrac{4}{7}+\dfrac{5}{14}}{1+\dfrac{45}{49}}$ | $\dfrac{\dfrac{4}{7}\times\dfrac{3}{14}}{1\div\dfrac{45}{49}}$ |

11.                               $x \neq 0$

| Quantity A | Quantity B |
|---|---|
| $\dfrac{1}{\left(\dfrac{1}{\dfrac{1}{x}}\right)}$ | $x$ |

12. $\dfrac{3}{7}$ of $\dfrac{21}{6}$ equals $\dfrac{5}{9}$ of what number?

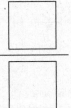

13. Two-thirds of the people in Lawrence County are eligible to vote. Only $\frac{4}{5}$ of the eligible people register to vote. Only $\frac{3}{4}$ of the registered voters actually vote on Election Day. What fraction of the county's population did not vote?

14. $2\frac{1}{2}$ pounds of steak cost the same as $1\frac{1}{4}$ pounds of lamb. If 4 pounds of lamb cost $18, what would 5 pounds of steak cost?

    (A) $5.75
    (B) $8
    (C) $11.25
    (D) $21
    (E) $27.25

15. If $S$ is the set of all fractions $\frac{a}{b}$, where $a$ and $b$ are integers so that $1 \leq a \leq 5$ and $2 \leq b < 4$, then

    (A) $S$ contains 10 distinct numbers
    (B) $S$ contains no integers
    (C) $S$ contains 3 fractions that are not integers
    (D) $S$ contains 3 fractions less than 1
    (E) $S$ contains 0

16. Northern Lights College has only three majors—music, education, and math (and each student has precisely one major). Half of the students are education majors. One-third of the students are math majors. Three-quarters of the music majors are female. If there are 120 male music majors, how many students attend the college?

17. If $\left(\frac{2}{x}\right)^3 = \left(\frac{x}{-2}\right)^2$, then what is $x$?

    (A) $-1$
    (B) 0
    (C) 1
    (D) $\sqrt{2}$
    (E) 2

18. A new scout troop started up in 2013 with 24 boys. In 2014, 8 new boys joined and then $\frac{1}{8}$ quit. In 2015, $\frac{1}{7}$ quit and then three boys joined. What fraction of the troop would have to leave to get back to the original start-up size?

Ⓐ $\frac{1}{9}$

Ⓑ $\frac{1}{8}$

Ⓒ $\frac{1}{6}$

Ⓓ $\frac{1}{4}$

Ⓔ $\frac{1}{3}$

19. A terrible flu has hit the students from Professor Murty's lecture. He can see that $\frac{5}{7}$ of them are absent and $\frac{1}{3}$ of the remaining students are looking pale. If the pale students leave early, he'll have only 12 students left. How many students are normally in Professor Murty's lecture?

20. The chief of police for Smalltown USA notices that, not including himself, $\frac{3}{5}$ of his police force carries firearms. If he includes himself, $\frac{5}{8}$ of his force carries firearms. How many people on his force do not carry firearms?

Ⓐ 5

Ⓑ 6

Ⓒ 11

Ⓓ 16

Ⓔ 24

## DECIMALS

Any number can be expressed as combination of powers of 10 and powers of $\left(\frac{1}{10}\right)$. For instance $\frac{777}{5} = 155\frac{2}{5}$ or $155\frac{4}{10}$, which can be expressed as $1 \times 10^2 + 5 \times 10^1 + 5 \times 10^0 + 4 \times \left(\frac{1}{10}\right)^1$. We typically write this as 155.4 where the period is called a decimal point and separates the powers of 10 (left of the decimal point) from the powers of $\frac{1}{10}$ (right of the decimal point). This is called the *decimal expansion*. Sometimes the expansion is infinite ($\sqrt{2} = 1.414\ldots$), sometimes it's finite $\left(\frac{7}{25} = 0.28\right)$, sometimes it has repeating patterns ($23/99 = 0.23232323\ldots$), and sometimes it has no patterns ($\pi = 3.141591\ldots$). Our system of decimal numbers relies on place value.

## Converting Between Fractions and Decimals

Simply type the fraction on your calculator, using the ÷ operation as the fraction bar. For example, to find $\frac{7}{25}$ as a decimal open the onscreen calculator and type "7 ÷ 25." The calculator will show 0.28, which is the decimal equivalent of $\frac{7}{25}$.

### EXAMPLE 1

Which of the following is equal to 0.021021021....?

(A) $\frac{7}{333}$

(B) $\frac{9}{25}$

(C) $\frac{33}{40}$

(D) $\frac{21}{99}$

(E) $\sqrt{3}$

**Solution 1:** $25 = 5 \times 5$ and $40 = 2 \times 2 \times 2 \times 5$ so by the tip $\frac{9}{25}$ and $\frac{33}{40}$ have finite decimals. Also $\sqrt{3}$ is irrational so it has an infinite nonrepeating decimal. Thus B, C, and E are not correct. Using long division we see that $\frac{21}{99} = 0.2121...$ and $\frac{7}{333} = 0.021021....$ So the answer is **A**.

$$
\begin{array}{r}
0.212... \\
99\overline{)21.000...} \\
\underline{198} \\
120 \\
\underline{99} \\
210 \\
\underline{198} \\
...
\end{array}
\qquad
\begin{array}{r}
0.02102... \\
333\overline{)7.00000...} \\
\underline{666} \\
340 \\
\underline{333} \\
70 \\
\underline{0} \\
700 \\
\underline{666} \\
...
\end{array}
$$

**Solution 2:** Test the answers, by entering each answer choice on the calculator. Typing 7 ÷ 333 shows the result 0.021021021, meaning that **A** is correct.

## Comparing Decimal Numbers

How do we compare decimal numbers? If one number has more digits to the left of the decimal than the other, it is larger.

---

**EXAMPLE 2**

Compare 322.95 and 99.1. We start by writing one above the other aligned at the decimal point: $\begin{array}{r}322.95\\99.1\end{array}$. Notice that 322.95 has three digits to the left of the decimal and 99.1 has two digits to the left of the decimal so 322.95 > 99.1.

---

If both numbers have the same number of digits to the left of the decimal, we compare digits in the same place starting from the left. The first place we find where the digits are not the same, the number with the larger digit is the larger number.

---

**EXAMPLE 3**

Compare 341.738 and 341.729.

```
3 4 1 . 7 3 8
↕ ↕ ↕ . ↕ ↑
3 4 1 . 7 2 9
```

Notice that 3 = 3, 4 = 4, 1 = 1, 7 = 7, 3 > 2 so 341.738 > 341.729. Note, the fact that 8 < 9 in the final digit is irrelevant.

---

## Operations on Decimals

To add (or subtract) decimals, line them up at the decimal point and add (or subtract) as you would integers. The answer will have a decimal point in the place directly below the other decimal points.

---

**EXAMPLE 4**

$\begin{array}{r}123.45\\+67.891\end{array}$ becomes $\begin{array}{r}\phantom{0}1\phantom{0}1\phantom{0}1\\123.450\\+67.891\\\hline191.341\end{array}$ and $\begin{array}{r}123.45\\-54.321\end{array}$ becomes $\begin{array}{r}1\phantom{0}13\phantom{00}4\phantom{0}10\\12\cancel{3}.4\cancel{5}\cancel{0}\\-54.321\\\hline69.129\end{array}$

---

To multiply you do not need to line up the decimals. Treat the numbers as if they are integers and multiply. Then count the number of total number of spaces after the decimals in the factors. There should be that many places after the decimal point in the product.

Examples 4 and 5 above illustrate how operations with decimals work. In practice when these situations arise, most students would do better to type the numbers directly on the calculator to minimize the chance of an arithmetic error.

## Multiplying or Dividing by Powers of Ten

Since decimal numbers are based on powers of ten it is extremely easy to multiply or divide by $10^n$, where $n$ is a positive integer. To multiply a number by $10^n$, just move the decimal place $n$ places to the right. For example, $24.345 \times 10^2 = 2{,}434.5$.

$$24.345 \times 10^2 \Rightarrow 2434.5$$

To divide a number by $10^n$, just move the decimal place $n$ places to the left. For example, $24.345 \div 10^2 = 0.24345$.

$$24.345 \div 10^2 \Rightarrow 0.24345$$

---
**EXAMPLE 6**

Choose the largest value.

(A) $0.123 \times 10^5$

(B) $1{,}230{,}000 \div 10^3$

(C) $0.00123 \times 10^6$

(D) $1{,}230 \div 10^2$

(E) $123{,}000{,}000 \div 10^7$

**Solution:** In A we move the decimal five places to the right to get 12,300. In B we move the decimal three places to the left to get 1,230. In C we move the decimal six places to the right to get 1,230. In D we move the decimal two places to the left to get 12.3. In E we move the decimal seven places to the left to get 12.3. The largest value is 12,300. The answer is **A**.

---

How can we divide or multiply by $10^n$ when $n$ is less than 0? For example, if you want to divide by $10^{-4}$ you may instead multiply by $10^4$, following the rules above. Likewise, if you are asked to multiply by $10^{-3}$ you may instead divide by $10^3$.

## PROBLEMS (Solutions on page 97)
## Basic Problems

1.
| Quantity A | Quantity B |
|---|---|
| $8.023 - 7.032$ | $0.401 + 0.5023$ |

2.
| Quantity A | Quantity B |
|---|---|
| $(0.5)^2$ | $5 \times 0.5$ |

3.
| Quantity A | Quantity B |
|---|---|
| $(0.1)^3$ | $1,000 \div 1,000,000$ |

4.
| Quantity A | Quantity B |
|---|---|
| $0.15 + 0.0032 - 8.2$ | $2.5 \div 1.75 \times 3.1$ |

5.
| Quantity A | Quantity B |
|---|---|
| $34.2 \times 10^5$ | $0.0342 \times 10^9$ |

6.
| Quantity A | Quantity B |
|---|---|
| $1.03 \div 10^4$ | $1,030 \div 10^7$ |

7. Choose the largest value.

   Ⓐ $45.6 \times 9$

   Ⓑ $0.465 \times 10^3$

   Ⓒ $2.33 \times 103.5$

   Ⓓ $646.003 - 1.254$

   Ⓔ $1,003 \div 1.5$

8. Choose the smallest value.

   Ⓐ $9.65 - 7.23$

   Ⓑ $0.00345 \times 10^3$

   Ⓒ $101 \div 50$

   Ⓓ $646.003 - 647.254$

   Ⓔ $1001.4 - 999.8$

## GRE Problems

9.
| Quantity A | Quantity B |
|---|---|
| $(0.99)^9$ | $(0.99)^{10}$ |

10.
| Quantity A | Quantity B |
|---|---|
| $0.00923 \times 10^8$ | $92,300,000 \div 10^2$ |

11. $39 \times 10^3$ is how many times larger than $1.3 \times 10^{-4}$?

   Ⓐ $10^{-1}$

   Ⓑ $10^7$

   Ⓒ $3,000$

   Ⓓ $30,000,000$

   Ⓔ $300,000,000$

12. 0.00015 is how many times smaller than 600?

 (A) 4,000

 (B) $4 \times 10^6$

 (C) $10^7$

 (D) 30,000

 (E) 400,000

13. Solve for $x$ if $16.44 \times 0.47223 \times x = 4{,}722.3 \times 1.644$ .

14. Solve for $x$ if $6.15 \times 723 \div x = 615 \times 0.0723$.

### TIP

- On the GRE you are likely to only encounter square roots, though knowing cube roots or other roots may help with some problems.
- Although $(-3)^2 = 9$, $\sqrt{9} \neq 3$. Square root is defined as the "principal radical" and only returns positive values or zero.
- The square root (and more generally $n$th root for $n$ even) is only defined for positive numbers. The square root of negative four, $\sqrt{-4}$, does not make sense[1] since there is no real number whose square is $-4$.
- The cube root (and more generally $n$th root for $n$ odd) is defined for all numbers. For example $\sqrt[3]{-8} = -2$ since $(-2)^3 = -8$.
- Although $(\sqrt{a})^2 = a$, it is not always true that $\sqrt{a^2} = a$. For example $\sqrt{(-3)^2} = \sqrt{9} = 3$ not $-3$. It is always true that $\sqrt{a^2} = |a|$.

## RADICALS AND EXPONENTS

We say that 3 is the square root of 9 and write $\sqrt{9} = 3$ because $3^2 = 9$. Similarly $\sqrt{25} = 5$ because $5^2 = 25$ and $\sqrt{100} = 10$ because $10^2 = 100$. More generally, we define $\sqrt[n]{a}$, the "$n$th root of $a$," to be $b$ when $b^n = a$. For example, the cube root of 8, $\sqrt[3]{8}$, is equal to 2 since $2^3 = 8$ and the fifth root of 243, $\sqrt[5]{243}$, is equal to 3 since $3^5 = 243$. Any expression of the form $\sqrt[n]{a}$ can be called a radical.

---

**EXAMPLE 1**

If $y^3 = 125$ and $x^2 = 16$, what is the greatest possible value of $y - x$?

**Solution:** The calculator does not have a cube root button, so solve for $y$ using a guess-and-check approach. We need $y \times y \times y = 125$. You should be able to find that $5 \times 5 \times 5 = 125$, so $y = 5$. Since $4^2 = 16$, it is tempting to assume $x = 4$, and then $y - x = 5 - 4 = 1$. But remember that $x^2 = 16$ has two solutions, 4 and $-4$, because a negative squared is positive. Then the greatest value of $y - x$ is $5 - (-4) = 5 + 4 = 9$. The answer is **9**. Note, $y$ cannot equal $-5$ because $(-5)^3 = -5 \times -5 \times -5 = -125$, not 125.

---

[1] *Complex numbers would allow you to solve this problem, but the GRE only concerns itself with real numbers.*

# Simplifying Radicals

Expressions involving radicals can be challenging to simplify. You can add or subtract *like* radicals. For instance, $2\sqrt{6} + 3\sqrt{6} = 5\sqrt{6}$ (think two apples plus three apples equals five apples).

When $a \geq 0$ and $b > 0$, we can simplify radicals using the rules $\sqrt{ab} = \sqrt{a}\sqrt{b}$ and $\sqrt{\frac{a}{b}} = \frac{\sqrt{a}}{\sqrt{b}}$.

For instance, $\sqrt{12} = \sqrt{4 \times 3} = \sqrt{4} \times \sqrt{3} = 2\sqrt{3}$ and $\sqrt{2.25} = \sqrt{\frac{9}{4}} = \frac{\sqrt{9}}{\sqrt{4}} = \frac{3}{2} = 1.5$.

Using the last rule, radicals are usually simplified to remove any squares under the radical sign. So, you will see $2\sqrt{3}$ and not $\sqrt{12}$, or $3\sqrt{2}$ and not $\sqrt{18}$ (note $\sqrt{18} = \sqrt{9 \times 2} = \sqrt{9} \times \sqrt{2} = 3\sqrt{2}$).

Before calculators were in common use, many answers involved radicals, and it was usually considered bad form to give an answer, like $\frac{2}{\sqrt{3}}$, with a radical in the denominator. To *rationalize a denominator*, simply multiply numerator and denominator by the same radical to get an equivalent fraction, without a radical in the denominator.

For example, $\frac{2}{\sqrt{3}} \times \frac{\sqrt{3}}{\sqrt{3}} = \frac{2\sqrt{3}}{3}$ or even $\frac{2}{3}\sqrt{3}$.

> **TIP**
>
> - You may not add or subtract different radicals. For example, $\sqrt{9} - \sqrt{4} \neq \sqrt{9-4}$ as $\sqrt{9} - \sqrt{4} = 3 - 2 = 1$, which is not $\sqrt{5}$. An expression like $\sqrt{6} + \sqrt{5}$ cannot be simplified at all.
>
> - Of course, the reverse of the first tip is also invalid. Note that $\sqrt{9-4} \neq \sqrt{9} - \sqrt{4}$ and $\sqrt{9+4} \neq \sqrt{9} + \sqrt{4}$. Still a very common mistake would be to calculate $\sqrt{9+4} = \sqrt{9} + \sqrt{4} = 3 + 2 = 5$. Clearly $\sqrt{13} \neq 5$. Beware—it's an easy trap to fall into!

---

**EXAMPLE 2**

If the area of a square is 60, what is the length of each side?

(A) 3,600

(B) 15

(C) $4\sqrt{15}$

(D) $2\sqrt{5}$

(E) $2\sqrt{15}$

**Solution:** The formula for the area of a square is $A = s^2$, where $s$ is the length of each side. So $60 = s^2$, and we have to solve for $s$. Taking the square root of each side, we get $s = \sqrt{60}$ (in this case we know $\sqrt{s^2} = s$ since $s$ is positive). We must simplify $\sqrt{60}$. We use a factor tree to factor 60 and discover that $\sqrt{60} = \sqrt{2^2 \times 3 \times 5} = \sqrt{2^2} \times \sqrt{3 \times 5} = 2\sqrt{15}$. The answer is **E**.

---

**EXAMPLE 3**

Simplify $\dfrac{5}{2}\sqrt{\dfrac{6}{15}}$.

(A) $\sqrt{\dfrac{3}{2}}$

(B) $2\sqrt{3}$

(C) $\dfrac{1}{2}\sqrt{10}$

(D) $\sqrt{\dfrac{2}{5}}$

(E) $\sqrt{2}+\sqrt{5}$

**Solution:** First, we'll factor the numbers under the square root sign and cancel the common factor, $\dfrac{5}{2}\sqrt{\dfrac{6}{15}}=\dfrac{5}{2}\sqrt{\dfrac{\cancel{3}\times 2}{\cancel{3}\times 5}}=\dfrac{5}{2}\sqrt{\dfrac{2}{5}}$. Second, we use the rule $\sqrt{\dfrac{a}{b}}=\dfrac{\sqrt{a}}{\sqrt{b}}$ to find that $\dfrac{5}{2}\sqrt{\dfrac{2}{5}}=\dfrac{5}{2}\dfrac{\sqrt{2}}{\sqrt{5}}$. Then, we rationalize the denominator (cancelling as needed) $\dfrac{5\sqrt{2}}{2\sqrt{5}}\times\dfrac{\sqrt{5}}{\sqrt{5}}=\dfrac{5\sqrt{2}\sqrt{5}}{10}=\dfrac{\sqrt{2}\sqrt{5}}{2}$. Finally, we combine the radicals using the rule $\sqrt{ab}=\sqrt{a}\sqrt{b}$ and bring the fraction in front to get $\dfrac{\sqrt{2}\sqrt{5}}{2}=\dfrac{\sqrt{10}}{2}=\dfrac{1}{2}\sqrt{10}$. The answer is **C**.

An alternate (challenging, but maybe quick) approach would be to estimate the value of the expression given as a decimal and compare it to each of the given answers.

## Defining Powers

An expression like $a^n$ is called a *power*. The *base* of the power is $a$ and the *exponent* is $n$. When $n$ is an integer, powers are a special notation for repeated multiplication. Pay careful attention to how powers are defined when $n$ is some other kind of number.

If $n$ is a positive integer then we define $a^n=\underbrace{a\times a\times a\times a\ldots\times a}_{n\,\text{times}}$. For instance, $2^5=2\times 2\times 2\times 2\times 2=32$. When $n=2$, we call the power a *perfect square*; for example, $9=3^2$, and if $n=3$, we call the power a *perfect cube*, for example, $8=2^3$.

If $n$ is a negative integer and $a$ is not zero, then we define $a^n=\dfrac{1}{a^{|n|}}=\underbrace{\dfrac{1}{a}\times\dfrac{1}{a}\times\dfrac{1}{a}\times\ldots\times\dfrac{1}{a}}_{n\,\text{times}}$. For instance, $3^{-2}=\dfrac{1}{3^2}=\dfrac{1}{3}\times\dfrac{1}{3}=\dfrac{1}{9}$. You may not see a negative exponent on the GRE, but they still can be helpful in solving GRE problems.

If $n$ is zero and $a\neq 0$, then define $a^n=1$. Yes, $4^0=1$ and $\pi^0=1$.

If $a$ is zero and $n>0$, then $a^n=0^n=0$. Yes, $0^4=0$ and $0^{100}=0$. Yet, $0^0$ and $0^{-7}$ are undefined.

**EXAMPLE 4**

Which of the following numbers are less than 1?

Indicate *all* that apply.

**A** $5^{-3}$

**B** $\left(\dfrac{1}{5}\right)^{-3}$

**C** $5^0$

**Solution:** For A we see that $5^{-3} = \dfrac{1}{5} \times \dfrac{1}{5} \times \dfrac{1}{5} = \dfrac{1}{125}$. Recall that $\dfrac{1}{\left(\frac{1}{5}\right)} = 5$, then

$\left(\dfrac{1}{5}\right)^{-3} = 5 \times 5 \times 5 = 125$. Finally $5^0 = 1$. So the only answer less than 1 is A. Choose **A**.

When $n$ is a fraction, $n = \dfrac{p}{q}$ with $q$ positive and $p$ positive or negative, then we define $a^n = a^{\frac{p}{q}} = \left(\sqrt[q]{a}\right)^p$. For instance, $81^{\frac{1}{4}} = \left(\sqrt[4]{81}\right)^1 = \sqrt[4]{81} = 3$ or $8^{\frac{2}{3}} = \left(\sqrt[3]{8}\right)^2 = 2^2 = 4$. As mentioned earlier, only square roots appear frequently on the GRE. So it would be reasonable to expect you to know that $4^{2.5} = 4^{\frac{5}{2}} = \left(\sqrt{4}\right)^5 = 2^5 = 32$, but it may be unreasonable to ask for $2{,}187^{\frac{3}{7}}$.

## Rules for Working with Powers

These rules help you simplify expressions with powers

**Rule 1:** $a^{m+n} = a^m a^n$. For example, $2^{2+3} = 2^2 \times 2^3$ since $32 = 4 \times 8$. This rule is used more often to combine products of powers into one power: "keep the base and add the exponents." For example, $5^4 \times 5^4 = 5^{4+4} = 5^8$.

**Rule 2:** $a^{m-n} = \dfrac{a^m}{a^n}$. This is just a variation of the previous rule combined with the definition of negative exponents. An example is $4^{5-3} = \dfrac{4^5}{4^3}$, which makes sense as

$4^{5-3} = 4^2 = 16$ and $\dfrac{4^5}{4^3} = \dfrac{4^2}{1} = 16$ (using cancellation). More often this rule is used for examples like $5^4 \div 5^5 = 5^{4-5} = 5^{-1} = \dfrac{1}{5}$.

**Rule 3:** $(ab)^n = a^n b^n$. For example, $(2 \times 5)^3 = (2 \times 5) \times (2 \times 5) \times (2 \times 5) = (2 \times 2 \times 2) \times (5 \times 5 \times 5) = 2^3 \times 5^3$.

**TIP**

- A common mistake would be "keep the exponent and add the bases." For instance, $2^4 \times 3^4$ is not equal to $5^4$, as $2^4 \times 3^4 = 16 \times 81 = 1{,}296$ but $5^4 = 625$. However, $2^4 \times 3^4 = (2 \times 3)^4 = 6^4$.

- Another common mistake would be to try to simplify when powers are added. For instance, $2^3 + 2^5$ is not equal to $2^8$, as $2^3 + 2^5 = 8 + 32 = 40$ and $2^8 = 256$.

- There is one special time when you can simplify the sum of powers. When you have two identical powers of two, three identical powers of three, or, generally, $n$ identical powers of $n$. For instance, $2^3 + 2^3 = 2 \times 2^3 = 2^4$ and $3^2 + 3^2 + 3^2 = 3 \times 3^2 = 3^3$.

**EXAMPLE 5**

Simplify $\dfrac{(10^3)^2 \div 10^5 \times 10^7}{2^3 2^2 5^7}$.

(A) 20

(B) 40

(C) 100

(D) $\dfrac{2}{5}$

(E) $\dfrac{25}{2}$

**Solution:** First $(10^3)^2 = 10^6$, so the numerator is $10^6 \div 10^5 \times 10^7$, which equals $10^{6-5+7} = 10^8$. Second, combining the powers of 2 in the denominator we get $2^{(3+2)}5^7$. So we are trying to simplify $\dfrac{10^8}{2^5 5^7}$. If we express 10 as $2 \times 5$, then we have $\dfrac{(2 \times 5)^8}{2^5 5^7}$, which equals $\dfrac{2^8 5^8}{2^5 5^7}$. Now using our rules for dividing powers we have $2^{8-5}5^{8-7} = 2^3 \times 5 = 40$. Choose **B**.

## PROBLEMS (Solutions on page 98)

## Basic Problems

| | Quantity A | Quantity B |
|---|---|---|
| 1. | $(5^2)^3$ | $5^5$ |
| 2. | $\left(\left(\dfrac{1}{2}\right)^3\right)^2$ | $2^{-6}$ |
| 3. | $10^5$ | $2^6 5^4$ |
| 4. | $\dfrac{8}{2^5}$ | $(2^{-2})^{-2}$ |
| 5. | $\sqrt{\dfrac{8}{9}}$ | $\dfrac{2}{3}$ |
| 6. | $\sqrt{4+9}$ | $\sqrt{4} + \sqrt{9}$ |

| | Quantity A | Quantity B |
|---|---|---|
| 7. | $\sqrt{9-4}$ | $\sqrt{9}-\sqrt{4}$ |
| 8. | $(2+3)^2$ | $2^2 + 3^2$ |
| 9. | $-\sqrt[3]{8}$ | $\sqrt[3]{-8}$ |
| 10. | $\sqrt{(-4)^2}$ | $-4$ |

11. If $2^a \times 16^2 = 4^5$ then what is $a$?

   (A) $-3$
   (B) $-1$
   (C) $0$
   (D) $1$
   (E) $2$

12. If $\dfrac{3^x}{9} = \sqrt{81}$, then $x = ?$

   (A) $0$
   (B) $2$
   (C) $4$
   (D) $6$
   (E) $8$

13. Choose the largest value.

   (A) $2^3$
   (B) $3^2$
   (C) $2^3 \times 3^2$
   (D) $2^3 \times 2^{-3}$
   (E) $(2^3)^2$

## GRE Problems

14. Solve for $a$ if $2^{a+6} 4^a = 8^3$.

   (A) $0$
   (B) $1$
   (C) $2$
   (D) $3$
   (E) $4$

15. If $\sqrt{6^n} = \dfrac{2^n}{\sqrt{2}} \times \dfrac{3^n}{\sqrt{3}}$, then what is $n$?

(A) $-1$
(B) $0$
(C) $1$
(D) $2$
(E) $3$

16. Simplify $\sqrt{\dfrac{x^{10}y^8z^5}{x^6y^7z^6}}$.

(A) $x\sqrt{yz}$

(B) $\dfrac{x^2\sqrt{xz}}{z}$

(C) $\dfrac{\sqrt{xyz}}{z}$

(D) $\dfrac{\sqrt{x^2yz}}{z}$

(E) $\dfrac{x^2\sqrt{yz}}{z}$

| | Quantity A | Quantity B |
|---|---|---|
| 17. | $\dfrac{\sqrt{40}}{2}$ | $\dfrac{20}{\sqrt{10}}$ |

18. A square and a circle have the same area

| | Quantity A | Quantity B |
|---|---|---|
| | Diameter of the circle | Diagonal length of the square |

| | Quantity A | Quantity B |
|---|---|---|
| 19. | $3^4 + 3^4 + 3^4$ | $3^5$ |

| | Quantity A | Quantity B |
|---|---|---|
| 20. | $2^4 + 2^4 + 2^4$ | $2^6$ |

| | Quantity A | Quantity B |
|---|---|---|
| 21. | Average of $2^0, 2^1, 2^2,$ and $2^3$ | Average of $3^0, 3^1,$ and $3^2$ |

| | Quantity A | Quantity B |
|---|---|---|
| 22. | Average of $3^1, 3^2,$ and $3^3$ | Sum of $3^0, 3^1,$ and $3^2$ |

# SOLUTIONS TO PRACTICE PROBLEMS
## Numbers (Problems on page 44)

1. **(79)** Try to picture this using old-fashioned long division. Because we are dividing by 9, put 9 to the left of the vertical bar. The quotient, 8, appears at the top:

$$9\overline{)n}^{\;8}$$

You would next multiply the quotient, 8, by the divisor, 9, and write the result under $n$. Then subtract:

$$
\begin{array}{r}
8 \\
9\overline{)n} \\
-72
\end{array}
$$

This implies that $n \geq 72$. Furthermore, we know that subtracting $n - 72$ leaves a remainder of 7, so $n$ must be 7 more than 72. Then $n = 72 + 7 = 79$.

2. **(B, C)** The reciprocal is $1 \div \left(\dfrac{2}{5}\right)$, which equals $1 \times \left(\dfrac{5}{2}\right) = \dfrac{5}{2} = 2.5$. So answers B and C are correct. Answer A is $1 \div \left(\dfrac{5}{2}\right) = 1 \times \left(\dfrac{2}{5}\right) = \dfrac{2}{5} = 0.4$ and is not the correct answer.

3. **(D)** The opposite of $a$ is $-a$. Without knowing the value of $a$, we can't tell which is larger. If $a < 0$, then $-a > 0$, and $-a$ is larger. If $a > 0$ then $-a < 0$, and $a$ is larger. If $a = 0$ then $-a = 0$, and they are equal.

4. **(D)** As $abc = 0$, then one of the three values $a$, $b$, or $c$ must equal zero. Since $b > 1$, $b$ is not equal to zero. Hence $a = 0$ or $c = 0$. If $a = 0$, $c$ could be anything including zero. That means $a$ and $c$ could be equal ($a = 0 = c$) or one could be larger than the other ($a = 0$ and $c = -3$).

5. **(A)** The expression in Quantity A looks complicated and is tedious to compute. Luckily we don't have to compute it. Since it is in absolute value signs, the result must be greater than or equal to zero. But $-1$, in Quantity B, is less than zero.

6. **(A)** This tests your knowledge of order of operations. In Quantity A, there are no parentheses or exponents, so we do multiplication and division in left to right order. In this case that means division, then multiplication. We finish with addition. $2 + 8 \div 4 \times 3 = 2 + 2 \times 3 = 2 + 6 = 8$. In Quantity B we do whatever is inside parentheses first proceeding from innermost to outermost. Hence we do addition, then division, and finally multiplication. $((2 + 8) \div 4) \times 3 = (10 \div 4) \times 3 = 2.5 \times 3 = 7.5$. Clearly $8 > 7.5$.

7. **(D)** Try testing a range of values for the variables within the given interval. If $a = 1$, $c = 9$, and $b = 5$, then $c \div a$ equals $9 \div 1 = 9$, which is greater than 5. But if $a = 4$, $c = 6$, and $b = 5$, then $c \div a$ equals $6 \div 4 = 1.5$, which is less than 5.

8. **(A)** Solve this challenging one by again testing a range of values for the variables within the given interval. If $x = 1.1$ and $y = 1.2$, the calculator shows that Quantity A, 2.3, is quite a bit larger than Quantity B, 1.32. If $x = 1.8$ and $y = 1.9$, then A is 3.7, while B is 3.42; again A is greater. Finally, try $x = 1.01$ and $y = 1.99$. Then A is $1.01 + 1.99 = 3$, while B is $1.01 \times 1.99$, which can be easily estimated without having to type it in: $1.01 \times 1.99 \approx 1 \times 2 = 2.0$.

Since Quantity A is greater all three times, choose A. You might also note that whenever $x = y$, then $x + y = 2x$, and again Quantity A is greater because the given $y < 2$ implies that $yx < 2x$ for positive $x$.

9. **(B)** What pairs of numbers add to 11? $1 + 10$, $2 + 9$, $3 + 8$, $4 + 7$, and $5 + 6$. The only product that equals 30 is $5 \times 6$. So the numbers are $a = 5$ and $b = 6$. Then $a - b = 5 - 6 = -1$ and $\frac{a}{b} = \frac{5}{6}$. Since $-1 < \frac{5}{6}$, B is larger. But wait, couldn't $a = 6$ and $b = 5$? Then $a - b = 1$ and $\frac{a}{b} = \frac{6}{5}$. $1 < \frac{6}{5}$ so again B is larger. In both cases B is larger.

10. **(B)** The opposite of $a$ is $-a$, and the reciprocal of $a$ is $\frac{1}{a}$. Their quotient is $\frac{-a}{\frac{1}{a}} = -a \times \frac{a}{1} = -a^2$.

The quotient of $a$ and the reciprocal of $a$ is $\frac{a}{\frac{1}{a}} = a \times \frac{a}{1} = a^2$. Even if we took the quotient in the opposite order, the result in Quantity A is always negative and the result in Quantity B is always positive.

11. **(B)** Since $a$ is an integer and $|a| \leq 2$, $a$ must be one of $-2$, $-1$, $0$, $1$, or $2$. That means that one of the terms in the product $(a + 2)(a + 1)(a)(a - 1)(a - 2)$ must be zero and hence the product is zero. As $4 > 0$, choose B.

12. **(A)** As with every absolute value problem, there are three cases: $b - a > 0$, $b - a = 0$, or $b - a < 0$. If $b - a > 0$, then $|b - a| = b - a$ and hence $b - a = a - b$. Add $a$ to both sides and then add $b$ to both sides to see that $2b = 2a$, or $b = a$. But that is impossible as we are told $a$ is not equal to $b$. If $b - a = 0$, then $b = a$, which is also impossible. Hence the remaining case, $b - a < 0$, must be true. If $b - a < 0$, then $b < a$.

## Integers (Problems on page 48)

1. **(A)** The easiest way to solve this problem is to subtract $x$ from both quantities to get $-y$ and $y$. Which is larger? $-y$ is larger than $y$, since $y$ is a negative number.

2. **(A)** Since both $x$ and $y$ are negative, their product is positive and their sum is negative.

3. **(A)** The product of two negative numbers is positive. But the difference of two negative numbers can also be positive, for example $-6 - (-8) = 2$. It's not hard to see the difference will be largest when $x = -1$ and then $x - y = |y| - 1$. When $x = -1$, $xy = |y|$. But $|y|$ is always greater than $|y|-1$.

4. **(C)** Since they are consecutive and increasing, for example $a = 3$, $b = 4$, and $c = 5$, then $a - b = -1$ and $b - c = -1$.

5. **(B)** In this case, $a - b = -1$ and $c - b = 1$.

6. **(D)** Which integers, $n$, have the property that $n^2 \leq n$? $1^2 \leq 1$. Also $0^2 \leq 0$, so $n$ could be 1 or 0 (or possibly other values).

7. **(D)** Which integers, $n$, have the property that $n^2 \geq 5$? Clearly $n = 3$ would do as $3^2 = 9 \geq 5$. But $-3$ is also an integer and $(-3)^2 = 9 \geq 5$. So $n$ could be greater or less than 2.

8. **(C)** At first glance you might decide to choose B since more numbers are being multiplied. That would be wrong. The consecutive integers from –5 to 5 include zero. Anything times 0 is 0. Hence the product of consecutive integers from –5 to 5 is zero. Likewise the product of consecutive integers from –5 to 10 is zero.

9. **(8)** The nine numbers must be –8, –6, –4, –2, 0, 2, 4, 6, 8, because –8 + –6 + –4 + –2 + 0 + 2 + 4 + 6 + 8 = 0. To see at a glance why this sum is zero, notice that each negative integer on the list can be paired with its opposite to form a sum of zero. For example, –6 + 6 = 0. Choose the greatest of these nine integers, 8. Here, do not set up the nine consecutive even integers as $x, x + 2, x + 4 \ldots$, because that is too cumbersome.

10. **(0)** Again, do not blindly represent the integers as $x, x + 1, x + 2 \ldots$, because it is easier to test specific values. For example, the five numbers might be 8, 9, 10, 11, and 12, or they might be 21, 22, 23, 24, and 25. Notice that in any set of five consecutive integers, one of the integers is a multiple of 5. When this multiple of 5 is then multiplied by the other numbers, the resulting product will also be a multiple of 5. Then $P$ is divisible by 5 and therefore leaves no remainder when divided by 5.

11. **(2,184)** Set up the equation $x + (x + 1) + (x + 2) = 39$. Combining like terms on the left shows $3x + 3 = 39$. Subtract 3 from each side: $3x = 36$. Dividing by 3 yields $x = 12$. This makes the three integers 12, 13, and 14. Find their product on the calculator: $12 \times 13 \times 14 = 2{,}184$.

12. **(27)** Use a guess-and-check approach on the calculator, multiplying three consecutive odd integers until you find a trio whose product is 693. For example, $5 \times 7 \times 9 = 315$ is too small, whereas $9 \times 11 \times 13 = 1{,}287$ is too large. The correct triple is 7, 9, and 11, because $7 \times 9 \times 11 = 693$. The sum of these is $7 + 9 + 11 = 27$.

13. **(E)** Test the positive integers $(1, 2, 3, \ldots)$ to see which satisfy the inequality. If $x = 1$, then $x^2 = 1 \leq 9$. If $x = 2$, then $x^2 = 4 \leq 9$. If $x = 3$, then $x^2 = 9 \leq 9$. If $x = 4$, then $x^2 = 16 \nleq 9$. There are three valid answers.

14. **(E)** The expression $x - y$ will be smallest when $x$ is the smallest and $y$ is the largest it can be. Take $x = -3$ and $y = 3$. Then $x - y = -6$.

15. **(72)** It seems that the answer should just be $7 \times 10 = 70$, obtained by choosing the greatest possible values for $x$ and $y$ individually. But recall that when multiplying two negatives the product is positive, so we must also consider the negative values of the variables. Notice that if $x = -9$ and $y = -8$, then $xy = 72$. This is the greatest possible value for $xy$.

16. **(D)** Let's test small values of $x$. If $x = 0$, $x^2 + x + 1 = 0 + 0 + 1 = 1 \leq 2$. If $x = 1$, $x^2 + x + 1 = 1 + 1 + 1 = 3 \nleq 2$. Clearly for $x > 1$, it will also be false. If $x = -1$, $x^2 + x + 1 = 1 - 1 + 1 = 1 \leq 2$. If $x = -2$, $x^2 + x + 1 = 4 - 2 + 1 = 3 \nleq 2$. Clearly for $x < -2$ it will also be false. So the inequality is only true when $x = 0$ or –1.

   Alternate solution: Subtract 1 from both sides of the inequality to get $x^2 + x \leq 1$. Then factor the left side to get $x(x + 1) \leq 1$. So this question is really asking when a product of two consecutive numbers is less than or equal to one. A quick inspection tells us this is impossible unless one of the factors is zero (i.e., $x = 0$ or $x + 1 = 0$). Hence $x = 0$ or $x = -1$ are the only solutions.

17. **(A)** The cube of a negative integer is always negative. For example, $(-2)(-2)(-2) = -8$. The square of a negative integer is always positive. A negative is never greater than or equal to a positive.

18. **(C)** The product of three numbers being negative means that either one is negative and two are positive or all three are negative. The first case is not possible with consecutive integers. To have both positive and negative in a set of consecutive integers you have to have zero where the product would be zero, not a negative. So all three numbers must be negative. The largest any one of them could be is $-1$, if we had the numbers $-3$, $-2$, and $-1$.

19. **(B)** The average of any two consecutive integers is not an integer. For example, $\frac{2+3}{2} = 2.5$.

    So A is not the answer. The average of three consecutive integers is always an integer. In fact, it is always the middle number! If the numbers are $n$, $n + 1$, and $n + 2$, then their average is $\frac{n+(n+1)+(n+2)}{3} = \frac{3n+3}{3} = n+1$. For example, the average of 2, 3, and 4 is 3.

    For more information on why the other answers cannot be correct see the section in Chapter 5 on averages.

20. **(A)** Five consecutive integers could be three odd and two even, where their sum is odd, or two odd and three even, where their sum is even. So C is not true. Consecutive integers can be negative (e.g., $-5, -4, -3, -2, -1$) so their sum can be less than 15. So B is not true. Thus A must be true.

    **Alternate solution:** If the middle number is $x$, then the sum of the five consecutive numbers is $5x$. Hence the sum is always a multiple of 5 and A is true. If $x$ is even the sum, $5x$, is also even, but if $x$ is odd, the sum is also odd. So C is not always true. And clearly if $x < 3$, then the sum, $5x$, is less than 15. So B is not always true either.

21. **(B)** We know from problem 20 that A is always true and C is true when the middle number is even. Thus the answer must be that B cannot be true. Note the smallest sum from five consecutive *positive* integers is $1 + 2 + 3 + 4 + 5 = 15$.

22. **(45)** Represent the consecutive integers as $x$, $x + 1$, $x + 2$, and $x + 3$. Setting the sum equal to 46 and combining like terms yields $4x + 6 = 46$. Then $4x = 40$, so $x = 10$. This makes our original four integers 10, 11, 12, and 13. The next three consecutive integers are 14, 15, and 16. Their sum is $14 + 15 + 16 = 45$.

23. **(C)** Try selecting three values for $a$, $b$, and $c$, such as 2, 3, 4, or 5, 6, 7. Notice that in both of these cases, the product $abc$ is even because one or more of the variables is even. This will always be the case when multiplying three consecutive integers. Then $abc + 1$ is odd, because one more than an even is always odd.

24. **(C)** Notice $a^2 - ab = a(a - b)$ and since $a,b$ are consecutive and decreasing, $a - b = 1$. Hence $a^2 - ab = a(a - b) = a \times 1 = a$.

25. **(C)** Notice that $a + ab = a(1 + b)$ and since $a,b$ are consecutive and decreasing $b + 1 = a$. Hence, $a + ab = a(1 + b) = a(a) = a^2$.

26. **(C)** At first glance, it seems B would be larger since there are more addends, but that is incorrect. Consider carefully that $(-5) + (-4) + (-3) + (-2) + (-1) + 0 + 1 + 2 + 3 + 4 + 5$, and by reordering $5 + (-5) + 4 + (-4) + 3 + (-3) + 2 + (-2) + 1 + (-1) + 0$ it is easy to see the sum is zero. Likewise, for the sum from $-10$ to $10$.

**Alternate Solution:** The sum of consecutive integers from $-5$ to $5$ is the sum of 11 consecutive integers so it is 11 times the middle number, which is $11 \times 0 = 0$. Likewise, the sum of consecutive integers from $-10$ to $10$ will be $21 \times 0 = 0$.

## Number Theory (Problems on page 60)

1. **(B)** The smallest positive factor of any number is 1. The largest factor of any positive number is the number itself—in this case 8.

2. **(C)** By testing all primes less than $\sqrt{91} \approx 9.5$, we find that 91 is divisible by 7, and $91 = 7 \times 13$. The smallest prime divisor of 91 is 7. It is easy to start factoring 63 as it is a multiple of 3: $63 = 3 \times 21 = 3 \times 3 \times 7$. The largest prime factor of 63 is 7.

3. **(B)** Many people will just assume there are an even number of odd and evens. Not so in this case. Positive single-digit even numbers are 2, 4, 6, and 8. Positive single-digit odd numbers are 1, 3, 5, 7, and 9. If we had included 0 there would have been an equal number of odds and evens.

4. **(C)** We know (see tips) that $\dfrac{ab}{\mathrm{GCF}(a,b)} = \mathrm{LCM}(a,b)$.

5. **(C)** As $\dfrac{ab}{\mathrm{GCF}(a,b)} = \mathrm{LCM}(a,b)$, if we multiply both sides of the equation by $\mathrm{GCF}(a,b)$, we get $ab = \mathrm{LCM}(a,b) \times \mathrm{GCF}(a,b)$.

6. **(B)** The only even prime number is 2 and $2 < 3$.

7. **(D)** All primes besides 2 are odd. An odd prime could be 3 or it could be larger, say 7.

8. **(C)** As $N$ is prime, it has only two factors, 1 and itself. So the product of its factors is $1 \times N$, which equals $N$.

9. **(E)** We factor 72 as follows: $72 = 2 \times 36 = 2 \times 2 \times 18 = 2 \times 2 \times 2 \times 9 = 2 \times 2 \times 2 \times 3 \times 3$. Using exponents this can be expressed as $2^3 \times 3^2$. Notice A does not equal 72, while B, C, and D all equal 72 but are not made up of primes.

10. **(C)** To be divisible by 9 the sum of the digits must be a multiple of 9. In this case the sum of the digits is $9 + 3 + 7 + D + 2 + 4 = 25 + D$. As $D$ is a digit from 0 to 9, the only multiple of 9 that $25 + D$ could equal is 27, when $D = 2$. Hence 937,224 is divisible by 9 and thus also divisible by 3. To be divisible by 8 the last three digits must be divisible by 8 and $224 = 28 \times 8$. As 937,224 is divisible by 8, it is also divisible by 4 and 2.

11. **(D)** The product of an even with any other number is even, so A, $xy$, is even and B, $8x$, is even. Any even number is divisible by 2, so C, $\dfrac{x}{2}$, is an integer, but it could be an odd or an even integer. For example $\dfrac{14}{2} = 7$ is odd, but $\dfrac{16}{2} = 8$ is even. The difference between

an even and an odd is always odd. Why? If $x - y = z$, then $y + z = x$. If $z$ was even then we would have odd ($y$) plus even ($z$) equal to even ($x$), which is not true. Note E is not necessarily odd for reasons similar to B.

12. **(D)** These are equal if $x$ does not have 2 as a factor. For instance, if $x = 25$ then it has three factors $(1, 5, 25)$ and Quantity A would be $2 \times 3 = 6$. Meanwhile $2x = 50$ has six factors $(1, 2, 5, 10, 25, 50)$. They are not equal if $x$ already has a factor of 2. For instance if $x = 10$, then it has four factors $(1, 2, 5, 10)$, and Quantity A would be $2 \times 4 = 8$. But $2x = 20$, which has only six factors $(1, 2, 4, 5, 10, 20)$.

13. **(D)** Note that $2x$ has the same prime factorization as $x$ except it has an extra factor of 2. If $x$ already has 2 as a prime factor, then $2x$ has no new prime factors. For example, if $x = 6 = 2 \times 3$, then $2x = 2 \times 6 = 2 \times 2 \times 3$. Both $x$ and $2x$ have two prime factors (2 and 3). If $x$ does not have 2 as a factor, then $2x$ has one more distinct prime factor than $x$. For example, if $x = 21 = 3 \times 7$, then $2x = 2 \times 21 = 2 \times 3 \times 7$. In this case $2x$ has three distinct prime factors, while $x$ has only two.

14. **(C)** The even two-digit positive integers are 10, 12, . . . , 98, while the odd two-digit numbers are 11, 13, . . . , 99. Each even number corresponds to an odd number one more than it, namely $10 \leftrightarrow 11$, $12 \leftrightarrow 13$, . . . , $98 \leftrightarrow 99$. Thus, there is an equal number of each.

15. **(D)** The GCF($a$,$ab$) is $a$. The GCF($b$,$ba$) is $b$. We do not know which is larger, $a$ or $b$.

16. **(A)** The LCM(7,3) is 21 since LCM(7,3) = $3 \times 7 \div$ GCF(7,3) = $3 \times 7 \div 1 = 21$. As the lowest common positive multiple of 7 and 3 is odd, any other positive multiple of 7 and 3 will be larger. In fact, the smallest even multiple is 42.

17. **(B)** The smallest number divisible by both 5 and 7 is the LCM(5,7). Now LCM(5,7) = $5 \times 7 \div$ GCF(5,7) = $5 \times 7 \div 1 = 35$. Since $35 < 70$, choose B.

18. **(A)** The largest number that is a factor of both 30 and 90 is the GCF(30,90). Since 30 is a factor of 90, GCF(30,90) = 30. As $30 > 15$, choose A.

19. **(A)** Try $N = 6$. Then the product of its factors is $1 \times 2 \times 3 \times 6 = 36$, while $2N = 2 \times 6 = 12$. Try $N = 8$. Then the product of its factors is $1 \times 2 \times 4 \times 8 = 64$, while $2N = 16$. It appears the B will be larger, but can we be certain? Since $N$ is not prime, it has one factor besides 1 and $N$. That factor must be at least 2. So the product of factors of $N$ is at least $1 \times 2 \times N = 2N$. Could the product ever be equal to $2N$? Only if the only factor of $N$ besides 1 and itself was 2. This only happens when $N = 4$. But $N > 4$. So the product of factors of $N$ is always larger than $2N$.

20. **(D)** Since 2 divides 8 and 4 divides 8, the smallest number divisible by 2, 3, 4, and 8 is the LCM(3,8), which is 24. But any multiple of 24, like 240, will also be divisible by 2, 3, 4, and 8.

21. **(A)** To be divisible by 8, the last three digits must be divisible by 8. 1,001 is not divisible by 8 since 1 is not divisible by 8. 1,002 is not divisible by 8 since 2 is not divisible by 8. Continue to see that 1,008 is the first number greater than 1,000 that is divisible by 8.

22. **(D)** $N$ always has 1 and $N$ as factors. If the sum of its positive factors is $N + 1$, then it has no other positive factors except $N$ and 1. Thus $N$ is a prime number.

23. **(D, F, G)** Examine each choice individually. The factors of 8 are 1, 2, 4, and 8. The factors of 12 are 1, 2, 3, 4, 6, and 12. The factors of 15 are 1, 3, 5, and 15. These three choices each have more than three positive factors, so eliminate A, B, and C. Notice that the three factors of 25 are 1, 5, and 25, so D is correct. In general, a prime number $p$ when squared will have exactly three factors, namely 1, $p$, and $p^2$. Then F and G are also correct, noting that $49 = 7^2$.

24. **(A)** To be divisible by 3, the sum of the digits must be divisible by 3. Hence $7 + 2 + 8 + D + 4 + 9 = 30 + D$. As 30 is a multiple of 3, $D$ must be a multiple of three. So $D$ could be 0, 3, 6, or 9. Which of those will make the number divisible by 7? We can check each individually by dividing. But we notice that if $D = 0$, then 728,049 is the sum of multiples of 7, 700,000 + 28,000 + 49; hence it is divisible by 7.

25. **(B)** We investigate each possible answer. A, $p^2$, is not prime because it has $p$ as a factor. C, $p + 3$, could not be prime because, as the sum of two odds, it is even and divisible by 2. D, $17 \times 23$, could not be prime as it has 17 or 23 as factors. Since $72 = 3 \times 24$, $71 \times 72 \times 73$ is a multiple of three and the sum of multiples of three is a multiple of three and thus not prime. That just leaves B. Could $p + 2$ be prime? If $p = 3$, an odd prime, then $p + 2 = 5$, which is also prime.

26. **(A, B, D)** By definition, if $b$ is a factor of $c$, then $c$ is a multiple of $b$, making A correct. Now try putting in numbers such as $a = 3$, $b = 6$, and $c = 12$. Since 12 is a multiple of 3, **B** is correct. In general, if $a$ divides $b$ (with no remainder), and $b$ divides $c$, then $a$ divides $c$. Choice C is not correct because 12 is not a multiple of $18 = 3 \times 6$. Choice D is correct because the sum of two multiples of a number is also a multiple of that number. Here, $6 + 12 = 18$ is a multiple of 3, meaning that 3 is a factor of 18.

## Fractions (Problems on page 72)

1. **(A)** We calculate $\dfrac{1}{1+\frac{1}{2}} = \dfrac{1}{\frac{2}{2}+\frac{1}{2}} = \dfrac{1}{\frac{3}{2}} = 1 \times \dfrac{2}{3} = \dfrac{2}{3}$, while $\dfrac{2}{2+\frac{2}{1}} = \dfrac{2}{2+2} = \dfrac{2}{4} = \dfrac{1}{2}$. As $\dfrac{2}{3}$ is greater than $\dfrac{1}{2}$.

   Alternate approach: $\dfrac{1}{1+\frac{1}{2}} = \dfrac{1}{1+\frac{1}{2}} \times \dfrac{2}{2} = \dfrac{2}{2+2\times\frac{1}{2}} = \dfrac{2}{2+1} = \dfrac{2}{3}$.

2. **(B)** First we convert the mixed fraction to a regular fraction: $2\frac{2}{3} = \dfrac{3\times2+2}{3} = \dfrac{8}{3}$. Put another way, $2\frac{2}{3} = 2 + \frac{2}{3} = 1 + 1 + \frac{2}{3} = \frac{3}{3} + \frac{3}{3} + \frac{2}{3} = \frac{8}{3}$. Now the reciprocal of $\dfrac{8}{3}$ is $\dfrac{3}{8}$ and $\dfrac{3}{8} < \dfrac{3}{7}$.

3. **(A)** We note that $\dfrac{3}{5} \div \dfrac{5}{7} \div \dfrac{7}{9} = \dfrac{3}{5} \times \dfrac{7}{5} \times \dfrac{9}{7}$ which is certainly larger than $\dfrac{3}{5}$ as $\dfrac{7}{5}$ and $\dfrac{9}{7}$ are larger than 1. Meanwhile, $\dfrac{3}{5} \times \dfrac{5}{7} \times \dfrac{7}{9}$ is less than $\dfrac{3}{5}$ since $\dfrac{5}{7}$ and $\dfrac{7}{9}$ are less than 1.

4. **(C)** Upon inspection we note that $\dfrac{2}{10} = \dfrac{1}{5}$, $\dfrac{3}{7} = \dfrac{6}{14}$, and $\dfrac{8}{6} = \dfrac{4}{3}$. So both quantities are adding the same numbers, just in different orders.

5. **(A)** It is possible to compute each and compare, but we will work on both quantities at once:

Add $\frac{1}{4}$ to both quantities:

$$\frac{1}{2}-\frac{1}{3}+\frac{1}{4}+\frac{1}{4} \qquad \frac{1}{3}-\frac{1}{4}+\frac{1}{5}+\frac{1}{4}$$
$$1-\frac{1}{3} \qquad\qquad \frac{1}{3}+\frac{1}{5}$$

Subtract $\frac{1}{3}$ from both quantities:

$$1-\frac{1}{3}-\frac{1}{3} \qquad \frac{1}{3}+\frac{1}{5}-\frac{1}{3}$$
$$\frac{1}{3} \qquad\qquad \frac{1}{5}$$

Clearly $\frac{1}{3} > \frac{1}{5}$.

6. **(C)** In Quantity A, white is 4 of 6 equal parts, or $\frac{2}{3}$. In Quantity B, shaded is 6 of 9 equal parts or $\frac{2}{3}$.

7. **(D)** You could convert them all to decimals or use common denominators to compare fractions but we demonstrate how to use some estimation. A, $\frac{11}{20}$, is greater than $\frac{10}{20}=\frac{1}{2}$. B, $\frac{5}{6}$, is close to $\frac{6}{6}=1$. C, $\frac{3}{8}$, is less than $\frac{4}{8}=\frac{1}{2}$ but more than $\frac{2}{8}=\frac{1}{4}$. D, $\frac{2}{7}$, is close to $\frac{2}{8}=\frac{1}{4}$. E, $\frac{1}{3}$, is less than $\frac{1}{2}$ but more than $\frac{1}{4}$. Clearly A and B are too large. Now, as $\frac{1}{7}<\frac{1}{6}$, we know $\frac{2}{7}<\frac{2}{6}=\frac{1}{3}$. So E is not the smallest. Also $\frac{1}{8}>\frac{1}{9}$, so $\frac{3}{8}>\frac{3}{9}=\frac{1}{3}$. So C is greater than E. That leaves D as the smallest.

**Alternate solution:** Look at each fraction and multiply the numerator by three. In all cases but D, three times the numerator is greater than or equal to the denominator. So D is the smallest.

8. **(C)** There are 22 + 18 = 40 kids in the class. As 22 out of 40 are girls, the fraction of the class that is girls is $\frac{22}{40}=\frac{11}{20}$.

9. **(12)** We know that $\frac{3}{8}x=6$. If we multiply both sides of the equation by 2 and cancel appropriately, $2\times\frac{3}{8}x=2\times6$, we find that $\frac{3}{4}x=\mathbf{12}$.

Alternatively, we could have found $x$: $\frac{3}{8}x=6 \Rightarrow \frac{8}{3}\times\frac{3}{8}x=\frac{8}{3}\times6^{2} \Rightarrow x=16$. Then $\frac{3}{4}x=\frac{3}{4}\times16^{4}=\mathbf{12}$.

10. **(A)** First, we simplify Quantity A and take a rough estimate of its value. $\frac{\frac{4}{7}+\frac{5}{14}}{1+\frac{45}{49}}=\frac{\frac{8}{14}+\frac{5}{14}}{\frac{49}{49}+\frac{45}{49}}=\frac{\frac{13}{14}}{\frac{94}{49}}\approx\frac{1}{2}$. Then we see that $\frac{\frac{4^2}{7}\times\frac{3}{14^7}}{1\div\frac{45}{49}}=\frac{\frac{6}{49}}{\frac{49}{45}}\approx\frac{\frac{6}{48}}{1}=\frac{1}{8}$. Although these are rough

approximations, it is clear that A will be larger.

11. **(D)** First simplify $\frac{1}{\left(\frac{1}{\frac{1}{x}}\right)}=\frac{1}{\left(1\div\frac{1}{x}\right)}=\frac{1}{\left(1\times\frac{x}{1}\right)}=\frac{1}{x}$. Now which is larger, $x$ or $\frac{1}{x}$? That depends

on $x$. If $x=2$, then $1/x=\frac{1}{2}<2=x$. If $x=\frac{1}{2}$, then $\frac{1}{x}=\frac{1}{\left(\frac{1}{2}\right)}=2>\frac{1}{2}=x$.

12. $\left(\boldsymbol{\frac{27}{10}}\right)$ As an equation, $\frac{3}{7}\times\frac{21}{6}=\frac{5}{9}\times x$. To solve for $x$, multiply both sides by $\frac{9}{5}$:
$\frac{9}{5}\times\frac{3}{7}\times\frac{\cancel{21}}{\cancel{6}^2}=\frac{\cancel{9}}{\cancel{5}}\times\frac{\cancel{5}}{\cancel{9}}\times x$. Then $\frac{27}{10}=x$.

13. $\left(\boldsymbol{\frac{3}{5}}\right)$ $\frac{3}{4}$ of the registered voters voted, registered voters are $\frac{4}{5}$ of those eligible to vote,

and those eligible are $\frac{2}{3}$ of the population. Hence those who voted are $\frac{3}{4}\times\frac{4}{5}\times\frac{2}{3}=\frac{2}{5}$ of

the population. Hence $\frac{3}{5}$ of the population did not vote.

14. **(C)** This is really a conversion problem: $(5\,\text{lb steak})\times\frac{1.25\,\text{lb lamb}}{2.5\,\text{lb steak}}\times\frac{\$18}{4\,\text{lb lamb}}$, which

equals $\cancel{5}^{\cancel{x}}\times\frac{1.25}{2.5}\times\frac{\cancel{18}^9}{\cancel{4}^{\cancel{x}}}=1.25\times9=11.25$ dollars.

Alternatively, if we say 4 lb of lamb is approximately 3 times $1\frac{1}{4}$ lb of lamb, then $1\frac{1}{4}$ lb

of lamb cost about $\$18/3=\$6$. Then 5 lb of steak is twice 2.5 lb of steak or twice the price

of $1\frac{1}{4}$ lb of lamb. That is $2\times\$6=\$12$. As C is the only answer near $12, choose C.

15. **(D)** First note that $a$ can be 1, 2, 3, 4, or 5 and $b$ can be 2 or 3. Then
$S=\left\{\frac{1}{2},\frac{1}{3},\frac{2}{2},\frac{2}{3},\frac{3}{2},\frac{3}{3},\frac{4}{2},\frac{4}{3},\frac{5}{2},\frac{5}{3}\right\}$. If we reduce these fractions to lowest terms we have
$S=\left\{\frac{1}{2},\frac{1}{3},1,\frac{2}{3},\frac{3}{2},1,2,\frac{4}{3},\frac{5}{2},\frac{5}{3}\right\}$, which is only nine distinct numbers. We see that A, B, C,
and E are not true. So the answer must be D.

16. **(2,880)** Since $\frac{1}{2}$ of the students major in education and $\frac{1}{3}$ major in math, the rest must

study music. That is $1-\frac{1}{3}-\frac{1}{2}=\frac{1}{6}$ study music. As $\frac{3}{4}$ of the music students are female,

only $\frac{1}{4}$ are male. That is $\frac{1}{4}$ of $\frac{1}{6}$, or $\frac{1}{24}$, of all students are male music majors. That

group is 120 students. So the college has $24\times120=2,880$ students. This is a good problem

to use a diagram:

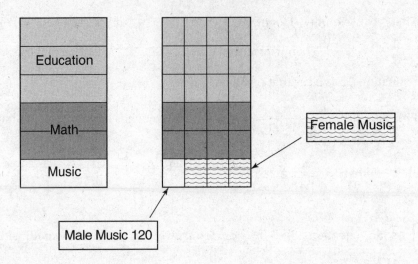

Education

Math

Music

Female Music

Male Music 120

17. **(E)** First we expand: $\left(\dfrac{2}{x}\right)^3 = \left(\dfrac{x}{-2}\right)^2 \Rightarrow \dfrac{8}{x^3} = \dfrac{x^2}{4}$. Then multiply both sides by $4x^3$ to clear

the denominators: $\dfrac{8}{x^3} = \dfrac{x^2}{4} \Rightarrow 4x^3 \times \dfrac{8}{x^3} = 4x^3 \times \dfrac{x^2}{4} \Rightarrow 32 = x^5$. This implies that $x = 2$.

18. **(A)** After the 8 joined in 2013, there were 32 boys in the troop. As $\dfrac{1}{8}$ of 32 = 4, after 4

quit there were 28 left. In 2014, $\dfrac{1}{7}$ of 28, or 4, left. There remained 24 until 3 joined, so

that 27 remained. To get back to the original size, 3 out of 27 would have to quit. As

$\dfrac{3}{27} = \dfrac{1}{9}$, choose A.

19. **(63)** Let $x$ be the class size. As $\dfrac{5}{7}$ of his students are absent, only $\dfrac{2}{7}$ are attending. $\dfrac{1}{3}$ of

those attending are getting sick, so $\dfrac{2}{3}$ of those attending are not getting sick and will

remain. Hence $\dfrac{2}{3}$ of $\dfrac{2}{7}$ of $x$ = 12. Solve for $x$: $\dfrac{2}{3} \times \dfrac{2}{7} \times x = 12 \Rightarrow \dfrac{4}{21} x = 12 \Rightarrow x = 12 \times \dfrac{21}{4} = 63$.

Normally, Professor Murty has 63 students in his class.

20. **(B)** Assume that the chief has $n + m$ officers; $n$ carry firearms and $m$ do not. Then

$\dfrac{n}{n+m} = \dfrac{3}{5}$ and $\dfrac{n+1}{n+m+1} = \dfrac{5}{8}$. If we cross multiply, we get the two equations $5n = 3n + 3m$

and $8n + 8 = 5n + 5m + 5$. The first equation simplifies to $n = 1.5m$, which we substitute

into the second equation to get $8(1.5m) + 8 = 5(1.5m) + 5m + 5$. This simplifies to $m = 6$.

Take $m = 6$ and thus $n = 1.5 \times 6 = 9$. Check: $\dfrac{9}{(6+9)} = \dfrac{9}{15} = \dfrac{2}{3}$ and $\dfrac{(9+1)}{(9+6+1)} = \dfrac{10}{16} = \dfrac{5}{8}$. There

are 6 officers on his force who do not carry firearms. Another way to look at

this problem is that you want a fraction equivalent to $\dfrac{3}{5}$ (like $\dfrac{6}{10}$, $\dfrac{9}{15}$, . . .) so that if you

add 1 to both numerator and denominator you get a fraction equivalent to $\dfrac{5}{8}$ (like $\dfrac{10}{16}$,

$\dfrac{15}{24}$, . . .). Then some guesswork could lead you to the answer.

# Decimals (Problems on page 79)

1. **(A)** Estimating, $8.02 - 7.03$ is $0.99$, while $0.40 + 0.50 = 0.90$.

2. **(B)** Straight calculation shows that $(0.5)^2 = (0.5)(0.5) = 0.25$, while $5 \times 0.5 = 2.5$. Alternatively, if we divide both quantities by $0.5$, we are left with $0.5$ in Quantity A and $5$ in Quantity B.

3. **(C)** $(0.1)^3 = (0.1)(0.1)(0.1) = 0.001$ since the product is 1 with three places to the right of the decimal point. Also to find $1,000 \div 1,000,000$, we move the decimal point in $1,000.0$ six places to the left and get $0.001$.

4. **(B)** Since $-8.2$ is so large compared to the other two values, the answer in Quantity A will be negative, while the answer in Quantity B will be positive.

5. **(B)** In Quantity A we move the decimal five places to the right to get $3,420,000$. In Quantity B we move the decimal nine places to the right to get $34,200,000$.

6. **(C)** Multiply both quantities by $10^4$ and now we have $1.03$ in A and $1,030 \div 10^3$ in B. To find $1,030 \div 10^3$, move the decimal three places to the left and get $1.03$.

7. **(E)** We use estimation. A is less than $50 \times 10 = 500$, B is $465$, C is approximately $2.33 \times 100 = 233$, D is approximately $645$, and E is approximately $1,000 \div \left(\dfrac{3}{2}\right) = 1,003 \times \dfrac{2}{3} \approx 667$.

   Because the last two approximations are very good, we can confidently say the answer is E.

8. **(D)** We use estimation. A is approximately 2, B is $3.45$, C is approximately $100 \div 50 = 2$, D is approximately $-1$, and E is approximately $1.5$. Only D is less than zero, so choose D.

9. **(A)** Divide both sides by $(0.99)^9$. Then Quantity A is 1 and Quantity B is $0.99$.

10. **(C)** In Quantity A move the decimal eight places to the right to find $923,000$. In Quantity B move the decimal two places to the left to find $923,000$.

11. **(E)** Another way to ask this question is, what do we have to multiply $1.3 \times 10^{-4}$ by to get $39 \times 10^3$? First, $1.3 \times 3 = 3.9$, so $1.3 \times 30 = 39$. Second, $10^{-4} \times 10^7 = 10^3$. So the answer is $30 \times 10^7$ or $300,000,000$.

    **Alternate solution:** $\dfrac{3.9 \times 10^3}{1.3 \times 10^{-4}} = \dfrac{39}{1.3} \times \dfrac{10^3}{10^{-4}} = 30 \times 10^{3-(-4)} = 30 \times 10^7$.

12. **(B)** Another way to ask this question is what do we multiply $0.00015$ by to get $600$? We note that $0.00015 \times 10^5 = 15$, that $15 \times 4 = 60$, and $60 \times 10 = 600$. In total we multiplied by $10^5 \times 4 \times 10 = 4 \times 10^6 = 4,000,000$. You could also check these answers with your calculator.

13. **(1,000)** To solve $16.44 \times 0.47223 \times x = 4,722.3 \times 1.644$, we divide. Then $x = 4,722.3 \times 1.644 \div 16.44 \div 0.47223 = (4,722.3 \div 0.47223) \times (1.644 \div 16.44)$. In the first set of parentheses the decimal moved four places, so the answer is $10^4$. In the second set of parentheses the decimal moved one place, so the answer is $10^{-1}$. Hence $x = 10^4 \times 10^{-1} = 10^3 = 1,000$.

14. **(100)** We'll approach this problem differently. First, solve $6.15 \div \underline{\hspace{1cm}} = 615$. Since the decimal moves two places to the right, the answer is $10^{-2}$. Second, solve $723 \div \underline{\hspace{1cm}} = 0.0723$. Since the decimal moves four places to the left the answer is $10^4$. Then $x = 10^{-2} \times 10^4 = 10^2 = 100$. You may find it easier to multiply both sides of the equation by $x$ and then approach this as a multiplication problem instead of a division problem.

## Radicals and Exponents (Problems on page 84)

1. **(A)** Many people incorrectly add the exponents and decide the answer is C. The rule is to multiply the exponents, so $(5^2)^3 = 5^6$.

2. **(C)** Much like problem 1, Quantity A is $\left(\left(\frac{1}{2}\right)^2\right)^3 = \left(\frac{1}{2}\right)^6 = \frac{1}{(2^6)}$. Quantity B is $2^{-6} = \frac{1}{(2^6)}$.

3. **(A)** Since $10 = 2 \times 5$, then $10^5 = (2 \times 5)^5 = 2^5 5^5$. Divide both quantities by what they have in common, $2^5 5^4$, and you'll have Quantity A is 5 and Quantity B is 2.

4. **(B)** As $8 = 2^3$, $\frac{8}{2^5} = 2^3 \div 2^5 = 2^{-2} = \frac{1}{2^2} = \frac{1}{4}$. Meanwhile $(2^{-2})^{-2} = 2^4 = 16$.

5. **(A)** The easiest way to solve this problem is to square both quantities. Then A is $\frac{8}{9}$ and B is $\left(\frac{2}{3}\right)^2 = \frac{2^2}{3^2} = \frac{4}{9}$.

6. **(B)** This is commonly mistaken to be a rule and thus believed equal when it is not. Note that $\sqrt{4+9} = \sqrt{13}$, which is between 3 and 4, since $3^2 < 13 < 4^2$. Meanwhile $\sqrt{4} + \sqrt{9} = 2 + 3 = 5$.

7. **(A)** This is also not a rule. Note that $\sqrt{9-4} = \sqrt{5}$, which is between 2 and 3 since $2^2 < 5 < 3^2$. Also $\sqrt{9} - \sqrt{4} = 3 - 2 = 1$.

8. **(A)** Here is another nonrule. We see $(2 + 3)^2 = 5^2 = 25$, while $2^2 + 3^2 = 4 + 9 = 13$.

9. **(C)** Note that $\sqrt[3]{8} = 2$ since $2^3 = 8$. Hence $-\sqrt[3]{8} = -2$. Also $\sqrt[3]{-8} = -2$ since $(-2)^3 = -8$.

10. **(A)** Be careful! These are not equal, as $\sqrt{(-4)^2} = \sqrt{16} = 4$.

11. **(E)** To solve for $a$ in $2^a \times 16^2 = 4^5$, it is best to change all powers to have a base of 2. Then $2^a \times 16^2 = 4^5 \Rightarrow 2^a \times (2^4)^2 = (2^2)^5 \Rightarrow 2^a \times 2^8 = 2^{10} \Rightarrow 2^{a+8} = 2^{10}$. Now that the bases are equal we can equate the exponents. As $a + 8 = 10$, then $a = 2$.

12. **(C)** We simplify and change all powers to have a base of 3: $\frac{3^x}{9} = \sqrt{81} \Rightarrow \frac{3^x}{3^2} = 9 \Rightarrow 3^{x-2} = 3^2$. Now we can equate exponents $x - 2 = 2$, and see that $x = 4$.

13. **(C)** As C is the product of A and B, which are both greater than 1, C is larger than either of them. Also as $3^2 = 9$ is larger than $2^{-3} = \frac{1}{8}$, C is larger than D. Now E is $(2^3)^2 = 2^6 = 64$, while C is $2^3 3^2 = 8 \times 9 = 72$.

14. **(B)** Change all powers to a base of two: $2^{a+6} 4^a = 8^3 \Rightarrow 2^{a+6} (2^2)^a = (2^3)^3 \Rightarrow 2^{a+6} 2^{2a} = 2^9 \Rightarrow 2^{(a+6)+2a} = 2^9 \Rightarrow 2^{3a+6} = 2^9$. Now we can equate exponents and solve for $a$: $3a + 6 = 9 \Rightarrow 3a = 3 \Rightarrow a = 1$.

15. **(C)** We write 6 as $2 \times 3$, change our radicals to exponents and simplify. $\sqrt{6^n} = \dfrac{2^n}{\sqrt{2}} \times \dfrac{3^n}{\sqrt{3}} \Rightarrow ((2 \times 3)^n)^{\frac{1}{2}} = \dfrac{2^n}{2^{\frac{1}{2}}} \times \dfrac{3^n}{3^{\frac{1}{2}}} \Rightarrow (2 \times 3)^{\frac{n}{2}} = 2^{n-\frac{1}{2}} 3^{n-\frac{1}{2}} \Rightarrow 2^{\frac{n}{2}} 3^{\frac{n}{2}} = 2^{n-\frac{1}{2}} 3^{n-\frac{1}{2}}$. Now we can see that we need to solve $\dfrac{n}{2} = n - \left(\dfrac{1}{2}\right)$. Multiply both sides by 2 to clear the fractions, and we get $n = 2n - 1 \Rightarrow -n = -1 \Rightarrow n = 1$.

16. **(E)** First we simplify under the radical: $\sqrt{\dfrac{x^{10}y^8z^5}{x^6y^7z^6}} = \sqrt{x^{10-6}y^{8-7}z^{5-6}} = \sqrt{x^4yz^{-1}}$. Since none of the answers have negative exponents, we move $z$ back into the denominator, $\sqrt{\dfrac{x^4y}{z}}$, and apply the radical to all parts: $\dfrac{\sqrt{x^4}\sqrt{y}}{\sqrt{z}} = \dfrac{x^2\sqrt{y}}{\sqrt{z}}$. Finally we rationalize the denominator: $\dfrac{x^2\sqrt{y}}{\sqrt{z}} \times \dfrac{\sqrt{z}}{\sqrt{z}} = \dfrac{x^2\sqrt{yz}}{z}$.

17. **(B)** First we rationalize the denominator in B: $\dfrac{20}{\sqrt{10}} \times \dfrac{\sqrt{10}}{\sqrt{10}} = \dfrac{20\sqrt{10}}{10} = 2\sqrt{10}$. Then we simplify the radical in A: $\dfrac{\sqrt{40}}{2} = \dfrac{\sqrt{4}\sqrt{10}}{2} = \dfrac{2\sqrt{10}}{2} = \sqrt{10}$. Clearly $2\sqrt{10}$ is greater than $\sqrt{10}$.

    **Alternate solution:** Since both quantities are positive, we can square both sides. A squared is $\left(\dfrac{\sqrt{40}}{2}\right)^2 = \dfrac{40}{4} = 10$. B squared is $\left(\dfrac{20}{\sqrt{10}}\right)^2 = \dfrac{400}{10} = 40$. So B is larger.

18. **(B)** Let $r$ be the radius of the circle, $d$, its diameter, and $s$, the side length of the square. The area of the circle is $\pi r^2$. Since $r = \dfrac{d}{2}$, the area of the circle is also $\pi\left(\dfrac{d}{2}\right)^2 = \dfrac{\pi d^2}{4}$. The area of the square is $s^2$. Then $s^2 = \dfrac{\pi d^2}{4}$ and thus $s = \sqrt{\dfrac{\pi d^2}{4}} = \sqrt{\dfrac{\pi}{4}}d$. But we want the diagonal of the square, which is $\sqrt{2}s$ (see Appendix). So $\sqrt{2}s = \sqrt{2}\sqrt{\dfrac{\pi}{4}}d = \sqrt{\dfrac{2\pi}{4}}d$. As $2\pi > 4$, $\sqrt{\dfrac{2\pi}{4}} > 1$, and thus $\sqrt{2}s > d$.

    **Alternate solution:** Draw a diagram so that the diameter of the circle and the diagonal of the square are equal. Then the square would fit inside the circle and hence not have equal area. To have equal area, the diagonal of the square would have to be increased. That is why the diameter is smaller.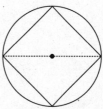

19. **(C)** $3^4 + 3^4 + 3^4 = 3 \times (3^4) = 3^5$.

20. **(B)** In Quantity A, $2^4 + 2^4 + 2^4 = 3 \times 2^4$. In Quantity B, $2^6 = 2^2 2^4 = 4 \times 2^4$. Since $4 > 3$, choose B.

21. **(B)** In Quantity A the average is $\dfrac{2^0 + 2^1 + 2^2 + 2^3}{4} = \dfrac{2^0 + 2^1 + 2^2 + 2^3}{2^2} = 2^{-2} + 2^{-1} + 2^0 + 2^1 = \dfrac{1}{4} + \dfrac{1}{2} + 1 + 2 = 3\dfrac{3}{4}$. In Quantity B the average is $\dfrac{3^0 + 3^1 + 3^2}{3} = 3^{-1} + 3^0 + 3^1 = \dfrac{1}{3} + 1 + 3 = 4\dfrac{1}{3}$.

22. **(C)** In Quantity A, the average is $\dfrac{3^1 + 3^2 + 3^3}{3} = 3^0 + 3^1 + 3^2$. So they are equal.

# Algebra

Algebra can be very helpful in solving some problems, but most problems on the GRE quantitative exam can be solved without any complicated algebra. The algebra that is required is much less than what is typically taught in your high school math classes. Use this chapter to brush up on your algebra skills and practice GRE-style questions that could involve algebra.

What is algebra? The essential concept is representing an unknown number with a symbol (usually a letter) that we call a *variable*. For example, in the expression $2x + 3$, $x$ is a variable representing an unknown number that we would like to double and add 3 to. It is called a variable because we can think of $x$ taking on different values (varying). If $x = 3$, then $2x + 3 = 9$. If $x = 5$, then $2x + 3 = 13$. If $x = 37$, then $2x + 3 = 77$.

## POLYNOMIALS AND FACTORING

A *monomial* is the product of a number with zero or more variables. A *binomial* is the sum (or difference) of two monomials; a *trinomial* is the sum (or difference) of three monomials, and so on. A *polynomial* is a sum (or difference) of one or more monomials.

| Name | Examples |
|------|----------|
| Monomial | $3x^2$, $-6st$, $\frac{1}{2}u^3v^5$, $8y$, $13$ |
| Binomial | $3x + 5$, $4y^3 - y$, $x^2 + y^2$, $4 + w$ |
| Trinomial | $x^2 + x + 1$, $3x + 2y + z$, $9 + x^2 - y^2$ |
| Polynomial | $23$, $4x + 5$, $3y^2 + y + 11$, $4x^5 + 3x^2 - x + 2$, $x^7 - x^6 + x^5 - x^4 + x^3 - x^2 - x + 1$ |

The number multiplied by the variables in a monomial is called the *coefficient*. The monomials in a polynomial are called the *terms* of the polynomial. In the polynomial $4x^5 + 3x^2 - x + 2$, the terms are $4x^5$, $3x^2$, $-x$, and 2. The coefficient of $x^5$ is 4 and the coefficient of $x$ is $-1$.

Although the GRE quantitative exam may never refer explicitly to polynomials by name, they do appear in a few questions. We'll first learn how to do basic operations with polynomials.

To *add polynomials* we collect like terms and add coefficients. That is, we put terms with the same variables together and add their coefficients. You can only add like terms—3 apples plus 2 apples equals 5 apples but you can't add 3 apples to 2 oranges.

EXAMPLE 1

Addition

$$(3x^2 - x + 5) + (2x^2 + 4x - 9) = (3x^2 + 2x^2) + (-x + 4x) + (5 - 9) = 5x^2 + 3x - 4$$

$$(4x^4 - x - 7) + (2x^3 + x^2 - 3x + 11) = (4x^4) + (2x^3) + (x^2) + (-x - 3x) + (-7 + 11)$$

$$= 4x^4 + 2x^3 + x^2 - 4x + 4$$

To *subtract polynomials* we simply distribute the negative and then add the results. When distributing, be sure every term in the second polynomial is multiplied by negative one.

EXAMPLE 2

Subtraction

$$(2x^2 - 2x + 5) - (2x^2 + 4x + 3) = 2x^2 - 2x + 5 - 2x^2 - 4x - 3 = (2x^2 - 2x^2) +$$

$$(-2x - 4x) + (5 - 3) = -6x + 2$$

$$(x - 7) - (2x^3 - 11) = x - 7 - 2x^3 + 11 = (-2x^3) + (x) + (-7 + 11) = -2x^3 + x + 4$$

To *multiply polynomials* we use the distributive property (sometimes multiple times).

EXAMPLE 3

A monomial times a binomial:

$$(3x)(2x^2 + 5) = (3x \times 2x^2) + (3x \times 5) = 6x^3 + 15x$$

EXAMPLE 4

A binomial times a binomial:

$$(2y + x)(3y^2 - 2x) = (2y + x)(3y^2) + (2y + x)(-2x)$$

$$= (2y \times 3y^2) + (x \times 3y^2) + (2y \times (-2x)) + (x \times (-2x))$$

$$= 6y^3 + 3xy^2 - 4xy - 2x^2$$

Notice we distributed the first binomial to each term, then we distributed again. Some people prefer to think of this as multiplying each term in the first polynomial times each term in the second polynomial.

EXAMPLE 5

A binomial times a binomial:

$$(2y + x)(3y^2 - 2x) = (2y \times 3y^2) + (x \times 3y^2) + (2y \times (-2x)) + (x \times (-2x))$$

$$= 6y^3 + 3xy^2 - 4xy - 2x^2$$

EXAMPLE 6

Simplify $(5x - 2)(x + 3) - (2x + 3)(x - 5)$

(A) $3x^2 + 5x - 21$

(B) $3x^2 + 20x + 9$

(C) $7x^2 + 5x - 21$

(D) $5x - 21$

(E) 0

**Solution:** First we compute $(5x - 2)(x + 3) = (5x)(x) + (-2)(x) + (5x)(3) + (-2)(3) = 5x^2 - 2x + 15x - 6 = 5x^2 + 13x - 6$. Then we compute $(2x + 3)(x - 5) = (2x)(x) + (2x)(-5) + (3)(x) + (3)(-5) = 2x^2 - 10x + 3x - 15 = 2x^2 - 7x - 15$. So the difference is $(5x - 2)(x + 3) - (2x + 3)(x - 5) = (5x^2 + 13x - 6) - (2x^2 - 7x - 15) = 5x^2 + 13x - 6 - 2x^2 + 7x + 15 = (5x^2 - 2x^2) + (13x + 7x) + (-6 + 15) = 3x^2 + 20x + 9$. Choose **B**. A common mistake would be to not distribute the negative to all parts of the second polynomial and result in the incorrect answer A.

Three products appear frequently when dealing with polynomials. In fact, they may be the only products that appear on the GRE. These are well worth memorizing.

The first is called the rule for squaring a binomial. We explain using multiplication.

$$(A + B)^2 = (A + B)(A + B) = (A + B)(A) + (A + B)(B) = (A \times A) + (B \times A) + (A \times B) + (B \times B) = A^2 + BA + AB + B^2 = A^2 + 2AB + B^2$$

Orally you might remember this as "To square a binomial, square the first term, multiply the first term by the second term and double it, square the last term."

The second is just the square of a difference. You really don't have to memorize it if you think of it as a variation on the first.

$$(A - B)^2 = (A + (-B))^2 = A^2 + 2(A)(-B) + (-B)^2 = A^2 - 2AB + B^2$$

The third is called the difference of squares since the product is a difference of perfect squares.

$$(A - B)(A + B) = (A - B)(A) + (A - B)(B) = (A \times A) + (-B \times A) + (A \times B) + (-B \times B) = A^2 - BA + AB - B^2 = A^2 - B^2$$

EXAMPLE 7

Expand each of the following: (i) $(2x + 4)^2$, (ii) $(3 - x)^2$, (iii) $(5x - 6y)(5x + 6y)$

**Solution:**

(i) $(2x + 4)^2 = (2x)^2 + 2(2x)(4) + (4)^2 = 4x^2 + 16x + 16$

(ii) $(3 - x)^2 = 3^2 - 2(3)(x) + x^2 = 9 - 6x + x^2$

(iii) $(5x - 6y)(5x + 6y) = (5x)^2 - (6y)^2 = 25x^2 - 36y^2$.

**TIP**

$(A + B)^2 = A^2 + 2AB + B^2$

$(A - B)^2 = A^2 - 2AB + B^2$

$(A - B)(A + B) = A^2 - B^2$

## EXAMPLE 8

Simplify $(3x + 7)^2 - (3x - 7)^2$

**(A)** 98

**(B)** $18x^2$

**(C)** $9x^2 + 42x + 49$

**(D)** $84x$

**(E)** $-18x^2$

**Solution:** Using our special multiplication rules $(3x + 7)^2 = (3x)^2 + 2(3x)(7) + 7^2 = 9x^2 + 42x + 49$, while $(3x - 7)^2 = (3x)^2 - 2(3x)(7) + 7^2 = 9x^2 - 42x + 49$. So $(3x + 7)^2 - (3x - 7)^2 = (9x^2 + 42x + 49) - (9x^2 - 42x + 49) = 9x^2 + 42x + 49 - 9x^2 + 42x - 49 = 84x$. Choose **D**.

The opposite of multiplying polynomials together is called factoring. In general this can be a difficult challenge, but for the GRE there are only a few types of problems you will encounter.

In *common factoring* you simply identify what the terms have in common and divide it out of each term. For example in the polynomial $4rst + 6r^2t - 2s^2t$, you can see that each term is divisible by 2 and by $t$. So we try to fill in the blanks $4rst + 6r^2t - 2s^2t = (2t)$ (___ + ___ + ___) to make the equation valid. By thinking about multiplication, we can see that $(2t)(2rs) = 4rst$, $(2t)(3r^2) = 6r^2t$, and $(2t)(-s^2) = -2s^2t$. Hence $4rst + 6r^2t - 2s^2t = (2t)(2rs + 3r^2 - s^2)$.

## EXAMPLE 9

Use common factoring to factor $3x^2y + 6x - 2xy$.

**Solution:** Note that $3x^2y + 6x - 2xy = 3xxy + (2)(3)x - 2xy$. In this form it should be clear that 3 is common to the first two terms, and 2 is common to the last two terms, but there is no constant common to all three terms. Also the second term has no $y$, so $y$ cannot be a common factor. But all three terms have one $x$. So the largest common factor is just $x$. Then $3x^2y + 6x - 2xy = x(3xy + 6 - 2y)$. Each term of the trinomial $3xy + 6 - 2y$ was chosen so that when multiplied by $x$ would result in the original expression $3x^2y + 6x - 2xy$.

The most common type of factoring on the GRE comes from *special factoring rules*– really the special multiplication rules used in reverse.

$$A^2 + 2AB + B^2 = (A + B)^2$$

$$A^2 - 2AB + B^2 = (A - B)^2$$

$$A^2 - B^2 = (A - B)(A + B)$$

**EXAMPLE 10**

Factor each of the following: (i) $x^2 + 2xy + y^2$, (ii) $x^2 - 6x + 9$, (iii) $4x^2 - 36$.

**Solution:** (i) $x^2 + 2xy + y^2 = (x + y)^2$, a straightforward application of the first special factoring rule. (ii) Because of the negative and the fact that $9 = 3^2$, we suspect it is the second special factoring rule. And indeed $-2(x)(3)$ does give the middle term $-6x$. Hence, $x^2 - 6x + 9 = (x - 3)^2$. (iii) Because we have a difference of squares, we see it is the third special factoring rule. $4x^2 - 36 = (2x)^2 - (6)^2 = (2x - 6)(2x + 6)$. We should recognize this factors further using common factoring. $(2x - 6)(2x + 6) = 2(x - 3)2(x + 3) = 4(x - 3)(x + 3)$.

Alternatively, you might also have common factored first to see that $4x^2 - 36 = 4(x^2 - 9) = 4(x^2 - 3^2) = 4(x - 3)(x + 3)$.

Using difference of squares, we can provide an alternate answer to Example 8:

Notice that $(3x + 7)^2 - (3x - 7)^2 = [(3x + 7) - (3x - 7)][(3x + 7) + (3x - 7)] = (3x + 7 - 3x + 7)(3x + 7 + 3x - 7) = 14(6x) = 84x$.

A common type of problem you may encounter on the GRE uses the special factoring rules to avoid ugly calculations.

## PROBLEMS (Solutions on page 140)
### Basic Problems

1. Add: $(2 - 3x + 5x^3) + (7 + 4x - x^5)$.

   **(A)** $9 - 7x + 4x^3$
   **(B)** $9 + x + 4x^3$
   **(C)** $9 + x + 5x^3$
   **(D)** $9 + x + 5x^3 - x^5$
   **(E)** $14 - 12x^2 - 5x^8$

2. Simplify: $(1 + 2x) - (3x + 4x^2) + (5x^2 + 6x^3) - (7x^3 + 8x^4)$.

   **(A)** $1 - 3x + 4x^2 + 6x^3 - 8x^4$
   **(B)** $1 - x + 9x^2 + 13x^3 + 8x^4$
   **(C)** $1 + 5x + 9x^2 + 13x^3 - 8x^4$
   **(D)** $1 - x + x^2 - x^3 - x^4$
   **(E)** $1 - x + x^2 - x^3 - 8x^4$

3. Multiply: $(2 + x)(3 - 2x)$.

   **(A)** $6 - x + 2x^2$
   **(B)** $6 - x - 2x^2$
   **(C)** $6 + 3x - 2x^2$
   **(D)** $6 + 3x + 2x^2$
   **(E)** $6 + x - 2x^2$

4. Which of the following is a correct use of the distributive property?

- (A) $(x^{100} - 1)(2 + x^{10}) = x^{10}(x^{100} + 2) - 1(x^{100} + 2)$
- (B) $(x^{100} - 1)(2 + x^{10}) = x^{100}(x^{10} + 2) + 1(2 + x^{10})$
- (C) $(x^{100} - 1)(2 + x^{10}) = 2(x^{100}) - x^{10}(x^{100} - 1)$
- (D) $(x^{100} - 1)(2 + x^{10}) = x^{100}(2 + x^{10}) - 1(2 + x^{10})$
- (E) $(x^{100} - 1)(2 + x^{10}) = 2(x^{100} - 1) + x^{100}(x^{10} - 1)$

| | |
|---|---|
| 5. | |

| Quantity A | Quantity B |
|---|---|
| $4 - y^2$ | $(2 - y)(2 + y)$ |

6.

| Quantity A | Quantity B |
|---|---|
| $t^2 + 9$ | $(t + 3)(t - 3)$ |

7.

| Quantity A | Quantity B |
|---|---|
| $3ab^2 - 2a^3b + 4ab$ | $ab(3b - 2a^2 + 2)$ |

8. When 1,000,000 is squared, the result is how much greater than $1,000,001 \times 999,999$?

## GRE Problems

9. Find the value of $\dfrac{x - y}{x^2 - y^2}$ if $x = 0.01$ and $y = 0.99$.

10. Find the value of $\dfrac{b^2 - a^2}{b + a}$ if $a = 43$ and $b = 57$.

11. We have 77 positive numbers and 44 negative numbers. Their sum is $77^2 - 44^2$. What is their average?

- (A) −33
- (B) 33
- (C) $-33^2$
- (D) $33^2$
- (E) $\dfrac{1}{121}$

| 12. | Quantity A | Quantity B |
|---|---|---|
| | $(x-1)(x)(x+1)$ | $(x-2)(x)(x+2)$ |

13.

$$ab = 2$$

| Quantity A | Quantity B |
|---|---|
| $(a+b)^2$ | $(a-b)^2$ |

14.

$$s > 0$$

| Quantity A | Quantity B |
|---|---|
| $(s+t)^2$ | $(s-t)^2$ |

15.

$$a - b = 24$$
$$a + b = 25$$

| Quantity A | Quantity B |
|---|---|
| $a^2 - b^2$ | $ab$ |

16.

$$x > 0 \text{ and } y > 0$$

| Quantity A | Quantity B |
|---|---|
| $\dfrac{x-y}{x+y}$ | $\dfrac{x^2-y^2}{(x+y)^2}$ |

17.

| Quantity A | Quantity B |
|---|---|
| $(0.63)^2 - (0.37)^2$ | $\dfrac{1}{4}$ |

$$x \neq 0$$

18.

| Quantity A | Quantity B |
|---|---|
| $\dfrac{1}{x} - \dfrac{1}{x^2}$ | $\dfrac{x-1}{x^2}$ |

19.

| Quantity A | Quantity B |
|---|---|
| $\left(x+\dfrac{1}{2}\right)^2 - \left(x-\dfrac{1}{2}\right)^2$ | $|x|$ |

20.

$$x + y = 3$$

| Quantity A | Quantity B |
|---|---|
| $x^2 + 2xy + y^2$ | $6 + x + y$ |

## SOLVING EQUATIONS

Equations show that two quantities are equal. For example, $3x = 4$, $a + b = a - b$, and $x^2 + 2x - 3 = 0$. An equation that involves only one variable can often be solved; this means to determine values of the variable that make the equation true.

The basic rule for solving equations is "whatever you do to one side of the equation, do to the other." If you start with two equal quantities and do the same thing to them, they remain equal.

| Rule in Words | Rule in Symbols | Example |
|---|---|---|
| Add the same number to both sides of the equation | If $a = b$, then $a + c = b + c$. | If $x - 3 = 4$, then $x - 3 + 3 = 4 + 3$ (i.e., $x = 7$). |
| Subtract the same number from both sides of the equation | If $a = b$, then $a - c = b - c$. | If $2x = 4 + x$, then $2x - x = 4 + x - x$ (i.e., $x = 4$). |
| Multiply both sides of the equation by the same nonzero number | If $a = b$ and $c \neq 0$, then $ac = bc$. | If $\dfrac{x}{2} = 3$, then $2\left(\dfrac{x}{2}\right) = 2(3)$ (i.e., $x = 6$). |
| Divide both sides of the equation by the same nonzero number | If $a = b$ and $c \neq 0$, then $\dfrac{a}{c} = \dfrac{b}{c}$. | If $3x = 15$, then $\dfrac{3x}{3} = \dfrac{15}{3}$ (i.e., $x = 5$). |
| Square both sides | If $a = b$, then $a^2 = b^2$. | If $\sqrt{x} = 3$, then $\left(\sqrt{x}\right)^2 = 3^2$ (i.e., $x = 9$). |

By combining the basic rules, you can solve many equations. Generally, you try to bring to one side all terms involving the variable you are solving for, and everything else to the other side.

**EXAMPLE 1**

Solve for $x$ if $3x - 2 = 5x + 8$.

**Solution:**

Add 2 to both sides

$$3x - 2 + 2 = 5x + 8 + 2$$
$$3x = 5x + 10$$

Subtract $5x$ from both sides

$$3x - 5x = 5x + 10 - 5x$$
$$-2x = 10$$

Divide both sides by $-2$

$$-\frac{2x}{-2} = \frac{10}{-2}$$
$$x = -5.$$

We have determined that $x = -5$. We can check our answer by substituting $x = -5$ into the original equation.

Check

$$3x - 2 = 5x + 8$$
$$3(-5) - 2 = 5(-5) + 8$$
$$-15 - 2 = -25 + 8$$
$$-17 = -17$$

It's correct!

**EXAMPLE 2**

If $(x + 2)5 = 3(x + 7)$, then solve for $x$.

**Solution:**

| | |
|---|---|
| First we expand to get rid of the parentheses | $(x + 2)5 = 3(x + 7)$ |
| | $5x + 10 = 3x + 21$ |
| Subtract $3x$ from both sides to get all $x$'s on one side. | $2x + 10 = 21$ |
| Subtract 10 from both sides. | $2x = 11$ |
| Divide by 2 to isolate $x$. | $x = 5.5$ |

---

### TIP

Squaring both sides of an equation can introduce invalid solutions. If $-\sqrt{x} = 3$, and we square both sides, we get $\left(-\sqrt{x}\right)^2 = 3^2$ or $x = 9$. Check this answer in the original equation, and we see that $-\sqrt{9} \neq 3$, so $x = 9$ is not a valid solution. In fact the original equation has no solutions. You can see that more easily if we multiply both sides of the original equation by $-1$. $-\left(-\sqrt{x}\right) = -(3)$ is equivalent to $\sqrt{x} = -3$. The result of any square root cannot be negative, so there are no solutions.

---

There are other rules for working with equations, but these require some special care when used.

| Rule in Words | Rule in Symbols | Example |
|---|---|---|
| If two nonzero values are equal, their reciprocals are equal. | $a = b$ and $a \neq 0$, then $\dfrac{1}{a} = \dfrac{1}{b}$ | $\dfrac{1}{x} = \dfrac{1}{2} \Rightarrow x = 2$ |
| If the squares of values are equal, then the values are equal or opposites. | $a^2 = b^2$ implies $a = b$ or $a = -b$ | $x^2 = 25 \Rightarrow x = 5$ or $x = -5$ |
| If the powers are equal and they have the same positive base (not equal to 1), then their exponents are equal. | $a^x = a^y$, $a > 0$, and $a \neq 1$ implies that $x = y$. | $2^{x+3} = 2^{2x-3} \Rightarrow x + 3 = 2x - 3 \Rightarrow x = 6$ |
| If the product of two values is zero, then one of the values has to be zero. | If $xy = 0$, then $x = 0$ or $y = 0$. | $(x + 1)x = 0 \Rightarrow x + 1 = 0$ or $x = 0 \Rightarrow x = -1$ or $0$ |

EXAMPLE 3

Solve for $x$, if $x^2 + 4 = 2x^2 - 5$.

(A) −3 only

(B) 3 only

(C) 1 only

(D) 3 or −3

(E) 0 or 3

**Solution:** First subtract $x^2$ from both sides:

$$x^2 + 4 - x^2 = 2x^2 - 5 - x^2$$
$$4 = x^2 - 5$$

Add 5 to both sides:

$$4 + 5 = x^2 - 5 + 5$$
$$9 = x^2$$

Now using the second rule above, we get $x = 3$ or $x = -3$. Choose **D**.

An alternate answer would be to continue from $4 = x^2 - 5$ by subtracting 4 from both sides to see $0 = x^2 - 9$. Now factor using difference of squares to see $(x - 3)(x + 3) = 0$. Since the product is zero, either $x - 3 = 0$ or $x + 3 = 0$. Hence $x = 3$ or $x = -3$.

EXAMPLE 4

If $5^{b+1} = 25^{2-b}$, then solve for $b$.

**Solution:** First represent 25 as $5^2$; then simplify using laws of exponents: $5^{b+1} = (5^2)^{2-b}$ $\Rightarrow 5^{b+1} = 5^{4-2b}$. Now we can equate the exponents and solve: $b + 1 = 4 - 2b \Rightarrow 3b = 3$ $\Rightarrow b = 1$.

### TIP

- You don't always have to solve for the variable in the problem. Sometimes you can solve directly for what is asked.

- As discussed in Chapter 2, for a multiple-choice question, you can check each of the five answers to find the correct one.

- If there are many variables in a problem and you have to solve for just one of them, treat the other variables as numbers.

- If an equation involves fractions, clear the denominators by multiplying both sides of the equation by the LCM of the denominators.

## EXAMPLE 5

$$x + 5 = 27$$

| Quantity A | Quantity B |
|------------|------------|
| $2x + 12$  | $3x - 10$  |

**Solution:** We could solve for $x$, but we will follow the tip above and try to directly find $2x + 12$ and $3x - 10$. Since $x + 5 = 27$, multiply both sides by 2 to get $2x + 10 = 54$. Now add two to both sides, and we have $2x + 12 = 56$. As $x + 5 = 27$, multiply both sides by 3 to get $3x + 15 = 81$. Subtract 25 from both sides and we have $3x - 10 = 56$. Surprisingly, $2x + 12 = 56 = 3x - 10$. Choose **C**.

## EXAMPLE 6

If $y < -2 < x$, solve for $x$ in terms of $y$: $\dfrac{x}{y + 2} = \dfrac{y}{x + 2}$

(A) $-y$

(B) $-y - 2$

(C) $y + 2$

(D) $y + 1$

(E) $y$

**Solution:** To clear fractions, we multiply both sides by $(x + 2)(y + 2)$ (this is the same as cross multiplying).

$$(x + 2)\cancel{(y + 2)} \frac{x}{\cancel{y + 2}} = \cancel{(x + 2)}(y + 2)\frac{y}{\cancel{x + 2}}$$

We are left with $(x + 2)x = (y + 2)y$, which expands to $x^2 + 2x = y^2 + 2y$. It's not clear how to proceed from here, but if we add one to both sides, we now have perfect squares, $x^2 + 2x + 1 = y^2 + 2y + 1$, which can be factored as $(x + 1)^2 = (y + 1)^2$. If we take square roots, we find that $x + 1 = y + 1$ or $x + 1 = -(y + 1)$. Solving both cases $x = y$ or $x = -y - 2$. But we were given that $y < x$ so the first case is not possible. Hence $x = -y - 2$. Choose **B**.

## Solving Systems of Linear Equations

Being able to solve a system of two linear equations in two unknowns is a useful basic skill. It is needed in many different types of math problems. While the technique is not always *required* to solve a GRE problem, it does give you a skill you can count on at all times. You may know it as the *substitution method*. We explain the technique with an example.

**EXAMPLE 7**

Find $x$ and $y$ so that $2x + 3y = 13$ and $x - 2y = 3$.

**Solution:**

| | |
|---|---|
| Number your equations. This helps us identify what happens in each step. | $2x + 3y = 13$ ① <br> $x - 2y = 3$ ② |
| First we choose an equation and isolate one of the variables. Since $x$ in equation 2 has no coefficient it is a good target. We add $2y$ to both sides. | Solve for $x$ in ② <br> $x = 3 + 2y$ |
| Now substitute that value for $x$ back into the other equation. This will eliminate one of the variables. | Substitute $x = 3 + 2y$ into ① <br> $2(3 + 2y) + 3y = 13$ |
| Solve for $y$. | $6 + 4y + 3y = 13$ <br> $6 + 7y = 13$ <br> $7y = 7$ <br> $y = 1$ |
| Now we use this solution for one variable to find the other. You can substitute into one of the original equations and solve for $x$. The easiest way to do this is to use the expression we found for $x$ in the second step. (Optional) Check your answer by substituting into the original equations. | Substitute $y = 1$ into $x = 3 + 2y$ <br> $x = 3 + 2(1) = 3 + 2 = 5$ <br><br> $x = 5, y = 1$ <br><br> Substitute $x = 5, y = 1$ into ① and ②. <br> $2(5) + 3(1) = 13$ <br> $(5) - 2(1) = 3$ |

Of course these problems are rarely so explicit. You will often find them as word problems or parts of other problems.

**EXAMPLE 8**

Three times a number plus a second number equals two. The sum of the numbers is four. What are the numbers?

(A) 1 and 5

(B) 1 and −5

(C) −1 and 5

(D) −1 and −5

(E) 1 and 2

**Solution:** Let $a$ be the first number and $b$ the second number. Then $3a + b = 2$ and $a + b = 4$.

We use the substitution method.

$$3a + b = 2 \quad ①$$
$$a + b = 4 \quad ②$$

Solving for $b$ in ②, we find $b = 4 - a$. Substitute $b = 4 - a$ into ① to find $3a + (4 - a) = 2 \Rightarrow 2a + 4 = 2 \Rightarrow 2a = -2 \Rightarrow a = -1$. Now substitute $a = -1$ into $b = 4 - a$, and $b = 4 - (-1) = 4 + 1 = 5$. Hence the numbers are −1 and 5. Choose **C**.

There is another standard technique for solving a system of linear equations. It involves adding or subtracting multiples of equations, and may be called the *elimination method*. We illustrate with an alternate solution to Example 7.

Number your equations. This helps us identify what happens in each step.

$2x + 3y = 13$ ①
$x - 2y = 3$ ②

We try to add (or subtract) a multiple of one equation to the other in order to get rid of one variable. In this case we multiply ② by 2 and subtract the result from ①.

Multiply ② by 2.
$2x - 4y = 6$
Subtract this from ①.

$$\begin{array}{r} 2x + 3y = 13 \\ -(2x - 4y = 6) \\ \hline 7y = 7 \end{array}$$

Now we can solve for $y$.
Now we use this solution for one variable to find the other. You can substitute into one of the original equations and solve for $x$.

$y = 1$
Substitute $y = 1$ into ②
$x - 2(1) = 3$
$x - 2 = 3$
$x = 5$

Now you have a solution.

$x = 5$ and $y = 1$

(Optional) Check your answer by substituting into the original equations.

Substitute $x = 5$, $y = 1$ into ① and ②.
$2(5) + 3(1) = 13$
$(5) - 2(1) = 3$

---

**EXAMPLE 9**

$$2x + 4y = 5$$
$$2x - y = -5$$

| Quantity A | Quantity B |
|:---:|:---:|
| $x$ | $y$ |

**Solution:** We follow the elimination method.

$2x + 4y = 5$ ①
$2x - y = -5$ ②

First we subtract ② from ①.

$$\begin{array}{r} 2x + 4y = 5 \\ -(2x - y = -5) \\ \hline 5y = 10 \end{array}$$

Hence $y = 2$. Now substitute $y = 2$ into ②, to get $2x - (2) = -5 \Rightarrow 2x = -5 + 2 \Rightarrow 2x = -3 \Rightarrow x = -1.5$.

Thus we have a solution, $x = -1.5$ and $y = 2$. Choose **B**.

**EXAMPLE 10**

**TIP**

If you are given two or more equations and are unsure of how to proceed, consider adding them or subtracting them. With surprising frequency, this produces a quick solution to the problem.

$$3x - 4y = 7$$
$$2y - x = 5$$

| Quantity A | Quantity B |
|------------|------------|
| $x - y$    | 10         |

**Solution:** You could solve for $x$ and $y$ using the substitution or elimination method. But let's follow the tip and just add the equations together to get $(3x - 4y) + (2y - x)$ = 7 + 5. This simplifies beautifully to $2x - 2y = 12$. Just divide by 2 to see $x - y = 6$. Choose **B**.

**EXAMPLE 11**

$a - b + c = 1$        What is $a + b + c$?
$b - c + a = 2$
$c - a + b = 3$

**Solution:** Just like our method for solving two linear equations in two unknowns, there is a method for solving three equations in three unknowns. Even if you know this method, you should suspect there is a simpler answer. Try adding all the equations together.

We get $(a - b + c) + (b - c + a) + (c - a + b) = 1 + 2 + 3$ and conveniently many variables cancel out to leave $a + b + c = $ **6**.

## PROBLEMS (Solutions on page 142)
### Basic Problems

1. If $2x + 3 = 6 - x$, then $x =$

2. Solve for $a$: $a(a - 3) = (a + 2)(a - 1)$.

3. Find all solutions for $(t + 2)(3 - t) = (t + 2)$.

   Indicate *all* that apply.

   A  4
   B  2
   C  0
   D  −2
   E  −4

4. Solve for $z$ in terms of $x$ and $y$ if $2x - y + 3z = 2 + y$.

   Ⓐ  $1 + y - x$

   Ⓑ  $\dfrac{2(y-x)}{3}$

   Ⓒ  $\dfrac{(2+2y-2x)}{3}$

   Ⓓ  $\dfrac{(1+y-x)}{3}$

   Ⓔ  $y + x$

5. Solve for $b$ if $2b^2 - 8 = 1 - b^2$.

   Indicate *all* that apply.

   A  −3
   B  0
   C  3
   D  $\sqrt{3}$
   E  $-\sqrt{3}$
   F  $3^2$

6. Solve for $x$ if $\dfrac{1}{x+1} = \dfrac{2}{x-1}$

   Ⓐ  −3

   Ⓑ  −1

   Ⓒ  0

   Ⓓ  1

   Ⓔ  $\dfrac{1}{2}$

7.                                  $m + n = 7$
                                    $3 - n = 6$

   | Quantity A | Quantity B |
   |------------|------------|
   | $m$        | 9          |

8.                                  $x - y = 3$
                                    $2x + 3y = 2$

   | Quantity A | Quantity B |
   |------------|------------|
   | $x$        | $y$        |

9. If $y \neq z$ and $(x + y)z = y(x + z)$, then solve for $x$ in terms of $y$ and $z$.

   (A) $0$

   (B) $\dfrac{xy}{z}$

   (C) $\dfrac{y(x+z)}{yz}$

   (D) $y - z$

   (E) $y + z$

10. If $2x - 3 = 17$, then $2x + 2 = ?$

11. If $RS$ and $TU$ are straight lines that meet at the center of the circle, find $a$.

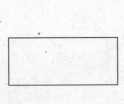

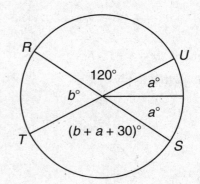

12. If $4^{b+1} = 2^{3b} \div 4$, then solve for $b$.

13. If $8^{a/3} = 2^{3}8^{1-a}$, then solve for $a$.

   (A) $0$

   (B) $2$

   (C) $4$

   (D) $1.5$

   (E) $-1$

14. The volume of a sphere is given by $V = \dfrac{4\pi r^3}{3}$. What is the radius, $r$, in terms of $V$?

(A) $\dfrac{3V}{4\pi}$

(B) $\sqrt[3]{\dfrac{3V}{4\pi}}$

(C) $\sqrt[3]{\dfrac{3\pi}{4V}}$

(D) $\sqrt[3]{\dfrac{4\pi}{3V}}$

(E) $\dfrac{4V}{3\pi}$

15.
$$x^2 - 4 = 0$$

| Quantity A | Quantity B |
|------------|------------|
| $x$ | 2 |

16.
$$x(2(x + 3) + 3) = 3(4 + 3x)$$

| Quantity A | Quantity B |
|------------|------------|
| $x$ | 6 |

17.
$$3x - 6 = 4$$

| Quantity A | Quantity B |
|------------|------------|
| $2x - 6$ | $x - 4$ |

18.
$$3x - y = 2$$
$$3x + y = 4$$

| Quantity A | Quantity B |
|------------|------------|
| $x$ | $y$ |

19.
$$3x + 2y + z = -2$$
$$2x + y + z = 10$$

| Quantity A | Quantity B |
|------------|------------|
| Average of $x$ and $y$ | $z$ |

20. If $r - s = 3$ and $t + s = 11$, what is the average of $r$ and $t$?

21. If $ax^2 - bx + c = 0$ and $-bx^2 + ax - c = 0$, then which of the following is true:

Indicate *all* that apply.

A  If $a \neq b$, then $x = 0$ or $-1$
B  If $x \neq 0$, then $a = b$.
C  If $x = 2$, then $a = b$.

22. Derek has twice as many marbles as Jason. Cornelia has one-third as many marbles as Derek. Together these three have 55 marbles. How many does Derek have?

23. Jillian doubled her favorite number, added 1, divided by 3, and subtracted 2. The result was her favorite number! What is Jillian's favorite number?

(A) 5

(B) 17

(C) 21

(D) –3

(E) –5

## INEQUALITIES

**EXAMPLE 1**

| Quantity A | Quantity B |
|:---:|:---:|
| $3x - 2$ | 4 |

The GRE exam will never ask you to directly solve an inequality problem like: "if $3x - 2 > 4$ solve for $x$." Yet, all quantitative comparison questions are implicitly asking you to work with inequalities. The example above is asking you to work with the inequality $3x - 2 > 4$.

**Solution:** Rather than solve the inequality directly, we will try some values of $x$. When $x = 0$, we have $3(0) - 2 = -2$, which is less than 4. When $x = 5$, we have $3(5) - 2 = 13$, which is greater than 4. Since there are no restrictions on $x$, A or B could be greater depending on $x$. The answer is **D**.

The classical solution you may have learned in high school might look like:

Since $3x - 2 > 4$, add 2 to both sides to get $3x > 6$. Now divide both sides by 3 to get $x > 2$. Thus $3x - 2$ is greater than 4 when $x$ is greater than 2. When $x > 2$, like $x = 5$, A > B and when $x < 2$, like $x = 0$, A < B. Since $x$ can be any real number, again the answer is **D**.

We'll discuss the standard rules for inequalities and then see how they are useful in solving quantitative comparison (and other) questions. They are very important whether you intend to try solving inequalities directly or use any of the other techniques we suggest.

- **Add or subtract the same number from both sides.** If $a < b$, then for any number $c$, $a + c < b + c$ and $a - c < b - c$. Consider the true inequality $-2 < 5$. Add 2 to both sides, and we have $-2 + 2 < 5 + 2$, which is $0 < 7$ (true). Subtract two from both sides and we have $-2 - 2 < 5 - 2$, which is $-4 < 3$ (also true).

- **Multiply or divide by a positive number.** If $a < b$ and $c > 0$, then $ca < cb$ and $\dfrac{a}{c} < \dfrac{b}{c}$.

  Consider the inequality $3 < 6$. If we multiply by 2, we get $3 \times 2 < 6 \times 2$, which is $6 < 12$ (true). If we divide by 3, we get $\dfrac{3}{3} < \dfrac{6}{3}$, which is $1 < 2$ (also true).

- **Multiply or divide by a negative number.** If $a < b$ and $c < 0$, then $ca > cb$ and $\dfrac{a}{c} > \dfrac{b}{c}$.

  It is very important to notice that the inequality reverses. Consider the inequality $-4 < 2$. If we multiply by $-1$, we get $-4 \times -1 > 2 \times -1$, which is $4 > -2$ (true). If we divide by $-2$, we get $\dfrac{-4}{-2} > \dfrac{2}{-2}$ which is $2 > -1$ (also true).

---

**EXAMPLE 2**

$$x < 1$$

| Quantity A | Quantity B |
|:---:|:---:|
| $5 - 2x$ | $3x + 1$ |

**Solution:** Let's solve $5 - 2x < 3x + 1$. First add $2x$ to both sides to get $5 < 5x + 1$. Now subtract 1 from both sides to get $4 < 5x$. Finally divide both sides by 5 to see that $\dfrac{4}{5} < x$ or $x > 0.8$. So A < B when $x > 0.8$, but it was assumed that $x$ must be less than 1. So if $x$ is between 0.8 and 1 (like 0.9), A < B. But if $x < 0.8$ (like 0), then A > B. So the answer is **D**.

---

There are other important rules for inequalities that are very useful on the GRE. Some will defy your intuition so study them carefully.

- **Squaring both sides.** If $a < b$, then $a^2 < b^2$ when $a$ and $b$ are nonnegative. For example, if $\sqrt{x} < \sqrt{2}$, then $x < 2$. When at least one of $a$ or $b$ is negative, other things can happen. For instance $-3 < 2$ but $(-3)^2 = 9$, which is not less than $2^2$. Also, $-3 < -2$ but $(-3)^2 = 9$, which is greater than $(-2)^2 = 4$.
- **Take the square root of both sides.** If $a < b$, then $\sqrt{a} < \sqrt{b}$, as long as $a$ and $b$ are non-negative. For example, if $x^2 < 4$, then $\sqrt{x^2} < \sqrt{4}$. Simplifying that means $|x| < 2$ or $x$ is between $-2$ and 2.
- **Take the reciprocal of both sides.** If $a < b$, then $\dfrac{1}{a} > \dfrac{1}{b}$ as long as $a$ and $b$ have the same sign (they are both positive or both negative). For instance, $2 < 3$ so $\dfrac{1}{2} > \dfrac{1}{3}$. Also $-3 < -2$ so $-\dfrac{1}{3} > -\dfrac{1}{2}$. What happens if $a < 0 < b$? Then $\dfrac{1}{a} < \dfrac{1}{b}$. Consider $-3 < 2$ and $-\dfrac{1}{3} < \dfrac{1}{2}$.

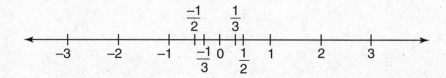

**EXAMPLE 3**

$$x < 0$$

| Quantity A | Quantity B |
|------------|------------|
| $4 - x$ | $\dfrac{x}{2} - 10$ |

**Solution:** The easiest solution is by careful observation. As $x$ is negative, $-x$ is positive. Hence $4 - x = 4 + (-x)$ is the sum of positive numbers and is thus positive. So A > 0.

As $x$ is negative, so is $\dfrac{x}{2}$. So a negative minus 10 is also negative. Hence B < 0. Clearly A > B. So the answer is A.

If we choose to solve the inequality directly, we would proceed as follows:

Assume A < B, that is, $4 - x < \dfrac{x}{2} - 10$.

Multiply both sides by 2 to clear the denominators.

$2(4 - x) < 2\left(\dfrac{x}{2} - 10\right)$ becomes $8 - 2x < x - 20$.

Add $2x$ to both sides and obtain $8 < 3x - 20$.

Add 20 to both sides: $28 < 3x$.

Divide both sides by 3: $\dfrac{28}{3} < x$. $\dfrac{28}{3}$ is approximately 9.3.

So A < B when $x > 9.3$. But $x < 0$ so A > B. The answer is **A**.

We can treat inequalities as objects and add them together to get true results. Be careful about subtracting, multiplying, or dividing inequalities; the results will usually be false (though occasionally true).

> *Add two inequalities together.* If $a < b$ and $c < d$, then $a + c < b + d$. If $x < 3$ and $y < 5$, then $x + y < 8$.

Some inequalities that you might think are obviously true are not always true. Try substituting numbers between 0 and 1 or negative numbers to get a counterexample.

- $a < a^2$ is not true for all $a$. When $a > 1$, then $a < a^2$ but when $0 < a < 1$, then $a > a^2$. For example, if $a = 2$, then $2 < 2^2 = 4$. If $a = \frac{1}{2}$, then $\frac{1}{2} > \frac{1^2}{2} = \frac{1}{4}$. Of course if $a = 1$, then $a = a^2$ $(1 = 1^2)$. If $a < 0$, then $a < a^2$. Any negative number will be less than its square since squares are always positive. For instance, $-2 < (-2)^2 = 4$.

- $a > \frac{1}{a}$ is not true for all $a$. When $a > 1$, then $a > \frac{1}{a}$, but when $0 < a < 1$, then $a < \frac{1}{a}$. For example, if $a = 2$, then $2 > \frac{1}{2}$. If $a = \frac{1}{2}$, then $\frac{1}{2} < \frac{1}{\frac{1}{2}} = 2$. Of course, if $a = 1$, then $a = \frac{1}{a}$ (as $1 = \frac{1}{1}$).

- $a > \sqrt{a}$ is not true for all $a$. When $a > 1$, then $a > \sqrt{a}$, but when $0 < a < 1$, then $a < \sqrt{a}$. For example, if $a = 4$, then $4 > \sqrt{4} = 2$. If $a = \frac{1}{4}$, then $\frac{1}{4} < \sqrt{\frac{1}{4}} = \frac{1}{2}$. Of course, if $a = 1$, then $a = a^2$, as $1 = 1^2$.

**EXAMPLE 4**

Given $\frac{1}{2} < a < 1$, choose the smallest value.

(A) $a^2$

(B) $a$

(C) $\sqrt{a}$

(D) $\frac{1}{a}$

(E) $a - a^2$

**Solution:** We know from our rules above that when $a$ is between 0 and 1 (and it is in this case) that $a^2 < a$, $a < \sqrt{a}$, $a < \frac{1}{a}$. So the answer is not B, C, or D. That leaves A and E. Which is smaller, $a^2$ or $a - a^2$? A picture helps, but remember, $a$ could be close to $\frac{1}{2}$ or very close to 1.

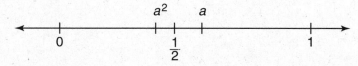

We'll solve directly. Assume $a^2 < a - a^2$. Divide by $a$ (a positive number) to get $a < 1 - a$. Add $a$ to both sides: $2a < 1$. Divide by 2: $a < \frac{1}{2}$. So $a^2 < a - a^2$ when $a < \frac{1}{2}$. But $a > \frac{1}{2}$ so $a^2 > a - a^2$. The answer is **E**.

## PROBLEMS (Solutions on page 145)

## Basic Problems

1.                           Assume $a - b > 0$

| Quantity A | Quantity B |
|------------|------------|
| $-a$ | $-b$ |

---

2.                           Let $a = 0.7$

| Quantity A | Quantity B |
|------------|------------|
| $(a^2)^2$ | $\sqrt{\sqrt{a}}$ |

---

3.                           Assume $x < y$

| Quantity A | Quantity B |
|------------|------------|
| $x - y$ | $y - x$ |

---

4.                           Let $x = -1$

| Quantity A | Quantity B |
|------------|------------|
| $x^4 - x^3$ | $x^3 - x^4$ |

---

5.                           Assume $x < 2$

| Quantity A | Quantity B |
|------------|------------|
| $4x - 3$ | $3x + 4$ |

---

6.

| Quantity A | Quantity B |
|------------|------------|
| $\left(\dfrac{1}{4}\right)^2$ | $\sqrt{\dfrac{1}{4}}$ |

---

7.                           Let $|-y| = 5$

| Quantity A | Quantity B |
|------------|------------|
| $y$ | $5$ |

---

8.

| Quantity A | Quantity B |
|------------|------------|
| $\sqrt{x^2}$ | $x$ |

9. If $x > 1$ and $y < -1$, which of the following must be true?

Indicate *all* that apply.

A $x + y < 0$

B $xy < 0$

C $x - y > 0$

D $x^2 > y^2$

10. Given $a > 2$, choose the smallest value.

(A) $a^2$

(B) $a$

(C) $\sqrt{a}$

(D) $\dfrac{1}{a}$

(E) $\dfrac{1}{a^2}$

## GRE Problems

11.

| Quantity A | Quantity B |
|---|---|
| $\left(\dfrac{1}{9}\right)^9$ | $\left(\dfrac{1}{9}\right)^{10}$ |

12.

| Quantity A | Quantity B |
|---|---|
| $5^6$ | $6^5$ |

13.

| Quantity A | Quantity B |
|---|---|
| $2^{10} - \left(\dfrac{1}{2}\right)^{10}$ | $2^9 + \left(\dfrac{1}{2}\right)^9$ |

14.

Let $x > 4$

| Quantity A | Quantity B |
|---|---|
| $\dfrac{2}{x} - \dfrac{3}{x^2}$ | $1$ |

15.

| Quantity A | Quantity B |
|---|---|
| $x^4 - x^2$ | $x^2 - x^4$ |

16.

Let $a^* = \dfrac{1}{a}$

| Quantity A | Quantity B |
|---|---|
| $(7^*)^*$ | $\left(\dfrac{1}{7^*}\right)^*$ |

17. If $0 < xy < 1$, which of the following is *not* possible?

(A) $x + y = 1$

(B) $x > 100$

(C) $x < 0 < y$

(D) $y < -100$

(E) $x - y = 1$

18. If $0 < xy < 1$, which of the following is possible?

   (A) $y < 0 < x$
   (B) $x < -2$ and $y > 2$
   (C) $x$ and $y$ are both integers
   (D) $x + y = 10$
   (E) $\dfrac{1}{x} < 0 < \dfrac{1}{y}$

19. Given $a > 1$, choose the largest value.

   (A) $a^2$
   (B) $a$
   (C) $\sqrt{a}$
   (D) $\dfrac{1}{a}$
   (E) $a - a^2$

## FUNCTIONS

A function is a rule that assigns to each input exactly one output. A simple example is "multiply the number by 3 and then add 1." Then an input of 5 returns an output of $3 \times 5 + 1$, which equals 16. In grade school you were often given a table of inputs and outputs and asked to find the rule. For the table on the right, you might guess the rule is "square the input," and you would be correct. Notice that although each input can have only one output you can have two inputs that have the same output. For instance, $2^2 = 4$ and $(-2)^2 = 4$.

| Input | Output |
|-------|--------|
| 0 | 0 |
| 1 | 1 |
| 2 | 4 |
| 3 | 9 |
| -2 | 4 |

A good application of this is the square root function. Many people say $\sqrt{9} = \pm 3$, that is, $\sqrt{9} = 3$ or $\sqrt{9} = -3$. As square root is a function, it cannot have two outputs for one input; square root is defined strictly as the nonnegative root, so $\sqrt{9} = 3$. (Yes, there are two numbers, 3 and $-3$, whose squares are equal to 9 but only one of them, 3, is the square root of 9.)

There is standard notation for defining functions. For the "multiply the number by 3 and then add 1" function, we write $f(x) = 3x + 1$. Here $x$ is the input, $f$ is the name of the function, and $3x + 1$ is the output.

EXAMPLE 1

Which function would produce the following table?

(A) $f(x) = 2x^2 + 1$

(B) $f(x) = 2x^2 - 1$

(C) $f(x) = -6x - 1$

(D) $f(x) = 3x + 1$

(E) $f(x) = 20 + x$

| x Input | f(x) Output |
|---------|-------------|
| −3 | 17 |
| −2 | 7 |
| −1 | 1 |
| 0 | −1 |
| 1 | 1 |
| 2 | 7 |

**Solution:** We could produce a table for each of the given functions but that would be very tedious. We'll just evaluate the functions at a few values and see which match the given table. It is easiest to evaluate a function at zero:

(A) $2(0)^2 + 1 = 1$

(B) $2(0)^2 - 1 = -1$

(C) $-6(0) - 1 = -1$

(D) $3(0) + 1 = 1$

(E) $20 + (0) = 20$

Only B and C agree with the table and produce a value of −1. Now we'll try evaluating at 1: (B) $2(1)^2 - 1 = 1$ while (C) $-6(1) - 1 = -7$. Only (B) agrees with the table. Choose **B**.

Functions appear implicitly in many mathematical problems and the GRE is no exception to that.

EXAMPLE 2

Orange, Inc., is a world-famous computer manufacturer. It costs them 240,000 + 300$L$ dollars to produce $L$ laptops at a new facility. These laptops are sold for 600 dollars each. How many do they have to sell in order to break even?

**Solution:** The function here is the profit, depending on the number of laptops produced and sold. Profit is revenue (600$L$) minus cost (240,000 + 300$L$). Hence $P(L)$ = 240,000 + 300$L$ − 600$L$ or $P(L)$ = 240,000 − 300$L$. The question is asking for the value of $L$ so that $P(L) = 0$. We can solve 240,000 − 300$L$ = 0 by adding 300$L$ to both sides, 240,000 = 300$L$ and dividing by 300, to get 800 = $L$. If they sell **800** laptops they will break even.

Functions are not often expressed explicitly using the standard notation on the GRE. If a function is defined, it is usually using some nonstandard notation. This can be very confusing for many students, so study the following examples carefully.

EXAMPLE 3

If $r* = \dfrac{1}{r}$, then what is $\left(1-\left(\dfrac{1}{2}\right)^*\right)^*$?

(A) $\dfrac{1}{2}$

(B) $-\dfrac{1}{2}$

(C) 0

(D) $-1$

(E) 2

**Solution:** First we find $\left(\dfrac{1}{2}\right)^* = \dfrac{1}{\left(\dfrac{1}{2}\right)} = 2$. So $\left(1-\left(\dfrac{1}{2}\right)^*\right)^* = (1-2)^* = (-1)^* = \dfrac{1}{(-1)} = -1.$

Choose **D**.

Functions of two or even more variables also appear on the GRE, though usually in some nonstandard guise. A standard function of two variables might be $f(x,y) = x^2 + y^2$. It takes two numbers as input and returns the sum of their squares. Here's one way this same function could appear on the GRE.

EXAMPLE 4

If $x \wedge y = x^2 + y^2$ then which of the following are valid rules?

Indicate *all* that apply.

A $\quad r(x \wedge y) = (rx) \wedge (ry)$

B $\quad (-x) \wedge (-y) = x \wedge y$

C $\quad x \wedge y = y \wedge x$

D $\quad r(x \wedge y) = (rx) \wedge y$

E $\quad r^2(x \wedge y) = (rx) \wedge (ry)$

**Solution:** Note $r(x \wedge y) = r(x^2 + y^2) = rx^2 + ry^2$ while $(rx) \wedge (ry) = (rx)^2 + (ry)^2 = r^2x^2 + r^2y^2$. Hence A is not valid. Also, $(-x) \wedge (-y) = (-x)^2 + (-y)^2 = x^2 + y^2$, which equals $x \wedge y$, so B is valid. We see that $x \wedge y = x^2 + y^2 = y^2 + x^2 = y \wedge x$; hence C is also valid. $(rx) \wedge y = (rx)^2 + y^2 = r^2x^2 + y^2$ but $r(x \wedge y) = rx^2 + ry^2$, as we saw above, so they are not equal. **D** is not valid. $r^2(x \wedge y) = r^2(x^2 + y^2) = r^2x^2 + r^2y^2$, which is equal to $(rx) \wedge (ry)$, as we saw above. So **E** is valid. Choose **B**, **C** and **E**.

## PROBLEMS (Solutions on page 147)

### Basic Problems

IN PROBLEMS 1 AND 2, $r^* = 1 - r$.

1.

| Quantity A | Quantity B |
|---|---|
| $(-2)^*$ | $2^*$ |

2.

| Quantity A | Quantity B |
|---|---|
| $3^*2^*1^*$ | $0^*(-1)^*(-2)^*$ |

3.

$$x_\clubsuit = \frac{1}{x}$$

| Quantity A | Quantity B |
|---|---|
| $\left(\dfrac{1}{10}\right)_\clubsuit$ | $10_\clubsuit$ |

4. If $x \odot y = \dfrac{x}{y}$, what is $(75 \odot 15)(15 \odot 75)$?

Ⓐ 25

Ⓑ 15

Ⓒ 5

Ⓓ 2.5

Ⓔ 1

5. For the function $F(x) = mx - 9$, what is $F(m)$?

Ⓐ $m - 9$

Ⓑ $(m - 3)(m + 3)$

Ⓒ $m^2 - 9m$

Ⓓ $m$

Ⓔ $(m + 3)^2$

6. If $G(x,y,z) = x + y - z$, what is $G(2,3,4) + G(3,4,2) + G(4,2,3)$?

### GRE Problems

7. If $[\![y]\!] = \dfrac{2}{y}$, then what is $\left[\!\left[\dfrac{1}{y}\right]\!\right] - [\![y]\!]$?

Ⓐ $\dfrac{2y-2}{y}$

Ⓑ $\dfrac{2(y-1)(y+1)}{y}$

Ⓒ $2 - \dfrac{2}{y}$

Ⓓ $\dfrac{1-y^2}{y}$

Ⓔ $2 - y$

8. If $r \odot t = r^2 - t^2$, then what is $(x - y) \odot (x + y)$?

(A) 0

(B) $-2y^2$

(C) $2x^2 - 4xy + 2y^2$

(D) $-4xy$

(E) $x^2 - y^2$

9. For the function $f(x) = Mx - 2$, $f(2) = 2$ and $f(3) = 4$. What is $f(5)$?

(A) 3

(B) 4

(C) 6

(D) 8

(E) 9

10. Define $\begin{vmatrix} a & b \\ c & d \end{vmatrix} = (a-b)(c-d)$. Which of the following are true?

Indicate *all* that apply.

$\boxed{A}$ $\begin{vmatrix} x & 1 \\ 1 & x \end{vmatrix} = (x-1)^2$

$\boxed{B}$ $\begin{vmatrix} 1 & x \\ x & 1 \end{vmatrix} = -(x-1)^2$

$\boxed{C}$ $\begin{vmatrix} x & x \\ 1 & 1 \end{vmatrix} = 0$

$\boxed{D}$ $\begin{vmatrix} -1 & x \\ x & -1 \end{vmatrix} = (x+1)^2$

$\boxed{E}$ $\begin{vmatrix} x & -1 \\ x & -1 \end{vmatrix} = (x+1)^2$

## COORDINATES AND LINES

On the GRE, there may be questions that require an understanding of graphs and points in the two-dimensional plane. On the number line, a point corresponded to a single real number. Similarly, in the plane, a point will correspond to a single *pair* of real numbers. This will allow us to use algebra to describe geometric objects.

Let's describe the so-called Cartesian coordinate system. What is needed are two perpendicular axes (number lines) and an origin at the point where they intersect. By convention, we'll specify that the $y$-axis is vertical and numbered from bottom to top, and that the $x$-axis is horizontal and numbered from left to right. The origin will be given the coordinate $(0, 0)$. To plot $(4, 3)$ you start at the origin $(0, 0)$, move right 4 units, move up 3 units, and then draw the point. To plot $(-2, -3)$, you start at the origin $(0, 0)$, move left 2 units, move down 3 units, and then draw the point.

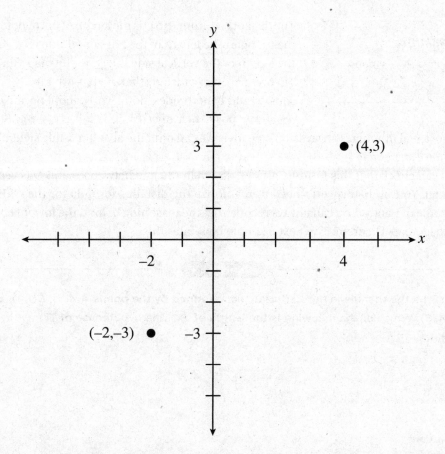

Now we can easily calculate the distance between two points in the plane. Here's how. Consider the two points $P(x_1, y_1)$ and $Q(x_2, y_2)$. For now, we'll assume that the line through $P$ and $Q$ is neither vertical nor horizontal. Using the line through $P$ and $Q$, we can form a right triangle, with sides parallel to the coordinate axes.

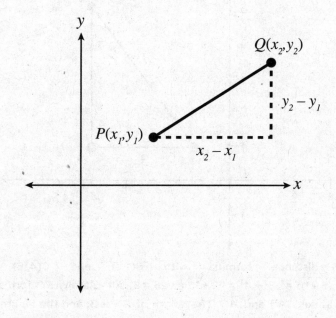

## DISTANCE FORMULA

The distance, $d$, between points $P(x_1, y_1)$ and $Q(x_2, y_2)$ is $d = \sqrt{(x_2 - x_1)^2 + (y_2 - y_1)^2}$.

The distance, $d$, from $P$ to $Q$ is the length of the hypotenuse of the triangle. The length of the horizontal side is $|x_2 - x_1|$, and the length of the vertical side is $|y_2 - y_1|$. By the Pythagorean Theorem, we can conclude that $d^2 = |x_2 - x_1|^2 + |y_2 - y_1|^2$. Taking square roots of both sides (don't worry about negatives since $d$ is always positive), we get $d = \sqrt{|x_2 - x_1|^2 + |y_2 - y_1|^2}$. Since the square of a real number is always non-negative, we can omit the absolute value signs above to get *distance formula*.

You can check that this formula also works when the line between $P$ and $Q$ is vertical or horizontal. You probably won't need to memorize the distance formula for the GRE, but it might come in handy. You can always reconstruct the reasoning behind the formula by using the Pythagorean Theorem. The next example illustrates this.

### EXAMPLE 1

Let $T$ be the triangle in the Cartesian plane formed by the points $A(4, 1)$, $B(1, 1)$, and $C(4, 5)$. Which of the following is the length of $\overline{BC}$, the hypotenuse of $T$?

- (A) 4
- (B) $\sqrt{5}$
- (C) 5
- (D) $\sqrt{3}$
- (E) 3

**Solution:**

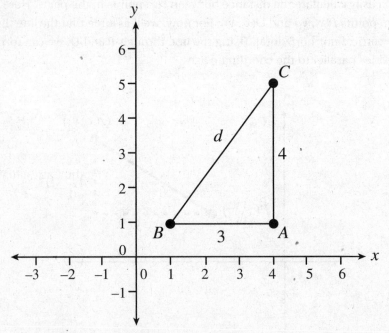

Using the distance formula with $B(1, 1)$ and $C(4, 5)$, we get $d = \sqrt{(4-1)^2 + (5-1)^2} = \sqrt{3^2 + 4^2} = \sqrt{9 + 16} = \sqrt{25} = 5$. Alternately, $\overline{BC}$ forms the hypotenuse of $T$, with legs $\overline{AB}$ and $\overline{AC}$. The length of $\overline{AB}$ is 3, and the length of $\overline{AC}$ is 4, so by the Pythagorean Theorem (or by remembering the 3-4-5 right triangle), the length of the hypotenuse is 5. Choose **C**.

To find the midpoint between two points in the Cartesian plane, simply take the average of each coordinate.

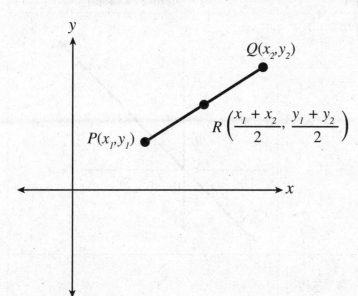

---

**EXAMPLE 2**

Select the option below that represents the midpoint between (2, −2) and (6, 4).

(A) (8, 2)

(B) (2, 4)

(C) (−2, 6)

(D) (4, 1)

**Solution:** Using the midpoint formula, we get $\left(\dfrac{2+6}{2}, \dfrac{-2+4}{2}\right) = \left(\dfrac{8}{2}, \dfrac{2}{1}\right) = (4, 1)$.

Choose **D**.

---

The *graph* of an equation or inequality is the set of all points *(x, y)* whose coordinates satisfy the equation or inequality. Usually, we represent these points on the Cartesian plane, so we associate a graph with a picture. Here are some examples you may know.

| Equation or Inequality | Graph | Picture of Graph |
|---|---|---|
| $y = x$ | $\{(0, 0), (1, 1), (2, 2),\ldots\}$ | <br><br><br> *y = x* |
| $x^2 + y^2 = 1$ | $\left\{(1, 0), (0, -1), \left(\dfrac{1}{\sqrt{2}}, \dfrac{1}{\sqrt{2}}\right), \ldots\right\}$ | $x^2 + y^2 = 9$ |
| $y \geq -1$ | $\{(-2, 1), (2, -1), (6, 0),$ $(-4, 1),\ldots\}$ | $y \geq 1$ |

**EXAMPLE 3**

Which of the following points lie *above* the graph of $y = x^2$?

Indicate *all* that apply.

A   (3, 9)

B   (2, 5)

C   (–1, 2)

D   (–3, –2)

E   (–2, 4)

**Solution:** If we plug a point into our equation and the equation is still valid, the point lies on the graph. For instance, $(9) = (3)^2$ is true, so $A(3, 9)$ lies *on* the graph. Similarly $(4) = (-2)^2$, so $D$ also lies on the graph. Now, for $B(2, 5)$, we find $(5) = (2)^2$ is not true, but our $y$ value of 5 is larger than the value of $2^2$, so $(2, 5)$ lies above the graph. For $C(-1, 2)$, we find $(2) = (-1)^2$ is again not true, and again our $y$ value of 2 is larger than $(-1)^2$, so $C$ lies above the graph. Finally, for $D(-3, -2)$, we find $-2 = (-3)^2$ is not true, but this time our $y$ value, $-2$, is less than $(-3)^2$, so $D$ lies below the graph. Choose **B** and **C**.

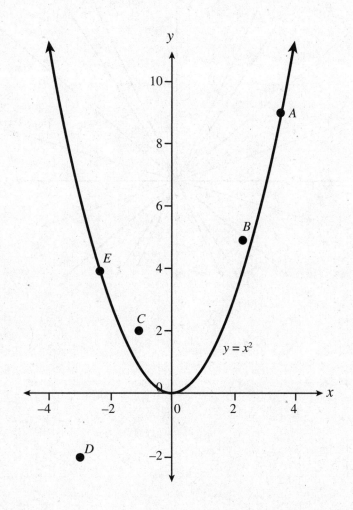

**ALGEBRA   133**

You may recall from previous experience that given two distinct points in the plane, there is a unique line through the two points. Given two points, we'll need the concept of slope to allow us to express the line algebraically.

$$\text{Slope} = \frac{\text{rise}}{\text{run}} = \frac{y_2 - y_1}{x_2 - x_1}$$

The slope of a line passing through the points $P(x_1, y_1)$ and $Q(x_2, y_2)$ is given by $\frac{\text{rise}}{\text{run}} = \frac{y_2 - y_1}{x_2 - x_1}$.

For a given line, this formula gives the same value, *regardless of the two points selected.* Remember that the slope of a vertical line is undefined (because we never divide by zero), and the slope of a horizontal line is 0. This makes sense since you wouldn't want a horizontal line to have any slope, since it is completely flat. The slope tells the direction (uphill, downhill) and steepness of the line. A line with a positive slope rises uphill to the right, and a line with a negative slope falls downhill to the right. The larger the absolute value of the slope, the more rapid the rise or fall.

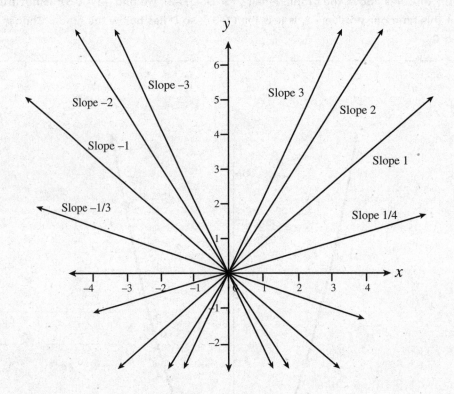

EXAMPLE 4

Consider the diagram shown below.

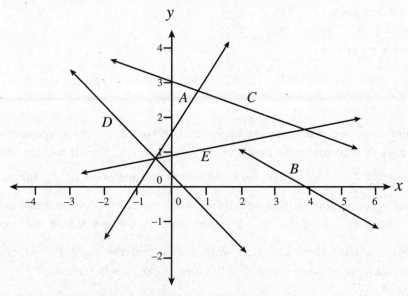

Select the largest and the smallest of the following.

(A) Slope of line *A*
(B) Slope of line *B*
(C) Slope of line *C*
(D) Slope of line *D*
(E) Slope of line *E*

**Solution:** The hardest part of this question is seeing past the clutter to the essential details. First, look only at the lines that are sloping up to the right: *A* and *E*. *A* is clearly the steepest, so *A* is the largest slope. Now, look at the lines sloping down to the right: *B*, *C*, and *D*. *D* is clearly the steepest, so *D* is the smallest slope. Remember, when it comes to negative numbers, smaller means it has a larger absolute value. For instance −10 is smaller than −3.

There are two commonly used forms of equations describing lines. We describe them both.

A line passing through the point $(x_1, y_1)$ and having slope *m* is given by the equation $y - y_1 = m(x - x_1)$. This is called the point-slope form for the equation of a line.

**POINT SLOPE FORM**

$$y - y_1 = m(x - x_1)$$

**EXAMPLE 5**

Which of the following represent an equation of the line through (3, 0) and (–1, 4).

Select *all* that apply.

- **A** $y + 1 = (-1)(x - 4)$
- **B** $y - 4 = (-1)(x + 1)$
- **C** $y = -x + 3$
- **D** $x + y = 3$
- **E** $x = y + 3$

**Solution:** There are many ways to approach this kind of problem. We use various techniques to illustrate some possibilities. To find an equation of the line, first find the slope: $\frac{4-0}{-1-3} = \frac{4}{-4} = -1$. Now, we'll use $m = -1$ and the point (3, 0), although the other point would work just as well. Here's what the point-slope equation gives us: $y - y_1 = m(x - x_1) \Rightarrow y - 0 = (-1)(x - 3)$, which gives us $y = -x + 3$. So **C** is correct.

Applying the point-slope equation with $m = -1$ and the point (–1, 4) gives us: $y - y_1 = m(x - x_1)$, which gives us $y - 4 = (-1)(x - (-1))$, so **B** is correct.

Plugging (3, 0) into A gives: $0 + 1 = (-1)(3 - 4)$, which simplifies to $0 = 0$. Then, plugging in (–1, 4) into A gives $5 = 5$. Thus, the first choice contains both points, and since the first choice is an equation of a line that contains both these points, it must be the same line. So **A** is also a correct choice.

Now, consider D. Subtracting $x$ from both sides will give us $y = -x + 3$, which is C. Thus, D is correct, too.

Finally, plugging in (–1, 4) into the last choice yields: $-1 = 4 + 3$, which is false. Thus, E is not correct. Choose **A**, **B**, **C**, and **D**.

---

A line that intersects the *y*-axis at the point (0, *b*) is said to have *y* intercept of *b*.

### SLOPE-INTERCEPT FORM

$$y = mx + b$$

A line with slope *m* and *y*-intercept *b* has the equation $y = mx + b$. This is called the slope-intercept form for the equation of a line. This equation form is popular since you can tell so much about the graph just from a quick read of the equation. For instance, if you were given the line $y = 2x + 6$, you can tell right away that the slope of that line is 2 and the line crosses the *y* axis at (0, 6).

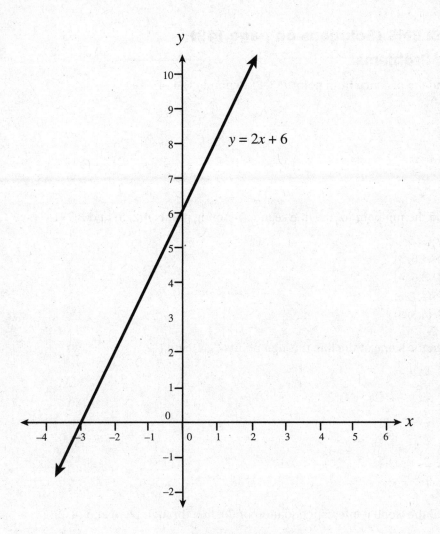

$y = 2x + 6$

---

**EXAMPLE 6**

| Column A | Column B |
| --- | --- |
| Slope of $3x + 2y = 7$ | $y$-intercept of $2x + 3y = -9$ |

**Solution:** First, put each into slope-intercept form. Column A becomes, by adding $-3x$ to both sides: $2y = -3x + 7$. Then, divide by 2 to get $y = \dfrac{-3}{2}x + \dfrac{7}{2}$. The slope is thus $\dfrac{-3}{2}$. For Column B, add $-2x$ to both sides to get: $3y = -2x - 9$. Then, divide both sides by 3 to get $y = \dfrac{-2}{3}x - 3$. The $y$-intercept is $-3$. Since $\dfrac{-3}{2} > -3$, select **A**.

## PROBLEMS (Solutions on page 149)

### Basic Problems

1. Find the distance from point $P(2, 8)$ to point $Q(-1, 4)$.

   (A) 2

   (B) 4

   (C) $\sqrt{5}$

   (D) 5

   (E) $\sqrt{6}$

2. Find the midpoint of the line segment joining points $A(2, 5)$ and $B(7, 1)$.

   (A) $(3, 5)$

   (B) $(4.5, 5)$

   (C) $(3.5, 4)$

   (D) $(4, 3.5)$

   (E) $(4.5, 3)$

3. Find the slope of the line through points $(3, 1)$ and $(-2, -3)$.

   (A) 1

   (B) 0.8

   (C) $\dfrac{3}{5}$

   (D) $\dfrac{2}{5}$

   (E) 0.2

4. Find the slope $y$-intercept equation of the line through $(2, 6)$ and $(8, 2)$.

   (A) $y = \dfrac{2}{3} + 8$

   (B) $y = \dfrac{2}{3}x + 8$

   (C) $y = -\dfrac{2}{3}x + \dfrac{2}{3}$

   (D) $y = -\dfrac{2}{3}x - \dfrac{22}{3}$

   (E) $y = -\dfrac{2}{3}x + \dfrac{22}{3}$

5. Which of the following could be the point slope equation for the line through $(1, 1)$ and $(5, 2)$?

   (A) $y - 1 = \left(\dfrac{1}{4}\right)(x - 1)$

   (B) $y + 1 = \left(-\dfrac{1}{4}\right)(x + 1)$

   (C) $y = \dfrac{1}{4}x + 1$

   (D) $y + 1 = 2(x - 1)$

   (E) $y - 1 = 2(x - 1)$

6. Find the slope of the line pictured below.

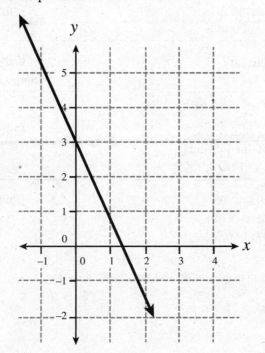

(A) 1.5
(B) 3
(C) −2
(D) −1
(E) 1

## GRE Problems

PROBLEMS 7 AND 8 ARE CONCERNED WITH THE DIAGRAM BELOW.

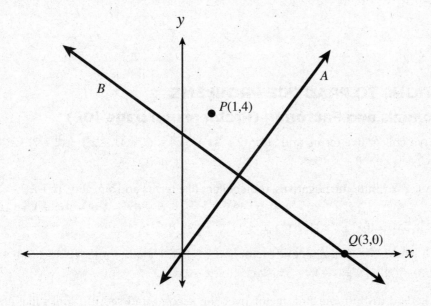

| 7. | Column A | Column B |
|----|----------|----------|
|    | Slope of line $A$ | 5 |

| 8. | Column A | Column B |
|----|----------|----------|
|    | −1 | Slope of line $B$ |

9. $$2 < t < 6$$

| Column A | Column B |
|----------|----------|
| Slope of line joining | 2 |
| $P(1, 1)$ and $Q(t, -2)$ | |

| 10. | Column A | Column B |
|-----|----------|----------|
|     | Distance from | 4 |
|     | $R(3, 3)$ to $S(t, -1)$ | |

11. Which of the following points is on the line $2x + 3y = -4$?

   Select *all* that apply.

   **A** (1, 1)

   **B** (−5, 2)

   **C** (−2, 0)

   **D** (0, −2)

   **E** (0, 0)

12. What is the slope of the line $4x = 2y + 5$?

   (A) 2

   (B) 1

   (C) $\dfrac{1}{2}$

   (D) $-\dfrac{1}{2}$

   (E) −2

## SOLUTIONS TO PRACTICE PROBLEMS
## Polynomials and Factoring (Problems on page 105)

1. **(D)** We collect like terms and add: $(2 - 3x + 5x^3) + (7 + 4x - x^5) = (2 + 7) + (-3x + 4x) + (5x^3) + (-x^5) = 9 + x + 5x^3 - x^5$.

2. **(E)** We distribute the negatives, then collect like terms and simplify. $(1 + 2x) - (3x + 4x^2) + (5x^2 + 6x^3) - (7x^3 + 8x^4) = 1 + 2x - 3x - 4x^2 + 5x^2 + 6x^3 - 7x^3 - 8x^4 = 1 + (2x - 3x) + (-4x^2 + 5x^2) + (6x^3 - 7x^3) - 8x^4 = 1 - x + x^2 - x^3 - 8x^4$.

3. **(B)** It's best to treat the second factor as $3 + (-2x)$. Then $(2 + x)(3 - 2x) = (2)(3) + (2)(-2x) + (x)(3) + (x)(-2x) = 6 - 4x + 3x - 2x^2 = 6 - x - 2x^2$.

4. **(D)** Let's distribute the first factor over the second and see if it looks like any of the answers. $(x^{100} - 1)(2 + x^{10}) = (x^{100} - 1)(2) + (x^{100} - 1)(x^{10})$. None of the answers seem to

match. We'll be careful to treat $(x^{100} - 1)$ as $x^{100} + (-1)$ and distribute the second factor over the first. $(x^{100} - 1)(2 + x^{10}) = (x^{100})(2 + x^{10}) + (-1)(2 + x^{10})$.

5. **(C)** Follow the rule for difference of squares to see that $4 - y^2 = 2^2 - y^2 = (2 - y)(2 + y)$.

6. **(A)** Using the rule for difference of squares $(t + 3)(t - 3) = t^2 - 9$, which is not equal to $t^2 + 9$. Is one always larger than the other? Yes, $(t^2 - 9) + 18 = t^2 + 9$. So $t^2 + 9$ is always 18 larger than $t^2 - 9$.

7. **(D)** Let's multiply out B: $ab(3b - 2a^2 + 2) = (ab)(3b) + (ab)(-2a^2) + (ab)(2) = 3ab^2 - 2a^3b + 2ab$, which is not the same as A. So which is larger? If $a = 0$, both are zero. If $a = b = 1$, then A is $3 - 2 + 4 = 5$ while B is $3 - 2 + 2 = 3$. So sometimes one is larger and sometimes they are equal.

8. **(1)** The number $1{,}000{,}001 \times 999{,}999$ equals $(1{,}000{,}000 + 1)(1{,}000{,}000 - 1) = 1{,}000{,}000^2 - 1$, by the difference of squares. This is exactly 1 less than $1{,}000{,}000^2$.

9. **(1)** We factor and simplify before substituting:

$$\frac{x-y}{x^2 - y^2} = \frac{\cancel{x-y}}{\cancel{(x-y)}(x+y)} = \frac{1}{x+y} . \text{ Then } \frac{1}{(x+y)} = \frac{1}{(0.01 + 0.99)} = \frac{1}{1} = 1 .$$

10. **(14)** We factor and simplify before substituting:

$$\frac{b^2 - a^2}{b+a} = \frac{(b-a)\cancel{(b+a)}}{\cancel{(b+a)}} = b - a . \text{ Then } b - a = 57 - 43 = 14 .$$

11. **(B)** There are a total of $77 + 44$ numbers so to find the average we divide: $\dfrac{(77^2 - 44^2)}{(77 + 44)}$. It

is easier to factor and cancel before simplifying. $\dfrac{77^2 - 44^2}{77 + 44} = \dfrac{(77 - 44)\cancel{(77 + 44)}}{\cancel{77 + 44}} = 77 - 44 = 33$.

Hence, the average is 33.

12. **(D)** It's clear that if $x = 0$, then both quantities are zero. If $x = 1$, then A is zero, while B is $(1 - 2)(1)(1 + 2) = -3$. Similarly, if $x = 2$, then B is zero, while A is $(2 - 1)(2)(2 + 1) = 6$. Clearly it depends on the value of $x$.

13. **(A)** First we know that $(a + b)^2 = a^2 + 2ab + b^2$ which, as $ab = 2$, equals $a^2 + 2(2) + b^2 = a^2 + b^2 + 4$. Meanwhile $(a - b)^2 = a^2 - 2ab + b^2$, which as $ab = 2$, equals $a^2 - 2(2) + b^2 = a^2 + b^2 - 4$. Since $a^2$ and $b^2$ are nonnegative, $a^2 + b^2 + 4 > a^2 + b^2 - 4$.

14. **(D)**

| | $(s + t)^2$ | $(s - t)^2$ |
|---|---|---|
| Expand | $s^2 + 2st + t^2$ | $s^2 - 2st + t^2$ |
| Subtract $s^2 + t^2$ | $-(s^2 + t^2)$ | $-(s^2 + t^2)$ |
| | $2st$ | $-2st$ |

Even knowing $s > 0$, since $t$ could be positive or negative, A or B could be larger.

15. **(A)** We see that $a^2 - b^2 = (a - b)(a + b) = (24)(25) = 600$. We know that $(a + b)^2 = a^2 + 2ab + b^2$ while $(a - b)^2 = a^2 - 2ab + b^2$, so $(a + b)^2 - (a - b)^2 = 2ab - (-2ab) = 4ab$. But $(a + b)^2 - (a - b)^2$ is also equal to $25^2 - 24^2 = (25 - 24)(25 + 24) = 1(49) = 49$. As $4ab = 49$, $ab = \dfrac{49}{4}$, clearly much less than 600.

An alternate solution would be to add the given equations together $(a - b) + (a + b) = 24 + 25 \Rightarrow 2a = 49$. Hence $a = 24.5$. As $a + b = 25$, this means that $b = 0.5$. Now we can evaluate $a^2 - b^2 = (24.5)^2 - (0.5)^2$ and $ab = (24.5)(0.5)$. Even without evaluating, we can see that A > B.

16. **(C)** Start by factoring and simplifying B, $\dfrac{x^2 - y^2}{(x + y)^2} = \dfrac{(x - y)\cancel{(x + y)}}{(x + y)\cancel{(x + y)}} = \dfrac{x - y}{x + y}$. As $x$ and $y$ are positive, we did not cancel zero. Hence A = B.

17. **(A)** Factor before simplifying: $(0.63)^2 - (0.37)^2 = (0.63 + 0.37)(0.63 - 0.37) = (1)(0.26) = 0.26$. This is greater than $\dfrac{1}{4} = 0.25$.

18. **(C)** One approach is to factor $\dfrac{1}{x} - \dfrac{1}{x^2} = \dfrac{1}{x}\left(1 - \dfrac{1}{x}\right) = \dfrac{1}{x}\left(\dfrac{x}{x} - \dfrac{1}{x}\right) = \dfrac{1}{x} \cdot \dfrac{x - 1}{x} = \dfrac{x - 1}{x^2}$. Another approach would be to start with B and split it into two fractions $\dfrac{x - 1}{x^2} = \dfrac{\cancel{x}}{x^{\cancel{2}}} - \dfrac{1}{x^2} = \dfrac{1}{x} - \dfrac{1}{x^2}$.

19. **(D)** One way to simplify A is to factor using difference of squares. $\left(x + \dfrac{1}{2}\right)^2 - \left(x - \dfrac{1}{2}\right)^2 = \left(\left(x + \dfrac{1}{2}\right) - \left(x - \dfrac{1}{2}\right)\right)\left(\left(x + \dfrac{1}{2}\right) + \left(x - \dfrac{1}{2}\right)\right) = (1)(2x) = 2x$. How does $2x$ compare to $|x|$? When $x = 0$, they are equal. When $x = 1$, they are not.

20. **(C)** As $x^2 + 2xy + y^2 = (x + y)^2$, A is equal to $3^2 = 9$. Meanwhile B is $6 + (x + y) = 6 + 3 = 9$.

## Solving Equations (Problems on page 114)

1. **(1)** We add $x$ to both sides: $2x + 3 + x = 6 - x + x \Rightarrow 3x + 3 = 6$. Then we subtract 3 from both sides: $3x + 3 - 3 = 6 - 3 \Rightarrow 3x = 3$. Now divide both sides by 3, $\dfrac{3x}{3} = \dfrac{3}{3}$, and we have $x = 1$.

2. $\left(\dfrac{1}{2}\right)$ First expand $a(a - 3) = (a + 2)(a - 1) \Rightarrow a^2 - 3a = a^2 + a - 2$. Then subtract $a^2$ from both sides: $a^2 - 3a - a^2 = a^2 + a - 2 - a^2 \Rightarrow -3a = a - 2$. Now add $3a$ to both sides: $-3a + 3a = a - 2 + 3a \Rightarrow 0 = 4a - 2$. Add 2 to both sides: $0 + 2 = 4a - 2 + 2 \Rightarrow 2 = 4a$. Finally divide both sides by 4: $\dfrac{2}{4} = \dfrac{4a}{4} \Rightarrow \dfrac{1}{2} = a$. $\dfrac{1}{2}$, or $\dfrac{2}{4}$, or any equivalent fraction.

3. **(B, D)** Expand $(t + 2)(3 - t) = (t + 2) \Rightarrow 3t + 6 - t^2 - 2t = t + 2 \Rightarrow t + 6 - t^2 = t + 2$. Subtract $t$ from both sides, $t + 6 - t^2 - t = t + 2 - t \Rightarrow 6 - t^2 = 2$. Subtract 6 from both sides $6 - t^2 - 6 = 2 - 6 \Rightarrow -t^2 = -4$, and divide by $-1$ to get $t^2 = 4$. This implies that $t = 2$ or $t = -2$.

Alternatively, notice that if $t + 2 = 0$, and hence $t = -2$, then both sides of the equation are zero and thus equal. Otherwise, we can cancel $t + 2$ from both sides to get $3 - t = 1$. Add $t$ to both sides to get $3 = 1 + t$, then subtract 1 from both sides, and we have $t = 2$. So the solutions are 2 and –2.

4. **(C)** To isolate $z$, we start by subtracting $(2x - y)$ from both sides, $2x - y + 3z - (2x - y) = 2 + y - (2x - y) \Rightarrow 3z = 2 + y - 2x + y \Rightarrow 3z = 2 + 2y - 2x$. Now divide by 3, and we have $z = \dfrac{2 + 2y - 2x}{3}$.

5. **(D, E)** First add $b^2$ to both sides, $2b^2 - 8 + b^2 = 1 - b^2 + b^2 \Rightarrow 3b^2 - 8 = 1$. Now add 8 to both sides, $3b^2 - 8 + 8 = 1 + 8 \Rightarrow 3b^2 = 9$. Divide by 3, $\dfrac{3b^2}{3} = \dfrac{9}{3} \Rightarrow b^2 = 3$. This implies that $b = \sqrt{3}$ or $b = -\sqrt{3}$.

6. **(A)** Multiply both sides by $(x + 1)(x - 1)$ to clear the denominators: $(x+1)(x-1)\dfrac{1}{x+1} = (x+1)(x-1)\dfrac{2}{x-1}$, which simplifies to $x - 1 = 2(x + 1)$. Expanded this is $x - 1 = 2x + 2$. Subtract $x$ from both sides $x - 1 - x = 2x + 2 - x \Rightarrow -1 = x + 2$. Then subtract 2 from both sides $-1 - 2 = x + 2 - 2 \Rightarrow -3 = x$.

7. **(A)** If we add the given equations, $(m + n) + (3 - n) = 7 + 6$, it simplifies nicely to $m + 3 = 13$. Subtract 3 from both sides, and we have $m = 10$.

8. **(A)** Multiply the first equation by 3, to get $3x - 3y = 9$. Add this to the second equation to get $(3x - 3y) + (2x + 3y) = 9 + 2 \Rightarrow 5x = 11 \Rightarrow x = \dfrac{11}{5} = 2.2$. If we substitute $x = 2.2$ back into the first equation, we have $(2.2) - y = 3$, so $y = 2.2 - 3 = -0.8$. As $2.2 > -0.8$, choose A.

   Alternate answer: as $x - y = 3$, $x = y + 3$. So $x$ is always 3 more than $y$, and hence larger than $y$.

9. **(A)** First we expand: $(x + y)z \Rightarrow y(x + z) \Rightarrow xz + yz = yx + yz$. We want to get all terms involving $x$ on one side of the equation. Subtract $yx$ from both sides, $xz + yz - yx = yx + yz - yx \Rightarrow xz - yx + yz = yz$. Then subtract $yz$ from both sides, $xz - yx + yz - yz = yz - yz \Rightarrow xz - yx = 0$. Now factor out an $x$ on the left side, $x(z - y) = 0$. Hence $x = 0$ or $z = y$. But we were given that $z \neq y$, so $x = 0$.

10. **(22)** A quick way to solve this problem is to notice that $2x + 2 = (2x - 3) + 5 = 17 + 5 = 22$.

11. **(30)** By comparing opposite (vertical) angles at the center of the circle we can get two nice equalities. First $b = 2a$ and second $120 = b + a + 30$. If we substitute the first in the second, we have $120 = 2a + a + 30 \Rightarrow 120 = 3a + 30 \Rightarrow 120 - 30 = 3a \Rightarrow 90 = 3a \Rightarrow a = 30$.

12. **(4)** First we use 2 as the base for all powers: $4^{b+1} = 2^{3b} \div 4 \Rightarrow (2^2)^{b+1} = 2^{3b} \div 2^2$. Now we use rules of exponents to simplify $2^{2b+2} = 2^{3b-2}$. For the equality to hold, we must have $2b + 2 = 3b - 2$. Subtract $2b$ from each side, $2b + 2 - 2b = 3b - 2 - 2b$, and we have $2 = b - 2$. Add 2 to each side, and we conclude that $b = 4$.

13. **(D)** First we change $2^3$ to 8, so that we may use 8 as the base for all the powers. Then $8^{a/3} = 2^3 8^{1-a} \Rightarrow 8^{a/3} = (8)8^{1-a}$. Now using rules for exponents we have $8^{a/3} = 8^{1+(1-a)} \Rightarrow 8^{a/3} = 8^{2-a}$. Since the bases are equal, we must have $\frac{a}{3} = 2 - a$. Multiply both sides by 3, $3\left(\frac{a}{3}\right) = 3(2-a) \Rightarrow a = 6 - 3a$. Add $3a$ to both sides, $a + 3a = 6 - 3a + 3a \Rightarrow 4a = 6$. Divide by 4 and we have $a = \frac{6}{4} = \frac{3}{2} = 1.5$.

14. **(B)** First multiply both sides by 3, to get rid of the fraction: $V \times 3 = \left(\frac{4\pi r^3}{3}\right) \times 3 \Rightarrow 3V = 4\pi r^3$.

Then we divide both sides by $4\pi$ to get $\frac{3V}{(4\pi)} = r^3$.

Finally, take cube roots to get $r = \sqrt[3]{\frac{3V}{4\pi}}$.

15. **(D)** As $x^2 - 4 = 0$, then $x^2 = 4$, which means that $x = 2$ or $x = -2$. In one case A and B are equal and in the other A < B.

16. **(B)** Start by expanding $x(2(x + 3) + 3) = 3(4 + 3x) \Rightarrow x(2x + 6 + 3) = 12 + 9x \Rightarrow x(2x + 9) = 12 + 9x \Rightarrow 2x^2 + 9x = 12 + 9x$. We subtract $12 + 9x$ to bring everything to one side: $2x^2 + 9x - (12 + 9x) = 0 \Rightarrow 2x^2 - 12 = 0$. Add 12 to both sides and then divide by 2 to get $x^2 = 6$. This means $x = \sqrt{6}$ or $x = -\sqrt{6}$. In either case it is less than 6.

17. **(A)** Starting with $3x - 6 = 4$, divide by 3 to get $\frac{(3x-6)}{3} = \frac{4}{3} \Rightarrow x - 2 = \frac{4}{3}$. Now multiply by 2 and $2(x-2) = 2 \times \frac{4}{3} \Rightarrow 2x - 4 = \frac{8}{3}$. Finally subtract 2 to get $2x - 4 - 2 = \frac{8}{3} - 2 \Rightarrow 2x - 6 = \frac{2}{3}$.

Going back to $x - 2 = \frac{4}{3}$, we subtract 2 to get $x - 2 - 2 = \frac{4}{3} - 2 \Rightarrow x - 4 = -\frac{2}{3}$.

**Alternate solution:** We start by solving for $x$ in $3x - 6 = 4$. First, add 6 to both sides to get $3x = 10$. Then, divide both sides by 3 to get $x = \frac{10}{3}$. If we substitute $x = \frac{10}{3}$ into the expression for A to get $2x - 6 = 2\left(\frac{10}{3}\right) - 6 = \frac{20}{3} - \frac{18}{3} = \frac{2}{3}$. If we substitute $x = \frac{10}{3}$ into the expression for B we get $x - 4 = \left(\frac{10}{3}\right) - 4 = \frac{10}{3} - \frac{12}{3} = \frac{-2}{3}$.

18. **(C)** If we add the two given equations, then $(3x - y) + (3x + y) = 2 + 4 \Rightarrow 6x = 6 \Rightarrow x = 1$. We can substitute $x = 1$ in the second equation $3(1) + y = 4 \Rightarrow 3 + y = 4$. Subtract 3 from each side, and we have $y = 1$. Since both $x$ and $y$ are 1, choose C.

19. **(D)** If we subtract the second equation from the first we get $(3x + 2y + z) - (2x + y + z) = -2 - 10 \Rightarrow x + y = -12$. Now divide both sides by 2 and we have $\frac{x+y}{2} = -6$. Thus the average of $x$ and $y$ is $-6$. What is $z$? $z$ can take on almost any value. Note $2x + y + z = 10$ can be rewritten as $x + (x + y) + z = 10$. As $x + y = -12$ this means $x + (-12) + z = 10 \Rightarrow x + z = 22$. When $x$ is very large, say 100, $z = -78$. When $x$ is small, say $x = 0$, then $z = 22$. So $z$ can be larger or smaller than $-6$.

20. **(7)** Add the two equations together, to get $(r - s) + (t + s) = 3 + 11 \Rightarrow r + t = 14$. Then divide by 2 to see that $\frac{r+t}{2} = 7$. Hence the average of $r$ and $t$ is 7.

21. **(A, C)** Not being certain what else to do, add the two equations together: $(ax^2 - bx + c)$ $+ (-bx^2 + ax - c) = 0$. Then collect like terms and simplify $(a - b)x^2 + (a - b)x = 0$. If we factor, then we have $(a - b)(x^2 + x) = 0 \Rightarrow (a - b)(x)(x + 1) = 0$. As the product is zero, $a - b = 0$, $x = 0$, or $x + 1 = 0$. Put another way, $a = b$ or $x = 0$ or $x = -1$. Now we can consider the options. A: if $a \neq b$, then $x = 0$ or $-1$ is true. B: If $x \neq 0$, then $a = b$ or $x = -1$. So B does not have to be true. C: If $x = 2$, then $(a - b)(x)(x + 1) = 0$ becomes $(a - b)(2)(2 + 1) = 0$ and hence $a - b = 0$, or $a = b$. C is true.

22. **(30)** Let Derek have $d$ marbles, Jason have $j$ marbles, and Cornelia have $c$ marbles. Then $d = 2j$, $c = \left(\frac{1}{3}\right)d$, and $d + c + j = 55$. As $d = 2j$, $j = \frac{d}{2}$. Then substitute $j = \frac{d}{2}$ and $c = \left(\frac{1}{3}\right)d$ into $d + c + j = 55$ to get $d + \left(\frac{1}{3}\right)d + \frac{d}{2} = 55$. Multiply both sides by 6 to clear the denominators, $6d + 2d + 3d = 330$. Hence $11d = 330$ or $d = 30$.

23. **(E)** Let Jillian's favorite number be $J$. Then Jillian doubled her favorite number, $2J$, added one, $2J + 1$, divided by three, $\frac{2J+1}{3}$, and subtracted two, $\frac{2J+1}{3} - 2$. This was her favorite number so $\frac{2J+1}{3} - 2 = J$. To solve we first multiply both sides by 3 to clear the denominators, whence $(2J + 1) - 6 = 3J$. Subtract $2J$ from both sides and $1 - 6 = J$, or $J = -5$.

# Inequalities (Problems on page 122)

1. **(B)** As $a - b > 0$, subtract $a$ from both sides: $(a - b) - a > 0 - a \Rightarrow -b > -a$.

2. **(B)** First note that $(a^2)^2 = a^4$, while $\sqrt{\sqrt{a}} = \left((a)^{\frac{1}{2}}\right)^{\frac{1}{2}} = a^{\frac{1}{4}}$. For numbers between 0 and 1 (like 0.7) taking the fourth power gives a smaller result, $a^4 < a$, but taking the fourth root gives a larger result, $a^{\frac{1}{4}} > a$. Hence $a^{\frac{1}{4}} > a > a^4$.

3. **(B)** As $x < y$, subtracting $y$ from both sides gives $x - y < y - y \Rightarrow x - y < 0$. If we multiply this inequality by $-1$ (reversing the inequality sign) we get $-1(x - y) > -1 \times 0 \Rightarrow y - x > 0$. Hence $x - y < 0 < y - x$.

4. **(A)** Remember that $-1$ raised to any even power is 1 and raised to any odd power is $-1$. If we evaluate A, $x^4 - x^3 = (-1)^4 - (-1)^3 = 1 - (-1) = 2$. Now $x^3 - x^4 = -1(x^4 - x^3) = -1(2) = -2$.

5. **(B)** One way to solve this problem is to ask when they are equal: $4x - 3 = 3x + 4 \Rightarrow 4x - 3 - 3x = 3x + 4 - 3x \Rightarrow x - 3 = 4 \Rightarrow x - 3 + 3 = 4 + 3 \Rightarrow x = 7$. Since they are equal when $x = 7$, when $x < 7$ (as in this case), one is always larger than the other. If $x = 1$, $4x - 3 = 4(1) - 3 = 1$ and $3x + 4 = 3(1) + 4 = 7$. So, when $x < 2$, $3x + 4$ is always larger.

   **Alternate solution:** Notice that $3x + 4 = (4x - 3) + (7 - x)$. As $x < 2$, $7 - x$ is always positive. So $3x - 4$ is always a positive number larger than $4x - 3$. Hence $3x + 4$ is larger.

6. **(B)** For a number between 0 and 1 (like $\frac{1}{4}$), squaring gives a smaller result, $\left(\frac{1}{4}\right)^2 < \frac{1}{4}$, but taking the square root gives a larger result $\sqrt{\frac{1}{4}} > \frac{1}{4}$. Hence $\left(\frac{1}{4}\right)^2 < \frac{1}{4} < \sqrt{\frac{1}{4}}$. In this case you could have computed the values and compared, $\left(\frac{1}{4}\right)^2 = \frac{1}{4} \times \frac{1}{4} = \frac{1}{16}$ while $\sqrt{\frac{1}{4}} = \frac{1}{2}$ since $\left(\frac{1}{2}\right)^2 = \frac{1}{4}$.

7. **(D)** As $|-y| = 5$, $-y = 5$, or $-y = -5$. In the first case, $y = -5$ and the second $y = 5$. Since we don't know which value $y$ has, we could have A < B or A = B.

8. **(D)** Remember that $\sqrt{x^2}$ is not always equal to $x$. If $x = -3$, then $\sqrt{x^2} = \sqrt{(-3)^2} = \sqrt{9} = 3$. If $x = 3$, then $\sqrt{x^2} = \sqrt{(3)^2} = \sqrt{9} = 3$.

9. **(B, C)** As $y < -1$, if we multiply by $-1$ (and switch the inequality sign), we have $-y > 1$. Now add this to $x > 1$, and we have $x + (-y) > 1 + 1 \Rightarrow x - y > 2$. So C is true. As $x > 1$ and $y < -1$, $x$ is positive and $y$ is negative. The product of a positive and a negative is negative. So $xy < 0$, and B is true. A is not true. If $x = 2$ and $y = -2$, then $x + y = 0$. D is not true. For example, if $x = 5$ and $y = -10$, then $x^2 = 25 < y^2 = 100$.

10. **(E)** First, we know that for numbers greater than 1 that $a^2 > a > \sqrt{a}$. So A and B are not the smallest. As $a > 2$, $\sqrt{a} > \sqrt{2} > 1$. We also know that as $a > 2$ that $\frac{1}{a} < \frac{1}{2} < 1$. So D is less than C. Finally as $a^2 > a > 0$, then $\frac{1}{a^2} < \frac{1}{a}$.

11. **(A)** The easiest way to solve this problem is to clear the denominators by multiplying both quantities by $9^{10}$. Then $A = 9^{10} \times \left(\frac{1}{9}\right)^9 = 9$ and $B = 9^{10} \times \left(\frac{1}{9}\right)^{10} = 1$. As 9 > 1 choose A. Alternatively, remember that $9^9 < 9^{10}$ implies that $\frac{1}{9^9} > \frac{1}{9^{10}}$.

12. **(A)** This is challenging as there is no way to avoid doing some calculations. We suggest you divide both quantities by $5^5$. Then A becomes 5 and B becomes $\left(\frac{6}{5}\right)^5 = (1.2)^5$. Since $12^2 = 144$, we know that $(1.2)^5 = (1.2)^2(1.2)^2(1.2) = (1.44)(1.44)(1.2)$. As $14^2 = 196$, $(1.44)^2$ is approximately 2. Thus B is approximately $2 \times 1.2 = 2.4$, nowhere near 5.

13. **(A)** Multiply both quantities by $2^{10}$ to clear the denominators. Then A becomes

$$\left[2^{10} - \left(\frac{1}{2}\right)^{10}\right]2^{10} = 2^{10}2^{10} - \frac{1}{2^{10}}2^{10} = 2^{20} - 1$$

while B becomes

$$\left[2^9 + \left(\frac{1}{2}\right)^9\right]2^{10} = 2^9 2^{10} + \frac{1}{2^9}2^{10} = 2^{19} + 2$$

Now $2^{20} - 1 = 2 \times 2^{19} - 1 = 2^{19} + 2^{19} - 1$. As $2^{19} - 1 > 2$, A is greater than B.

14. **(B)** First clear the denominators by multiplying both quantities by $x^2$. As $x > 4$ there is no possibility that this would change the inequality between A and B. Then A is $2x - 3$, while B is $x^2$. Then $2x - 3 = 2(x - 1.5) < 2x < 4x < x^2$. So B is greater than A.

   Alternate answer: $\dfrac{2}{x} - \dfrac{3}{x^2} = \dfrac{2}{x}\left(1 - \dfrac{3}{2x}\right)$. As $x > 4$, $\dfrac{2}{x}$ is between 0 and 1. As $x > 4$, $2x > 8$, so $\dfrac{3}{2x}$ is also between 0 and 1. The product of numbers between 0 and 1 is between 0 and 1.

15. **(D)** Note that $-1(x^4 - x^2) = -x^4 + x^2 = x^2 - x^4$. So these numbers are opposites. Except when $x = 0$, both are nonzero. So sometimes A = B, and sometimes not.

16. **(A)** $(7^*)^* = \left(\dfrac{1}{7}\right)^* = \left(\dfrac{1}{\frac{1}{7}}\right) = 1 \times \left(\dfrac{7}{1}\right) = 7$. Put another way, $*$ takes the reciprocal of a number and the reciprocal of the reciprocal is the original number. Now $\left(\dfrac{1}{7^*}\right)^* = \left(\dfrac{1}{\frac{1}{7}}\right)^* = 7^* = \dfrac{1}{7}$.

17. **(C)** A is possible as $\left(\dfrac{1}{2}\right) + \left(\dfrac{1}{2}\right) = 1$ and $0 < \left(\dfrac{1}{2}\right)\left(\dfrac{1}{2}\right) < 1$ since $\left(\dfrac{1}{2}\right)\left(\dfrac{1}{2}\right) = \dfrac{1}{4}$. B is possible as we can make $y$ very small so that $x$ can be large and their product still be small. Let $x = 200$ and $y = \dfrac{1}{400}$. Then $x > 100$ and $0 < (200)\left(\dfrac{1}{400}\right) < 1$ as $(200)\left(\dfrac{1}{400}\right) = \dfrac{1}{2}$. C is not possible. If $x < 0 < y$, then $x$ is negative and $y$ is positive. Then $xy$ would be negative and hence not between 0 and 1. D is possible if $y = -200$ and $x = -\dfrac{1}{400}$. Then $xy = \dfrac{1}{2}$. E is possible if $x = \dfrac{3}{2}$ and $y = \dfrac{1}{2}$.

   Then $x - y = \dfrac{3}{2} - \dfrac{1}{2} = 1$ and $\left(\dfrac{3}{2}\right)\left(\dfrac{1}{2}\right) = \dfrac{3}{4}$, which is between 0 and 1.

18. **(D)** The product of positive and negative cannot be positive so A, B, and E are not possible. The product of integers is an integer and there are no integers between 0 and 1, so C is not possible. If $x = 10 - \dfrac{1}{1,000}$ and $y = \dfrac{1}{1,000}$, then $xy$ is greater than zero and less than $10\left(\dfrac{1}{1,000}\right) = \dfrac{1}{100} < 1$.

19. **(A)** First we know that for numbers greater than 1, that $a^2 > a > \sqrt{a}$. So B and C are not the largest. Also when $a > 1$, $0 < \dfrac{1}{a} < 1 < a$. So D is not the largest. Finally as $a^2 > a$, $a - a^2 < 0 < a$. So E is not the largest.

## Functions (Problems on page 127)

1. **(A)** Since $r^* = 1 - r$, $(-2)^* = 1 - (-2) = 3$. Also $2^* = 1 - 2 = -1$.

2. **(B)** You can compute this answer directly: $3^*2^*1^* = (1 - 3)(1 - 2)(1 - 1) = (-2)(-1)(0) = 0$, while $0^*(-1)^*(-2)^* = (1 - 0)(1 - (-1))(1 - (-2)) = 1(2)(3) = 6$.

3. **(A)** Notice that this function just takes reciprocals of numbers. The reciprocal of $\frac{1}{10}$ is $\frac{10}{1} = 10$. The reciprocal of 10 is $\frac{1}{10}$.

4. **(E)** Because of cancellation you don't have to calculate $(75 \odot 15)$ completely. You just need to notice we are taking the product of reciprocals: $(75 \odot 15)(15 \odot 75) = \frac{75}{15} \times \frac{15}{75} = 1$.

5. **(B)** To evaluate the function, we simply put $m$ everywhere that $x$ was, so $F(m) = m(m) - 9 = m^2 - 9$. Unfortunately $m^2 - 9$ is not an option. But remembering our difference of squares, $m^2 - 9 = (m - 3)(m + 3)$.

6. **(9)** $G(2,3,4) + G(3,4,2) + G(4,2,3) = (2 + 3 - 4) + (3 + 4 - 2) + (4 + 2 - 3) = (2 + 2 - 2) + (3 + 3 - 3) + (4 + 4 - 4) = 2 + 3 + 4 = 9$.

7. **(B)** $\left[\!\left[\frac{1}{y}\right]\!\right] - [\![y]\!] = \frac{2}{\left(\frac{1}{y}\right)} - \frac{2}{y} = 2y - \frac{2}{y}$. This is not an option so we combine the fractions.

$$2y - \frac{2}{y} = 2y\frac{y}{y} - \frac{2}{y} = \frac{2y^2}{y} - \frac{2}{y} = \frac{2y^2 - 2}{y}$$

This is still not an option so we factor the numerator.

$$\frac{2y^2 - 2}{y} = \frac{2(y^2 - 1)}{y} = \frac{2(y - 1)(y + 1)}{y}$$

8. **(D)** $(x - y) \odot (x + y) = (x - y)^2 - (x + y)^2$, which we can factor using difference of squares, into $((x - y) + (x + y))((x - y) - (x + y))$. Simplifying, we have $(2x)(-2y) = -4xy$.

9. **(D)** Since $f(2) = 2$, we know that $M(2) - 2 = 2$. Since $f(3) = 4$ we know that $M(3) - 2 = 4$. Let's add these two equations together: $(2M - 2) + (3M - 2) = 2 + 4 \Rightarrow 5M - 4 = 6$. Add 2 to both sides, and we have $5M - 2 = 8$. But $f(5) = M(5) - 2$. So $f(5) = 8$.

10. **(B, C, E)** First $\begin{vmatrix} x & 1 \\ 1 & x \end{vmatrix} = (x - 1)(1 - x) = (x - 1)(-1)(x - 1) = -(x - 1)^2$. So A is not true. Now $\begin{vmatrix} 1 & x \\ x & 1 \end{vmatrix} = (1 - x)(x - 1) = -(x - 1)(x - 1) = -(x - 1)^2$. So B is true. Now $\begin{vmatrix} x & x \\ 1 & 1 \end{vmatrix} = (x - x)(1 - 1) = 0 \times 0 = 0$. Thus C is true. $\begin{vmatrix} -1 & x \\ x & 1 \end{vmatrix} = (-1 - x)(x - (-1)) = -(1 + x)(x + 1) = -(x + 1)^2$. So D is not correct. $\begin{vmatrix} x & -1 \\ x & -1 \end{vmatrix} = (x - (-1))(x - (-1)) = (x + 1)(x + 1) = (x + 1)^2$. So E is correct.

# Coordinates and Lines (Problems on page 138)

1. **(D)** We use the distance formula:

$$= \sqrt{(x_2 - x_1)^2 + (y_1 - y_2)^2} = \sqrt{(-1-2)^2 + (4-8)^2} = \sqrt{(-3)^2 + (-4)^2} = \sqrt{9+16} = \sqrt{25} = 5.$$

2. **(E)** We use the midpoint formula: $\left( \dfrac{x_1 + x_2}{2}, \dfrac{y_1 + y_2}{2} \right) = \left( \dfrac{2+7}{2}, \dfrac{5+1}{2} \right) = (4.5, 3).$

3. **(B)** We use the slope formula: $\dfrac{\text{rise}}{\text{run}} = \dfrac{y_2 - y_1}{x_2 - x_1} = \dfrac{-3-1}{-2-3} = \dfrac{-4}{-5} = \dfrac{4}{5}.$

4. **(E)** First, we find the slope: $\dfrac{\text{rise}}{\text{run}} = \dfrac{y_2 - y_1}{x_2 - x_1} = \dfrac{2-6}{8-2} = \dfrac{-4}{6} = \dfrac{-2}{3}.$ Now, we use the point (8, 2)

   and slope $\dfrac{-2}{3}$ and the point slope form: $y = y_1 = m(x - x_1) \Rightarrow y - 2 = \left( -\dfrac{2}{3} \right)(x - 8).$ Now, we

   simplify with some algebra and change to slope $y$-intercept form.

   $$y = \left( -\dfrac{2}{3} \right)(x) - \left( -\dfrac{2}{3} \right)(8) + 2 \Rightarrow y = \left( -\dfrac{2}{3} \right)(x) + \dfrac{16}{3} + \dfrac{6}{3}, \text{ and we get } y = \left( -\dfrac{2}{3} \right)x + \left( \dfrac{22}{3} \right).$$

5. **(A)** First, we find the slope: $\dfrac{\text{rise}}{\text{run}} = \dfrac{y_2 - y_1}{x_2 - x_1} = \dfrac{2-1}{5-1} = \dfrac{1}{4}.$ Now, we use the point (1, 1) and

   slope $\dfrac{1}{4}$ and the point slope form $y - y_1 = m(x - x_1) \Rightarrow y - 1 = \left( \dfrac{1}{4} \right)(x - 1).$ If you had used

   point (5, 2), you may have found other correct answers that are not shown. You could
   also note that A is the only choice with the correct slope and in point slope form.

6. **(C)** We first identify two points on the line (intercepts are often easiest). We'll use (0, 3)

   and (1, 1). To find the slope, we use the formula $\dfrac{\text{rise}}{\text{run}} = \dfrac{y_2 - y_1}{x_2 - x_1} = \dfrac{1-3}{1-0} = \dfrac{-2}{1} = -2.$

7. **(B)** Line $A$ is fixed by the origin, (0, 0) and must be below the point (1, 4). If it could go

   through (1, 4), its slope would be $\dfrac{\text{rise}}{\text{run}} = \dfrac{y_2 - y_1}{x_2 - x_1} = \dfrac{4-0}{1-0} = \dfrac{4}{1} = 4.$ In fact, it must be less steep

   and, thus, have a lower slope than 4.

8. **(D)** Line $B$ must pass through (3, 0) and must also be below the point (1, 4). If it could

   go through (1, 4), its slope would be $\dfrac{\text{rise}}{\text{run}} = \dfrac{y_2 - y_1}{x_2 - x_1} = \dfrac{4-0}{1-3} = \dfrac{4}{-2} = -2.$ In fact, it must decline

   less quickly, so its slope must be higher than −2. Unfortunately, that is not conclusive.
   How does the slope compare to −1? If it passed through (1, 1), the slope would be
   $\dfrac{\text{rise}}{\text{run}} = \dfrac{y_2 - y_1}{x_2 - x_1} = \dfrac{1-0}{1-3} = \dfrac{1}{-2} = -0.5,$ which is more than −1. If it passed through (1, 3), the

   slope would be $\dfrac{\text{rise}}{\text{run}} = \dfrac{y_2 - y_1}{x_2 - x_1} = \dfrac{3-0}{1-3} = \dfrac{3}{-2} = -1.5.$ So the slope can be more or less than −1.

9. **(B)** No matter what the $x$-values are, the $y$-values are 1 and −2, making the slope negative; therefore, 2 is greater.

10. **(D)** The point $S$ is somewhere along the line segment that joins $(2, -1)$ and $(6, -1)$. If $S$ is at $(3, -1)$, then the distance between $S$ and $R$ is exactly 4 units (no need to use a formula). If $S$ is at $(5, -1)$, then the distance between $S$ and $R$ is clearly more than 4. So we cannot determine which is larger.

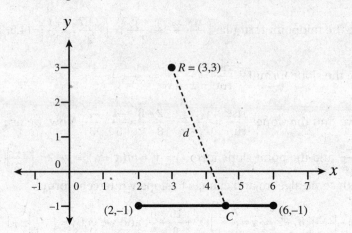

11. **(B, C)** There is no easy way to answer this other than to check.

| Answer | Substitute into 2x + 3y = –4 | Result |
|--------|------------------------------|--------|
| (1, 1) | 2(1) + 3(1) = –4 or 5 = –4 | Not on line |
| (–5, 2) | 2(–5)+3(2) = –4 or –4 = –4 | On line |
| (–2, 0) | 2(–2) + 3(0) = –4 or –4 = –4 | On line |
| (0, –2) | 2(0) + 3(–2) = –4 or –6 = –4 | Not on line |
| (0,0) | 2(0) + 3(0) = –4 or 0 = –4 | Not on line |

12. **(A)** First, we solve for $y$ to change $4x = 2y + 5$ into slope-intercept form. Subtract 5 from each side to get $4x - 5 = 2y$. Then, divide by 2 to get $2x - 2.5 = y$ or $y = 2x - 2.5$. In this form, the slope is the coefficient of $x$. So the slope is 2.

# Data Analysis

**5**

## PERCENTAGES

Percents are needed to understand any business report, political poll, or medical drug dosage. A percent expresses a number of parts per hundred. For instance, 4 apples is 8% of 50 apples since if we divide 50 apples into 100 parts (each part will be half an apple) then 4 whole apples will be 8 half apples or 8 parts. We could also note that 4 out of 50 apples is the fraction 4/50, which is equivalent to 8/100 so 4 apples is 8% of 50 apples.

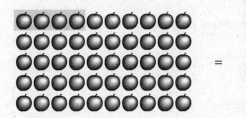 =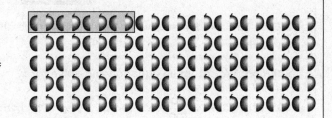

Typically we calculate percentages using fractions or decimals.

$$8\% \text{ of } 50 = \frac{8}{100} \times 50 = 0.08 \times 50 = 4$$

You'll note that $8\% = 0.08 = \frac{8}{100}$.

If asked to compute a fixed percentage of a number we just multiply.

**TIP**

What is *b*% of *c*?
$\frac{b}{100} \times c$

**EXAMPLE 1**

Bob saved 10% of his paycheck for his Friday night date. If his paycheck was $435 how much can he spend on the date?

**Solution:** 10% of $435 = \frac{10}{100} \times 435 = 43.5$. If you prefer decimals, 10% of 435 = 0.10 × 435 = 43.5. Bob has $43.50 for his date.

If asked to find a percentage we can set up a fraction and convert to a decimal.

**TIP**

*a* is what percentage of *c*?
$a = b\% \text{ of } c$
$a = \frac{b}{100} \times c$

$b = \frac{100a}{c}$

---

**EXAMPLE 2**

Ellen paid $14 of the $35 dinner bill on a date with Bob. What percentage of the bill did she pay? Was the bill split equally?

**Solution:** You might directly compute $\dfrac{14}{35} = 0.4$, which is $\dfrac{40}{100}$ or 40%. Why does this work? We need to find what percentage of 35 will equal 14, that is *x*% of 35 = 14.

$\dfrac{x}{100} \times 35 = 14$ so $x = 14 \times \dfrac{100}{35} = \dfrac{14}{35} \times 100 = 40$. Thus Ellen paid only 40% of the bill—not an equal share.

If asked to find a number so that a fixed percentage of it will be a given number, we can divide.

---

**EXAMPLE 3**

If Ellen has only $14 and wants to pay 50% of the dinner bill, what should they spend on dinner?

**Solution:** We set up an equation and solve for *x*.

50% of *x* = $14 so $\dfrac{50}{100} \times x = \$14$ or $\dfrac{1}{2} \times x = \$14$, hence $x = 2 \times \$14 = \$28$. If you prefer decimals, $0.50 \times x = \$14$ so $x = \dfrac{\$14}{0.50} = \$28$. Thus Ellen can afford 50% of the bill if it is $28 (or less).

We often use percentages to describe changes to a value. The percentage involved might compare the change (increase or decrease) to the old value or it might compare the new value to the old value. You must read a question carefully to distinguish between these two situations.

---

**EXAMPLE 4**

Ellen's salary was increased by 150% from 2014 to 2015. If she earned $50,000 in 2014, what does she earn in 2015?

(A) $65,000

(B) $75,000

(C) $125,000

(D) $150,000

(E) $200,000

**Solution:** In this case, we compare the *increase* in Ellen's salary to her original (2014) salary. So the increase (new–old) is 150% of $\$50,000 = \dfrac{150}{100} \times \$50,000 = \$75,000$.

Thus Ellen's salary was increased by $75,000. Ellen's new salary is $50,000 + $75,000 = $125,000. Choose **C**.

---

EXAMPLE 5

Bob's salary for 2014 is 150% of his 2013 salary. If he earned $50,000 in 2013, what does he earn in 2014?

(A) $65,000

(B) $75,000

(C) $125,000

(D) $150,000

(E) $200,000

**Solution:** In this case we compare Bob's 2014 salary with his 2013 salary. His 2014 salary is 150% of $50,000 = $\dfrac{150}{100} \times \$50{,}000 = \$75{,}000$. Bob's salary in 2014 is $75,000. Choose **B**.

EXAMPLE 6

Ellen was given a raise of x%. Her salary increased from $80,000 to $85,000.

| Quantity A | Quantity B |
|------------|------------|
| x% | 6% |

**Solution:** Let's compare the raise to her salary. She got a raise of $5,000. That is what percentage of $80,000? x% of $80,000 = $5,000 so $\dfrac{x}{100} \times \$80{,}000 = \$5{,}000$. Hence x = $5,000/$80,000 × 100 = 6.25. So Ellen received a 6.25% raise. Choose **A**.

Alternatively, 6% of $80,000 = $\dfrac{6}{100} \times \$80{,}000 = 6 \times \$800 = \$4{,}800$. Her raise was more than $4,800 so x% must be more than 6%.

EXAMPLE 7

| Quantity A | Quantity B |
|------------|------------|
| 25% of $40 | 40% of $25 |

**Solution:** First, 25% of $40 = $0.25 \times \$40 = \dfrac{1}{4} \times \$40 = \$10$. Second, 40% of $25 = $0.40 \times \$25 = 0.40 \times \$25 = \dfrac{4}{10} \times \$25 = \$10$. In either case, we get the same value, so 25% of $40 = 40% of $25. Choose **C**.

**TIP**

*a*% of *b* is equal to *b*% of *a*.

To calculate prices with tax at *a*% just multiply by $1 + \dfrac{a}{100}$. For example, if the tax is 5%, multiply by $1 + \dfrac{5}{100} = 1.05$.

EXAMPLE 8

A shirt costs $20 and sales tax is 7%. What is the total cost including tax?

(A) $27.00

(B) $21.40

(C) $21.07

(D) $21.04

(E) $20.07

**Solution:** The tax paid is 7% of $20 = 0.07 × $20 = $1.40. The total cost is $20 + $1.40 = $21.40. Choose **B**. Alternatively, multiply by $1 + \dfrac{7}{100} = 1.07$. The total cost is 1.07 × $20 = $21.40. The techniques are equivalent because of the distributive property: $21.40 = $20 + $1.40 = $20 + ($20 × 0.07) = $20 × (1 + 0.07) = $20 × 1.07.

It does not matter if you add tax before or after a percentage cut in price.

EXAMPLE 9

If there was a 20% discount, what would the total paid for the shirt be?

(A) $16.00

(B) $16.07

(C) $16.13

(D) $17.12

(E) $17.40

**Solution:** If we calculate tax first, we get $21.40 and then discount it by 20% to get $21.40 less 20% of $21.40 = $21.40 − (0.2 × $21.40) = $21.40 − $4.28 = $17.12. If we calculate the discount first, we get $20 less 20% of $20, which is $20 − (0.2 × $20) = $20 − $4 = $16. We then add 7% tax by multiplying $16 × 1.07 = $17.12. It may seem surprising, but either way you get the same result. Why? Because 0.8 × (1.07 × $20) = 1.07 × (0.8 × $20). Choose **D**.

If a number is decreased by a percentage and then increased by the same percentage, the result is LESS than the original number. The larger the percentage the greater the difference will be.

EXAMPLE 10

Norma accepted a 10% pay cut rather than lose her job.
One year later the company gave her a 10% raise.

| Quantity A | Quantity B |
|---|---|
| Norma's original salary | Norma's final salary |

**Solution:** Assume Norma made $100 (it's a nice easy number to deal with even if it is unrealistic). After the pay cut her salary was $90. Then they increased her salary by 10%. But 10% of $90 is just $9. So now her salary is $99, which is less than her original salary of $100. Generalizing we can see that her salary will be only 99% of its original value. Choose **A**.

## PROBLEMS (Solutions on page 182)

1.
$$35 \text{ is } x\% \text{ of } 50$$

| Quantity A | Quantity B |
|------------|------------|
| $x\%$ of 100 | $2x$ |

2.
| Quantity A | Quantity B |
|------------|------------|
| 6% of 60 | 60% of 6 |

3.
| Quantity A | Quantity B |
|------------|------------|
| 200% of $35,000 | 35% of $180,000 |

4. Mary's salary was $50,000. She now earns $75,000. The percentage increase in her salary was $n$ percent. What is the value of $n$?

```
┌─────────────┐
│             │
│             │
└─────────────┘
```

5. Mary's old salary was $60,000. Her new salary is 150% of her old salary. What is her new salary?

```
┌─────────────┐
│             │
│             │
└─────────────┘
```

6.
| Quantity A | Quantity B |
|------------|------------|
| $10 less 20% plus 8% tax | $8 less 10% plus 20% tax |

7.
$$62\% \text{ of } x = 84$$

| Quantity A | Quantity B |
|------------|------------|
| $x$ | 84% of $x$, plus 10% |

8. If Ellen invested $5,000 in a real estate deal and was repaid $5,700, what percentage profit did she earn?

(A) 5%
(B) 7%
(C) 10%
(D) 14%
(E) 15%

9. The first 50 questions on the exam were multiple-choice and worth 80% of the grade. The last four questions were essay style and worth 20% of the grade. Questions of each type are weighted equally. If Bob scored 73% on the exam and answered only one essay question, how many multiple-choice questions could he have answered correctly?

(A) 30
(B) 34
(C) 40
(D) 45
(E) 46

10. A "Wake Me Up" is made up of six ounces of cola (1% caffeine), 3 ounces of coffee (3% caffeine), and 1 ounce of espresso (10% caffeine). What percentage of a "Wake Me Up" is caffeine?

 %

11. Malik's business revenue for each of the past five years has been from $60,000 to $80,000 annually. For each of the past five years his business expenses have been from 12% to 18% of revenue. Which of the following could be the amount of profit Malik earned in one of the past five years? Note: *profit* is defined as revenue minus expenses.

Indicate *all* that apply.

- A  $42,000
- B  $44,000
- C  $48,000
- D  $50,000
- E  $60,000
- F  $70,000
- G  $71,000

12. Joe invested $X in a mutual fund. His investment increased in value by 6% in the first year, by 10% in the second year, and by *n*% in the third year. If his investment over the three-year period increased in value by at least 35% and at most 45%, which of the following could be *n*?

Indicate *all* that apply.

- A  15
- B  17
- C  19
- D  21
- E  23
- F  25
- G  27

## AVERAGES

How can you describe a large set of numbers with only one value? There are three common ways to describe the "central tendencies" of a set of values: *mean*, *median*, and *mode*.

The *mean* is the sum of the values divided by the number of values. This is more commonly called the average of the numbers. To be clear, on the GRE this is always referred to as the "average (arithmetic mean)." For example, 6 is the average (arithmetic mean) of 4, 8, 5, and 7 since $\frac{4+8+5+7}{4} = \frac{24}{4} = 6$.

If you list a set of values in order (from lowest to highest), the value in the middle is the *median*. For instance $200K is the median price among this list of home sale prices: $145K, $190K, $200K, $201K, $205K. If there is an even number of values, there is no middle value so we take the average of the two middle values as the median.

EXAMPLE 1

Six homes were sold in Canton, New York, in January for the prices $95K, $110K, $84K, $68K, $145K, and $98K.

|  Quantity A  |  Quantity B  |
|---|---|
| Median price | Average (arithmetic mean) price |

**Solution:** First we list the values in order: $68K, $84K, $95K, $98K, $110K, and $145K. We see that there is no middle value so we average the middle values $\frac{\$95K + \$98K}{2} = 96.5K$. Thus the median price was $96,500. The average price was $\frac{\$68K + \$84K + \$95K + \$98K + \$110K + \$145K}{6} = \frac{\$600K}{6} = \$100K$. So the average price was $100,000, which is greater than the median price of $96,500. Choose **B**. Interestingly, K could stand for 1,000 or any positive number and the result is the same.

In a list of values the *mode* is the most frequently occurring value. For example 6 is the mode for the set of values: {2, 3, 7, 6, 6, 8, 2, 6} since 6 occurs three times. The value 2 only occurs twice, and all other values occur once. Unlike mean and median, the mode of a set may not be unique. All of the values that occur most frequently can be called the mode. In the worst case, like {1, 2, 3, 4}, every value is the mode.

EXAMPLE 2

Consider the set of values $S$ = {1, 1, 2, 3, 3, 4, 4, 5, 5}

|  Quantity A  |  Quantity B  |
|---|---|
| Median of $S$ | Mode of $S$ |

**Solution:** The median is 3, but the mode is not unique. All of 1, 3, 4, and 5 are the mode. The median could be greater than the mode, 3 > 1, equal to the mode, 3 = 3, or less than the mode, 3 < 4. Choose **D**.

The average of 83, 84, and 85 is 84 because

$$\frac{83+84+85}{3} = \frac{(84-1)+84+(84+1)}{3} = \frac{84+84+84}{3} = 84$$

If there are an even number of values in the sequence of consecutive numbers, the average is the mean of the two middle values.

TIP

**The average of any sequence of consecutive numbers with an old number of terms is always the middle value.**

**EXAMPLE 3**

What is the average of the integers from 9 through 16 inclusive?

**Solution:** In this case there are eight summands: 9, 10, 11, 12, 13, 14, 15, and 16. The middle terms are 12 and 13 whose mean is $\frac{12+13}{2} = 12.5$. So the average of the integers 9 through 16 is **12.5**.

This property is also true for any arithmetic sequence—one where values are separated by a fixed value.

**EXAMPLE 4**

What is the average of 81, 85, 89, 93, and 97?

(A) 87
(B) 88
(C) 89
(D) 90
(E) 91

**Solution 1:** This is an arithmetic sequence since there is a common difference of 4. Thus the average is the middle term, 89. Choose **C**.

**Solution 2:** The average of five numbers is their sum divided by 5. Add the numbers on your calculator: 81 + 85 + 89 + 93 + 97 = 445. Then, 445 ÷ 5 = 89. Choose **C**.

It is easy to understand this property and other properties of averages if you think of averaging as sharing. When you average a set of numbers, you redistribute their values so that they all will have equal values. It is easy to see why this works for an arithmetic sequence but is also valid in general.

**EXAMPLE 5**

Find the average of 305, 310, and 315.

**Solution:** Think of sharing—take 5 from 315 and give it to 305.

| 305 | 310 | 315 |
|-----|-----|-----|
| +5  |     | −5  |
| 310 | 310 | 310 |

Now all three values will be the same—310. Thus **310** is the average.

## EXAMPLE 6

Mary earned 80, 83, 84, 89, and 89 on five tests. What is her average?

**Solution:** First we take 4 from 89 and give it to 80. Then we take 1 from the other 89 and give it to 83. Now we have 84, 84, 84, 88, and 85. We take three from 88 and share it among the 84's, giving each one. Now we see that Mary's average is **85**.

| 80 | 83 | 84 | 89 | 89 |
|----|----|----|----|----|
| +4 | +1 |    | −1 | −4 |
| 84 | 84 | 84 | 88 | 85 |
| +1 | +1 | +1 | −3 |    |
| 85 | 85 | 85 | 85 | 85 |

This technique is not good in all situations. But it can be useful for values that are relatively close in value and values that would be tedious to add.

## EXAMPLE 7

$$2x + y = 8 \text{ and } x + 2y = 10$$

| Quantity A | Quantity B |
|------------|------------|
| Average (arithmetic mean) of $x$ and $y$ | 4 |

**Solution:** Adding the two equations together, we find that $3x + 3y = 18$. If we divide by 3 we see that $x + y = 6$. We want to find the average of $x$ and $y$, that is $\frac{x+y}{2}$. So we divide $x + y = 6$ by 2 to get $\frac{x+y}{2} = 3$. Thus the average of $x$ and $y$ is 3. Choose **B**.

**TIP**

To find the average of unknown values don't try to solve for the values. Try adding the equations together and look for the average.

Sometimes you do not need to find the average—rather you are asked to find the total of the values. Knowing that Average = $\frac{\text{Total}}{n}$ we see that the Total = Average × $n$.

## EXAMPLE 8

If the average weight of a U.S. penny is 2.5 g, what is the weight of $1,000 in pennies?

(A) 2,500 g
(B) 25 kg
(C) 25,000 g
(D) 250 kg
(E) 1,000 kg

**Solution:** $1,000 equals 100,000 pennies. The total weight is the average weight times the number of pennies. Then 2.5 g × 100,000 = 250,000 g, which is 250 kg. Choose **D**.

A very common type of problem on the GRE involves completing a data set to get a desired average. Knowing how to get the total from the average is the key skill to solving this kind of problem.

Harold has caught three bass at the fishing tournament. They weigh 4 lb, 6 lb, and 4.5 lb. If he needs four fish with an average weight of 5 lb each to win the tournament, how big a fish does he need to catch?

> [                    ] lb

**Solution:** If he had four fish with an average of 5 lb, their total weight is the average times the number of fish, that is 4 × 5 = 20 lb. His current three fish weigh a total of 4 + 6 + 4.5 = 14.5 lb. He needs 20 − 14.5 = **5.5 lb** more.

**Alternate Solution:** If you prefer algebra, let $F$ be the weight of Harold's fourth fish.

We need $\frac{(F + 4 + 4.5 + 6)}{4} = 5$. Multiply both sides by 4 to get $F + 4 + 4.5 + 6 = 20$.

Subtract and we have $F = \mathbf{5.5}$. It's really the same computations—we just think about it differently.

## PROBLEMS (Solutions on page 184)

1.
| Quantity A | Quantity B |
|---|---|
| Average (arithmetic mean) of 4, 7, 9 | Average (arithmetic mean) of 4, 7, 10 |

2.
$$A = \{1, 1, 1, 2, 2, 3, 3, 3, 3, 5, 7, 9\}$$
| Quantity A | Quantity B |
|---|---|
| Mode of $A$ | Median of $A$ |

3.
| Quantity A | Quantity B |
|---|---|
| Average (arithmetic mean) of $A$ | 3 |

4. Mary received 82, 84, 90, and 88 on her first four tests. What score on test five would give her at least an 85 average?

Indicate *all* that apply.

- [A] 79
- [B] 80
- [C] 80.5
- [D] 81
- [E] 83
- [F] 85

5. Seven houses were sold last month in Potsdam, New York. The sale prices in thousands of dollars were $85K, $57K, $104K, $90K, $x$, $y$, and $99K. If the mode was $57K and the median price was $90K, then which of the following could be $x$ and $y$?

 (A) $x = $57K$ and $y = $75K$
 (B) $x = $88K$ and $y = $75K$
 (C) $x = $57K$ and $y = $95K$
 (D) $x = $88K$ and $y = $75K$
 (E) $x = $98K$ and $y = $107K$

6. If the average (arithmetic mean) of seven consecutive odd integers is 21, what is the smallest of the seven odd integers?

7. If the average (arithmetic mean) of six consecutive integers is 9.5, then what is the largest of the six integers?

 (A) 8
 (B) 9
 (C) 10
 (D) 12
 (E) 14

8. Mary needs an average of at least 85 in her math class to keep her scholarship. She received 82, 84, 90, and 88 on her first four tests. She expects to do poorly on test five but do well on test six—the final test. What is the lowest grade she could get on test five and still possibly keep her scholarship, assuming 100 is the maximum possible score on any test?

9. Susan received the same grade on her first four tests and 10 points better on her fifth test. If her test average is 82, what score did she receive on her fifth test?

10. The average score on the surprise quiz was 7 out of 10. Three students earned a 0, two earned only 1, and one earned a 2. No student earned a perfect score. What is the least number of students there could have been in the class? (Assume all quiz scores are whole numbers.)

 (A) 5
 (B) 11
 (C) 23
 (D) 25
 (E) 100

11. The average score on a 10-point surprise quiz was 8.5. If no one earned a perfect score and there are 10 students in the class, what is the lowest score a student could have earned? (Assume all quiz scores are whole numbers.)

12. Let $a$ and $b$ be real numbers so that $0 < a < 10$ and $20 < b < 30$. Which of the following must be true?

Indicate *all* that apply.

A $\boxed{\phantom{A}}$ $a + b > 21$
B $\boxed{\phantom{B}}$ The average of $a$ and $b$ is greater than 12.
C $\boxed{\phantom{C}}$ $ab < 300$
D $\boxed{\phantom{D}}$ $ab > 20$
E $\boxed{\phantom{E}}$ $a + b < 35$
F $\boxed{\phantom{F}}$ $b - a > 10$

## CHARTS AND GRAPHS

Look at any business report and you will find it full of many tables, charts, and diagrams. People find it easier to understand data when presented graphically. Questions on the GRE regarding data analysis test whether you can read those diagrams carefully to obtain reasonably precise information. The main types of diagrams used are pie charts, tables, line graphs, and bar graphs.

Data are usually summarized in tables by tallying which data elements belong to each of several categories.

| North America Population (in millions) | United States | Canada | Mexico | Guatemala | Cuba | Others |
|---|---|---|---|---|---|---|
| 519 | 300 | 33 | 106 | 15 | 11 | 54 |

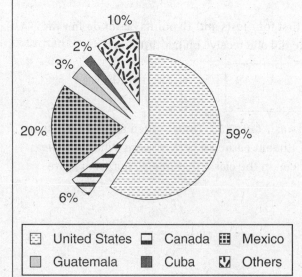

**North American Population—519 Million**

An alternative to the table, pie charts can be used to show what percentage of the data belong to each category. In the chart on the left it is easy to see that the United States has more than half the population of the continent or that Canada and Mexico together do not have as many people as the United States. Notice the title often includes important information—in this case the total population. This would allow you (using the percentages) to determine the population of each country. For instance, the population of Mexico is $519 \times 20\% = 519 \times 0.2 = 103.8$ million people. (Notice this value is not exactly the same as the figure in the table. Rounding in the pie chart places Mexico at 20% when in actual fact they are 106/519 = 20.42%. This kind of discrepancy can affect all data analysis questions. In most cases, a good estimate is sufficient—exact values may be difficult to provide.)

Pie charts can also just be labeled with the data values though you can estimate the percentages just by looking at the pie. Notice the title indicates the units.

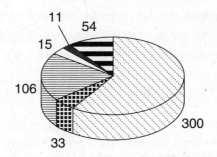

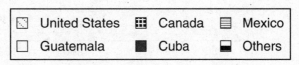

**North American Population (in millions)**

---

**EXAMPLE 1**

Which countries have more than 20% of the North American Population?

Indicate *all* that apply.

A  United States

B  Cuba

C  Mexico

**Solution:** Let's estimate. 25% of the whole would be represented by a quarter pie. The United States has more than a quarter of the pie. The only other country close to a quarter pie is Mexico, so it is the only other country with more than 20% of the North American population. Choose **A** and **C**.

---

Especially when the categories are years, a bar graph is a useful way to compare data from category to category. The following graph shows how the population of all three countries is distributed. It is clear that Mexico has a larger portion of the population in 2000 than 1960, since their bar is larger in 2000. Meanwhile, Canada seems to occupy roughly the same percentage of the population in the last 50 years—since their bar is about the same size in all five graphs. Note that this graph does not tell us how the overall population has been growing. The population may even be shrinking!

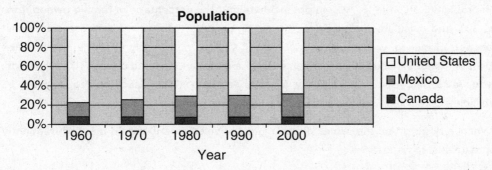

Line graphs provide the information in a way that emphasizes the trends or rates of change. Again this is most often used for categories that are years. First of all we note that population is growing in all three countries. More precisely, the rate of growth in the United States and Mexico is similar, but the rate of growth in Canada is slower. This is clear because the *slope* of the Canada line is less than the slope of the others.

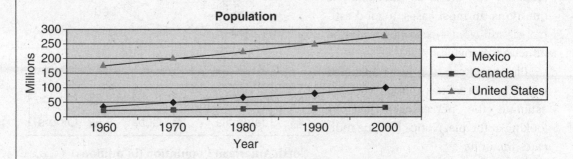

**Watch for totals.** In most pie charts it is important to know what the whole pie represents. If it is a pie of U.S. voters, you want to know how many U.S. voters there are. If it is a pie of world countries, you want to know how many countries there are. In some cases, the information is given somewhere on the chart; in other cases, you may need to total the values of each category to get the total. For example on page 163 you would have to total the populations of each country (300 + 33 + 106 + 15 + 11 + 54 = 519) to see that the North American population is 519 million.

**Watch for percentages as opposed to values.** In many charts, you are given percentages, not actual values. In "All U.S. Companies Ownership" chart (see problems 5–8 at end of this section) you can see from the right bar that female-owned companies have around 5% of all company revenues. That does not tell you how much revenue they have. To determine actual revenues, you would need to know the total revenue as well. If the total revenue is $22 trillion, then female-owned companies have revenue of 22 × 5% = 22 × 0.05 = $1.1 trillion.

**Watch for connecting tables.** When given multiple tables, information from one table is often connected to information from other tables. Some questions cannot be answered by using just one of the tables but requires information from both tables to find a solution. See problem 12 on page 169.

**Estimate, don't calculate.** It is impossible to determine precise figures from the given charts. Try to make good estimates and quick calculations. That is usually sufficient to determine the correct answer. Be careful though—a very loose estimate may lead you to an incorrect answer.

In problem 5 on page 167, you might estimate that the percentage of female-owned firms is 30% and calculate 23 million × 0.30 = 6.9 million. If you were to choose the closest answer, 7.1 million, you would be incorrect. If you were to wisely infer the answer must be less than 6.9 million since the percentage is less than 30% and choose (D) 6.4 million, you would be correct. Alternatively, a better estimate of 28% leads one to calculate 23 million × 0.28 = 6.64 million and choose the correct answer of D.

When in doubt, type the values directly into the calculator. It should be used frequently in data analysis questions.

**EXAMPLE 2**

In the year 2013, a company produced 120,000 units of a certain product. The next year the company doubled production of the product. In the year 2015, the company reduced production by 90,000 units. The number of units produced in 2015 is what percent greater than the number produced in 2013?

$$\boxed{\phantom{000000000000}} \%$$

**Solution:** Production in 2014 was 120,000 × 2 = 240,000 units, while in 2015 it was 240,000 − 90,000 = 150,000 units. The percent increase from 120 thousand to 150 thousand is given by: $\dfrac{150-120}{120} \times 100 = 25\%$ . (Difference over original value.)

## PROBLEMS (Solutions on page 185)

PROBLEMS 1–4 AND 9 AND 10 CONCERN THE FOLLOWING DIAGRAM.

**Australian Population 2002**
**21 Million**

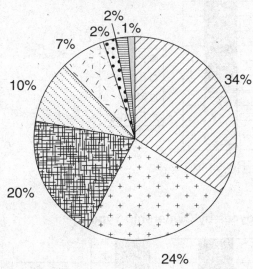

- ⊘ New South Wales
- ▢ Victoria
- ▦ Queensland
- ▨ Western Australia
- ◹ South Australia
- ◖ Tasmania
- ▤ Australian Capital Territory
- ▢ Northern Territory

| 1. | Quantity A | Quantity B |
|---|---|---|
| | Population of Queensland | Population of New South Wales |

| 2. | Quantity A | Quantity B |
|---|---|---|
| | Population of Victoria | 7,000,000 |

| 3. | Quantity A | Quantity B |
|---|---|---|
| | 500,000 | Population living in Territories |

4. If the population of Queensland doubles (while all other regions remain the same), what will be Queensland's percentage of the Australian population?

- (A) 20%
- (B) 30%
- (C) 33%
- (D) 40%
- (E) 50%

PROBLEMS 5–8 CONCERN THE FOLLOWING DIAGRAMS.

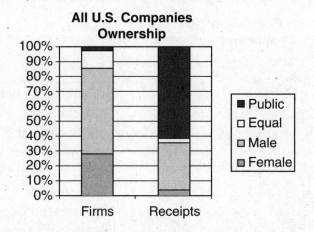

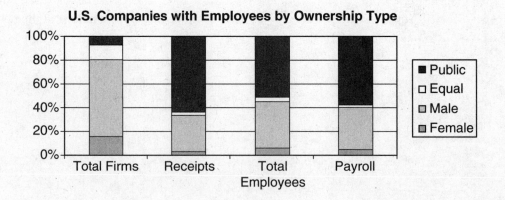

5. If there are 23 million companies in the United States, how many of them have totally female ownership?

  (A) 1.15 million
  (B) 3.8 million
  (C) 5 million
  (D) 6.4 million
  (E) 7.1 million

6. If 17.5 million U.S. companies do not have employees, then how many U.S. firms with employees have totally female ownership?

  (A) 500,000
  (B) 650,000
  (C) 1 million
  (D) 3.5 million
  (E) 5 million

7.

| Quantity A | Quantity B |
| --- | --- |
| Average receipts per female company | Average receipts per male company |

8.

| Quantity A | Quantity B |
| --- | --- |
| Average salary in public company | Average salary in nonpublic company |

9. Forecasts predict the population of Australia will grow by 10% in the next 10 years, but the population of Queensland will remain the same. What percentage of the Australian population will reside in Queensland in 2012?

  (A) 10%
  (B) 15%
  (C) 18%
  (D) 20%
  (E) 30%

10. A political restructuring is proposed where 25% of New South Wales citizens will become citizens of Queensland, and South Australia and Victoria will merge to become New Victoria. If the restructuring goes forth, what will be the most populous of the new states?

  (A) Queensland
  (B) New South Wales
  (C) New Victoria
  (D) Western Australia
  (E) South Australia

PROBLEMS 11–14 REFER TO THE FOLLOWING CHARTS DESCRIBING MARIJUANA USE AMONG 12- TO 17-YEAR-OLDS.

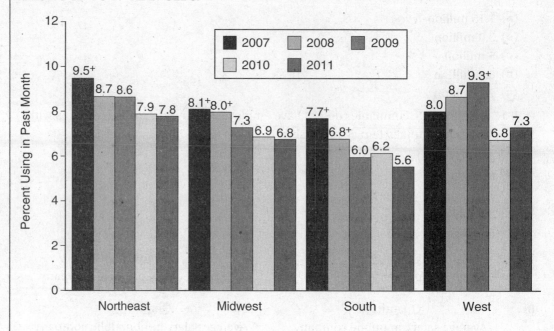

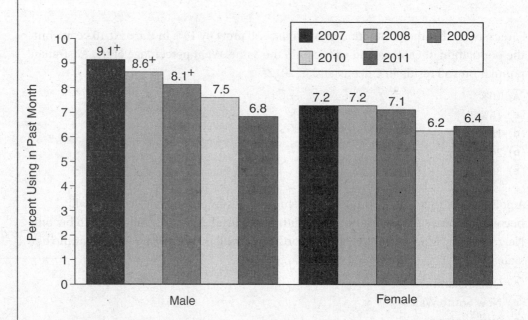

11. Marijuana use is generally decreasing, except in which of the following instances?

(A) 2009–2010 in the West
(B) 2007–2008 among males
(C) 2010–2011 in Midwest
(D) 2010–2011 among females
(E) 2008–2009 in Northeast

12. Male marijuana use in all regions is higher than female marijuana use. In which of the following is the marijuana use higher than the national male marijuana use for that year.

   (A) 2007 Midwest
   (B) 2008 Northeast
   (C) 2009 South
   (D) 2010 West
   (E) 2011 South

FOR PROBLEMS 13 AND 14 ASSUME THE NUMBER OF 12- TO 17-YEAR-OLDS IN 2011 WERE AS FOLLOWS:

| Northeast | Midwest | South | West |
|-----------|---------|-------|------|
| 7 million | 4 million | 17 million | 13 million |

13. *Nationally*, what would be the percentage of 12- to 17-years-olds that had tried marijuana in the past month for 2011?

   (A) 5.6%
   (B) 6.0%
   (C) 6.5%
   (D) 6.6%
   (E) 6.8%

14.             Quantity A                              Quantity B
        2011 marijuana users in West         2011 marijuana users in South

# COUNTING

There are many problems that ask how many ways something can happen. Although it's not as simple as what you learned in kindergarten, we call that counting. The most fundamental problems involve combining situations.

## BASIC COUNTING PRINCIPLE

If there are $m$ ways to do $X$ and $n$ ways to do $Y$, then there are $m \times n$ ways to do $X$ and $Y$.

EXAMPLE 1

A combination door lock has a two symbol access code. The first digit is A, B, C, or D. The second is 1, 2, 3, 4, or 5. How many different access codes are there?

How many access codes have only consonants and even numbers in them?

(A) 20

(B) 16

(C) 12

(D) 9

(E) 6

**Solution:** According to the counting principle, since there are four choices for the first symbol (A, B, C, or D) and five choices for the second symbol (1, 2, 3, 4, 5) there are $4 \times 5 = $ **20** possible access codes. We list them all in the hopes you see why this principle works.

|  |  | 2nd Symbol | | | | |
|---|---|---|---|---|---|---|
|  |  | 1 | 2 | 3 | 4 | 5 |
| 1st Symbol | A | A1 | A2 | A3 | A4 | A5 |
| | B | B1 | B2 | B3 | B4 | B5 |
| | C | C1 | C2 | C3 | C4 | C5 |
| | D | D1 | D2 | D3 | D4 | D5 |

If the first symbol has to be a consonant, there are only three choices (B, C, or D). The second symbol has to be even so there are two choices (2 or 4). Hence, there are $3 \times 2 = 6$ possible access codes that are made of a consonant and an even number. Choose **E**.

EXAMPLE 2

Gary has 4 pairs of pants, 4 ties, and 4 shirts.

| Quantity A | Quantity B |
|---|---|
| Number of outfits if he loses a tie and a shirt | Number of outfits if he loses 2 pants |

**Solution:** The counting principle applies even to more than two situations. Here Gary has $4 \times 4 \times 4$ outfits to begin with, since he has a choice of 4 pants, 4 ties, and 4 shirts. In both cases he loses two articles of clothing so the result is the same, right? Wrong. If he loses a tie and a shirt he now has $4 \times 3 \times 3 = 36$ outfits. If he loses two pants, he now has $2 \times 4 \times 4 = 32$ outfits. Choose **A**.

**TIP**

Watch out for double counting. It is easy to overestimate the result by counting some values twice (or more).

**EXAMPLE 3**

If $x$ and $y$ are integers so that $1 \le x < 5$ and $2 < y < 7$, how many possible values could $xy$ have?

(A) 30

(B) 25

(C) 20

(D) 16

(E) 13

**Solution:** Since $1 \le x < 5$ and $x$ is an integer, there are four choices for $x$: 1, 2, 3, and 4. Since $2 < y < 7$ and $y$ is an integer, there are 4 choices for $y$: 3, 4, 5, and 6. So by the counting principle, we expect there are $4 \times 4 = 16$ possible values for $xy$. Unfortunately, this is wrong. There are 16 possible products, but some of them have the same value. Let's see:

| | | | |
|---|---|---|---|
| $1 \times 3 = 3$ | $2 \times 3 = 6$ | $3 \times 3 = 9$ | $4 \times 3 = 12$ |
| $1 \times 4 = 4$ | $2 \times 4 = 8$ | $3 \times 4 = 12$ | $4 \times 4 = 16$ |
| $1 \times 5 = 5$ | $2 \times 5 = 10$ | $3 \times 5 = 15$ | $4 \times 5 = 20$ |
| $1 \times 6 = 6$ | $2 \times 6 = 12$ | $3 \times 6 = 18$ | $4 \times 6 = 24$ |

As you can see from the table, some values are repeated. So we actually have only 13 different possible values for $xy$. You don't actually have to check all these possible values. After determining there were at most 16 possible values and knowing that some of them were repeated, you would know the actual answer was less than 16. Thus the only possible answer is **E**.

## Venn Diagrams

There are 100 students at Baltimore High School—60 ride the bus and 60 walk. How is that possible? Wouldn't that make 120 students? No, because 20 do both. They walk in the morning but take the bus after school.

Often we count objects in groups, instead of individually. When we do so, some groups overlap and we can, unintentionally, over-count the objects. Venn diagrams are a way to avoid this. Each circular region inside the diagram represents the objects with a given trait. In this case we have a region (A) for bus riders and a region (B) for walkers. The overlap of regions represents those who do both. The area outside the regions represents those who do neither, in this case—none.

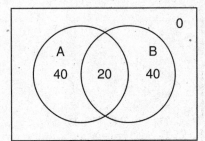

**EXAMPLE 4**

Of the 120 students at Regina High School, 70 own a PC, 20 own both a Mac and a PC, and 30 own neither. How many own a Mac but not a PC?

(A) 0

(B) 10

(C) 20

(D) 30

(E) 50

**Solution:** We use a Venn diagram. As 70 people own a PC and 20 own a PC and a Mac, we conclude that 50 own just a PC. And 30 own neither. Now we can count those distinct groups to see that 30 + 20 + 50 = 100 students are accounted for, of the 120 students at the school. That leaves 120 − 100 = 20 students who must own a Mac but not a PC. Choose **C**.

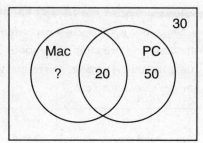

## Partitions

A common counting problem is to find out how many ways a given positive integer can be represented as the sum of smaller positive integers. For the number 5, there are six different "partitions": $5 = 4 + 1$, $5 = 3 + 2$, $5 = 3 + 1 + 1$, $5 = 2 + 2 + 1$, $5 = 2 + 1 + 1 + 1$, and $5 = 1 + 1 + 1 + 1 + 1$. If you think of a chocolate bar with five pieces, this is asking how you can share the bar with others, if the smallest portion is one piece.

Sometimes you are asked to partition a number into just two parts (share with only one other person). Sometimes you are asked to partition into only certain size parts. All these restrictions can cause wrinkles but the basic principle remains the same. Break the analysis down into small cases and take it one at a time, being sure not to miss any possibilities.

EXAMPLE 5

How many different ways are there to write 11 as the sum of three positive integers? Order does not matter: $x + y + z = 11$ and $y + x + z = 11$ count as just one way.

**Solution:** I always organize my sums by the largest part. There is no way for the largest part to be 11, $0 + 0 + 11 = 11$ but each part has to be at least 1. Similarly the largest part cannot be 10.

Largest Part Nine: $9 + 1 + 1$

Largest Part Eight: $8 + 2 + 1$

Largest Part Seven: $7 + 3 + 1$, $7 + 2 + 2$ Notice that once you fix 7 as the largest part you are really looking at finding all the ways to write $11 - 7 = 4$ as the sum of two parts: $4 = 3 + 1$ and $4 = 2 + 2$.

Largest Part Six: $6 + 4 + 1$, $6 + 3 + 2$

Largest Part Five: $5 + 5 + 1$, $5 + 4 + 2$, $5 + 3 + 3$

Largest Part Four: $4 + 4 + 3$

It's impossible to have three numbers add to 11 if the largest is 3 or less. So there are 10 different ways to write 11 as the sum of three positive integers.

EXAMPLE 6

José has a total of 58¢ in 7¢ and 4¢ stamps.

| Quantity A | Quantity B |
|---|---|
| Number of stamps José has | 11 |

**Solution:** This question really asks you to write 58 as the sum of two positive integers, one a multiple of 4 and the other a multiple of 7. Since 58 is even, we cannot use an odd multiple of 7. For example, we use one 7, then some multiple of 4 would have to be $58 - 7 = 51$, which is impossible. I suggest proceeding according to the number of sevens used.

Zero: There cannot be zero 7's since 58 is not divisible by 4.

Two: If we have two 7's, then we need $58 - (2 \times 7) = 44$ as a multiple of 4. As $44 = 11 \times 4$, take 2 seven-cent stamps and 11 four-cent stamps.

Four: If we have four 7's, then we need $58 - (4 \times 7) = 30$ as a multiple of 4. But 30 is not divisible by 4. No answer in this case.

Six: If we have six 7's, then we need $58 - (6 \times 7) = 16$ as a multiple of 4. As $16 = 4 \times 4$, take 6 seven-cent stamps and 4 four-cent stamps.

Eight: If we have eight 7's, then we need $58 - (8 \times 7) = 2$ as a multiple of 4. Impossible. And clearly more than 8 seven-cent stamps is also impossible.

So there are only two possibilities—$(2 \times 7¢) + (11 \times 4¢) = 58¢$ or $(6 \times 7¢) + (4 \times 4¢) = 58¢$. That is a total of 13 or 10 stamps, respectively. In one case this is greater than 11 and in the other less than 11. Chose **D**.

## Counting Commas

How many integers are there from 1 to 10? Anyone would say 10, which is correct. How many integers are there from 3 to 10? Since $10 - 3 = 7$, most people would say 7, which is incorrect. There are actually 8. Let's investigate further.

| Number to Count | Number Listed | End–Start | Actual Count | Count of Commas |
|---|---|---|---|---|
| 1 to 10 | 1, 2, 3, 4, 5, 6, 7, 8, 9, 10 | $10 - 1 = 9$ | 10 | 9 |
| 3 to 10 | 3, 4, 5, 6, 7, 8, 9, 10 | $10 - 3 = 7$ | 8 | 7 |

When you subtract the starting number from the ending number you are actually counting the number of commas! If you prefer, think of it as the number of spaces between the numbers. The count of numbers in the list is always one more than the number of commas.

### EXAMPLE 7

In a 200-page book, photos appear on pages 50 through 150

| Quantity A | Quantity B |
|---|---|
| Number of pages without photos | Number of pages with photos |

**Solution:** At first glance, most people would think that 100 pages have photos and thus $200 - 100 = 100$ do not. Of course pages 50 through 150 means $150 - 50 + 1 = 101$ pages with photos. Thus there are $200 - 101 = 99$ pages without photos. Choose **B**.

### EXAMPLE 8

On the first day of his Vegas vacation, Jerry lost $100 gambling. On the second day, he lost $200. On the third day, he lost $300. If the pattern continues for 9 days in total, how much does he need to win on the tenth day to break even for the trip?

$ [            ]

**Solution:** Jerry lost $\$100 + \$200 + \cdots + \$900 = \$100(1 + 2 + 3 + \cdots + 9) = \$100 \times \dfrac{(9)(10)}{2} = \$100 \times 45 = \$4,500.$

- The sum of the first $n$ positive integers is $\dfrac{n(n+1)}{2}$. For example, $1 + 2 + 3 + \cdots + 17 = \dfrac{17(18)}{2} = 153.$
- The sum of the first $n$ odd numbers is $n^2$. For example, $1 + 3 + 5 + 7 + 9 = 5^2 = 25.$

## PROBLEMS (Solutions on page 186)
## Basic Problems

1.

| Quantity A | Quantity B |
|---|---|
| Sum of first 25 positive integers | 250 |

2.

| Quantity A | Quantity B |
|---|---|
| Sum of first 25 odd positive integers | 600 |

3.　　　　　　A lock has a three-digit combination from 000 to 999

| Quantity A | Quantity B |
|---|---|
| Combinations with no zeros | Combinations with no ones |

4. Rice costs $2 per serving and curry costs $5 per serving at a certain restaurant. A family spends $39 on curry and rice at the restaurant. Servings may be ordered only in whole-number increments; that is, partial servings may not be ordered. Which of the following could be the number of servings of rice that the family ordered?

Indicate *all* that apply.

- [A] 2
- [B] 3
- [C] 5
- [D] 6
- [E] 7
- [F] 12
- [G] 16
- [H] 17

5. Theresa's wardrobe has seven blouses, four pairs of pants, and three belts. How many different outfits can she make? Assume each outfit consists of one of each item.

6. At Brebeuf College, there are 124 students in the band and 78 students who play rugby. If 12 students do both and 44 students do neither, how many students attend Brebeuf?

- (A) 156
- (B) 200
- (C) 202
- (D) 204
- (E) 234

## GRE Problems

7.
| Quantity A | Quantity B |
|---|---|
| Sum of first 50 positive integers | Sum of first 35 odd positive integers |

QUESTIONS 8–10 CONCERN A BOOK THAT HAS PAGES NUMBERED FROM 1 TO 999.

8.
| Quantity A | Quantity B |
|---|---|
| Total number of digits used to number pages | 2,800 |

9.
| Quantity A | Quantity B |
|---|---|
| Number of pages numbered with a 0 | Number of pages numbered with a 1 |

10.
| Quantity A | Quantity B |
|---|---|
| Number of pages numbered with a 2 | Number of pages numbered with a 1 |

11.
| Quantity A | Quantity B |
|---|---|
| Number of integers from −4 through 37 inclusive | Number of integers from 1 through 41 inclusive |

12.
| Quantity A | Quantity B |
|---|---|
| Number of ways to make 85¢ from 3¢ and 10¢ stamps | Number of ways to make 85¢ from 4¢ and 15¢ stamps. |

13. If $4 < x \leq 7$ and $2 \leq y < 6$, then how many different values are there for the sum $x + y$, if $x$ and $y$ are integers?

(A) 6
(B) 9
(C) 12
(D) 20
(E) 42

14. In a freshman calculus class of 34, students study in either the library or the math lab. 25 students study in the library and 15 study at the math lab. If all students study, what is the minimum number of students who study in both places?

(A) 2
(B) 3
(C) 6
(D) 8
(E) 15

15. Chris is 12th in line and Sara is 27th in line for concert tickets. After Chris purchases his tickets, he informs Sara there are 114 tickets left for sale. If each person buys the maximum of 8 tickets, how many tickets will Sara get?

# PROBABILITY

Probability is the study of chance or the likelihood of an event occurring. If there are four equally likely outcomes to an experiment, we say each of them has a one in four chance of occurring. We also say the probability of each outcome is $\frac{1}{4}$.

---

**EXAMPLE 1**

George buys a raffle ticket from a local charity. They sell only 50 tickets. What is the probability George wins the grand prize?

**Solution:** Since each ticket is equally likely to be the winner, George has a one in fifty chance of winning. The probability of his winning is $\frac{1}{50}$.

---

In any experiment, if all the possible outcomes are equally likely, the probability of an event, $X$, occurring is

$$P(X) = \frac{\text{Number of outcomes where } X \text{ occurs}}{\text{Total number of outcomes}}$$

$P(X)$ is 0 exactly when $X$ cannot occur. $P(X)$ is 1 exactly when $X$ always occurs. Otherwise $P(X)$ is between 0 and 1. The probability that an event will not occur is $1 - P(X)$. The sum of all probabilities must be 1.

---

**EXAMPLE 2**

A number is drawn randomly from 1 to 100. Find the probability of each of the following: (a) 105 is drawn, (b) an even number is drawn, (c) a number with zero in it is drawn, (d) a number without zero in it is drawn.

**Solution:**

(a) This is impossible—you can't draw 105 if only the numbers 1 to 100 are used. So the probability is zero.

(b) There are 50 even numbers and 100 possible outcomes so $P(\text{even}) = \frac{50}{100} = \frac{1}{2}$.

(c) There are 10 numbers with a zero in them (10, 20, . . . , 80, 90, 100). So the probability is $\frac{10}{100} = 0.1$.

(d) The answer is one minus the probability of drawing a number with zero in it. That is $1 - 0.1 = 0.9$. Why? If 10 out of 100 numbers have a zero in them, then 90 have no zero in them. So the probability is $\frac{90}{100} = 0.9$.

---

**TIP**

When independent experiments are repeated, the probability of getting event $X$ and then event $Y$ is the product of their probabilities.

**EXAMPLE 3**

Roll one six-sided die and flip a coin. What is the probability of getting heads and a number greater than 3?

(A) $\dfrac{1}{6}$

(B) $\dfrac{1}{4}$

(C) $\dfrac{1}{3}$

(D) $\dfrac{1}{2}$

(E) $\dfrac{2}{3}$

**Solution:** There are six possible die rolls and three of them are greater than 3, namely 4, 5, and 6. So when rolling the die, three of the outcomes are favorable. Thus $P$(die $> 3$) is $\dfrac{3}{6} = \dfrac{1}{2}$. The probability of getting heads when flipping a coin is $\dfrac{1}{2}$. So the probability of getting heads and a number greater than 3 is the product $\dfrac{1}{2} \times \dfrac{1}{2} = \dfrac{1}{4}$.

Alternatively this can be solved by listing all possible outcomes:

| | | | | | |
|---|---|---|---|---|---|
| 1H | 2H | 3H | 4H | 5H | 6H |
| 1T | 2T | 3T | 4T | 5T | 6T |

Clearly 3 of the possible 12 outcomes are desired (4H, 5H, or 6H). So the probability is $\dfrac{3}{12} = \dfrac{1}{4}$. Choose **B**.

**EXAMPLE 4**

Roll two six-sided dice. What is the probability of getting a *total* of 7?

**Solution:** There are six possible outcomes for the first die and six possible outcomes for the second die, so there are $6 \times 6 = 36$ possible outcomes. We list them below. Which of these outcomes give a total of seven? Only the boxed ones on the off-diagonal. Thus the probability of rolling a total of seven is $\dfrac{6}{36} = \dfrac{1}{6}$.

| | | | | | |
|---|---|---|---|---|---|
| 1,1 | 1,2 | 1,3 | 1,4 | 1,5 | 1,6 |
| 2,1 | 2,2 | 2,3 | 2,4 | 2,5 | 2,6 |
| 3,1 | 3,2 | 3,3 | 3,4 | 3,5 | 3,6 |
| 4,1 | 4,2 | 4,3 | 4,4 | 4,5 | 4,6 |
| 5,1 | 5,2 | 5,3 | 5,4 | 5,5 | 5,6 |
| 6,1 | 6,2 | 6,3 | 6,4 | 6,5 | 6,6 |

Alternatively we could find $P(1,6) + P(2,5) + P(3,4) + P(4,3) + P(5,2) + P(6,1)$. For instance, $P(1,6) = P(1) \times P(6) = \dfrac{1}{6} \times \dfrac{1}{6} = \dfrac{1}{36}$. Similarly, $P(2,5) = P(3,4) = P(4,3) = P(5,2) = P(6,1) = \dfrac{1}{36}$. Thus $P(1,6) + P(2,5) + P(3,4) + P(4,3) + P(5,2) + P(6,1) = 6 \times \dfrac{1}{36} = \dfrac{1}{6}$ or equivalent fraction.

## PROBLEMS (Solutions on page 189)

FOR PROBLEMS 1–3: IN BIOLOGY CLASS, MARY IS ASSIGNED A LAB PARTNER RANDOMLY. THE OTHER PEOPLE IN THE CLASS ARE ALICE, FRED, JAMAL, SARA, TOM, VERA, AND ZOE.

1.

| Quantity A | Quantity B |
|---|---|
| Probability her partner is Tom | Probability her partner is Zoe |

2.

| Quantity A | Quantity B |
|---|---|
| Probability her partner has a four-letter name | Probability her partner has a five-letter name |

3.

| Quantity A | Quantity B |
|---|---|
| Probability her partner is John | Probability her partner is male |

For problems 4 and 5, John rolls a fair six-sided die.

4.

| Quantity A | Quantity B |
|---|---|
| Probability of rolling an even number | Probability of not rolling 6 |

5.

| Quantity A | Quantity B |
|---|---|
| Probability of rolling a number greater than 2 | Probability of rolling a prime number |

6. Cole chooses a marble randomly from a jar that contains five white marbles, eight red marbles, and seven blue marbles. What is the probability he chooses a non-white marble?

$$\frac{\boxed{\phantom{XX}}}{\boxed{\phantom{XX}}}$$

7. Cole rolls two ten-sided dice (each has numbers 1–10). What is the probability that the sum of his numbers is 18 or greater?

(A) $\dfrac{2}{9}$

(B) $\dfrac{3}{50}$

(C) 0.04

(D) 0.05

(E) 0.18

8. Veronica is flipping three fair coins. What is the probability that she ends up with more heads than tails?

$$\frac{\boxed{\phantom{XX}}}{\boxed{\phantom{XX}}}$$

9. Marg designed a very unusual spinner for a game she created. What is the probability of spinning a 1 on this spinner?

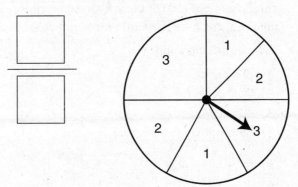

FOR QUESTIONS 10 AND 11, A JAR CONTAINS EIGHT MARBLES: TWO RED, TWO GREEN, AND FOUR WHITE.

10.  
| Quantity A | Quantity B |
| --- | --- |
| Probability of choosing two white marbles | Probability of choosing two green marbles |

11.  
| Quantity A | Quantity B |
| --- | --- |
| Probability of choosing white | Probability of choosing red or green |

12.  An experiment consists of flipping a fair coin three times.
Results are heads (H) or tails (T).

| Quantity A | Quantity B |
| --- | --- |
| Probability of flipping HHH | Probability of flipping HTH |

13. The probability that team A wins its game in New York is .6. The independent probability that team B wins its game in Hawaii is equal to $p$. If the probability that both teams win their games is at least .5, or $\frac{1}{2}$, which of the following could be $p$?

Indicate *all* that apply.

[A] .5
[B] .6
[C] .7
[D] .8
[E] .9
[F] $\frac{5}{6}$

14. A jar contains 8 red chips, 20 blue chips, and $x$ green chips (and no other chips). When a chip is drawn at random from the jar, a green chip is at least twice as likely to be chosen as a red chip but less likely to be chosen than a blue chip. Which of the following could be the *total* number of chips in the jar?

Indicate *all* that apply.

- A 40
- B 42
- C 44
- D 45
- E 46
- F 47
- G 48

# SOLUTIONS TO PRACTICE PROBLEMS
## Percentages (Problems on page 155)

1. **(B)** You do not need to solve for $x$ to answer this problem. We know that $x$ % of 100 is always $x$. And $x$ is less than $2x$ (as long as $x$ is positive, which it is in this case). If you want to solve for $x$, ask "35 is what percentage of 50?" So $x\% = \dfrac{35}{50} = \dfrac{70}{100}$. Thus $x = 70$. Clearly 70 is less than $2 \times 70 = 140$.

2. **(C)** 6% of $60 = 0.06 \times 60 = 3.6$ and 60% of $6 = 0.6 \times 6 = 3.6$. See example 7.

3. **(A)** 200% of $\$35,000 = \dfrac{200}{100} \times \$35,000 = \$70,000$. 35% of $\$200,000$ would also equal $\$70,000$ so 35% of $\$180,000$ must be less than $\$70,000$.

4. **(50%)** The increase is $\$25,000$. Compared to her original salary, $\dfrac{\$25,000}{\$50,000} = 0.5 = 50\%$.

5. **($90,000)** 150% of $\$60,000 = \dfrac{150}{100} \times \$60,000 = \$90,000$.

6. **(C)** 20% of $10 is $2. So $10 less 20% plus 8% tax is $1.08 \times \$8 = \$8.64$. 10% of $8 is $0.80. $8 less 10% plus 20% tax is $1.20 \times \$7.20 = \$8.64$. This does not follow directly from $a\%$ of $b = b\%$ of $a$, but it is the same principle.

7. **(A)** You do not need to solve for $x$ to answer this problem. 84% of $x$, plus 10% is $(0.84x) \times 1.10 = 0.924x = 92.4\%$ of $x$, which is clearly less than $x$ (as long as $x$ is positive, which it is since 62% of $x$ is 84.)

8. **(D)** Ellen earned $700 compared with an investment of $5,000. The percentage profit is $\dfrac{\$700}{\$5,000} = 0.14 = 14\%$.

9. **(D)** Bob earned at most 5 points on the essay question ($\frac{1}{4}$ of 20%). So he earned between 68 (if he got five on the essay) and 73 (if he got zero on the essay) out of 80 on the multiple-choice questions. Solving $\frac{x}{50} = \frac{68}{80}$, we find $x = 42.5$ so he got at least 42.5 multiple-choice questions correct. Solving $\frac{x}{50} = \frac{73}{80}$, we find $x = 45.6$ so he got at most 45.6 multiple-choice questions correct. Thus Bob got 43, 44, or 45 multiple-choice questions correct.

10. **(2.5%)** The cola contributes 1% of 6 oz = $0.01 \times 6$ oz = 0.06 oz of caffeine. The coffee contributes 3% of 3 oz = $0.03 \times 3$ oz = 0.09 oz of caffeine. The espresso contributes 10% of 1 oz = $0.10 \times 1$ oz = 0.1 oz of caffeine. That is a total of $0.06 + 0.09 + 0.1 = 0.25$ oz of caffeine in a 10 oz drink. As $\frac{0.25\,\text{oz}}{10\,\text{oz}} = 0.025 = 2.5\%$, the "Wake Me Up" is 2.5% caffeine.

11. **(D, E, F)** Malik earned the maximum possible profit in a year when he had the highest revenue, $80,000, *and* the least expenses, 12%. In such a year, he would have retained 88% of the $80,000, because $100\% - 12\% = 88\%$. Type $.88 \times 80,000 = \$70,400$.

    The minimum profit would be in a year when Malik earned the minimum revenue, $60,000, *and* had the highest expenses, 18%. When he paid 18% of 60,000, he retained $100 - 18 = 82\%$ of $60,000 = .82 \times 60000 = \$49,200$. Choose answers from $49,200 to $70,400.

12. **(B, C, D, E)** Joe's cumulative increase for the first two years can be thought of as 1.10 (1.06x). This equals 1.166X. His combined three-year appreciation can be represented by $\left(1 + \frac{n}{100}\right)$, times this quantity, so we have $1.35x \leq 1.166x \left(1 + \frac{n}{100}\right) \leq 1.45X$. The values 1.35 and 1.45 in this inequality come from the given percent increases of 35% to 45%, respectively. Divide all three branches of the inequality 1.166X to obtain $1.16 \leq 1 + \frac{n}{100} \leq 1.24$, roughly. Subtracting 1 yields $.16 \leq \frac{n}{100} \leq .24$ and $16 \leq n \leq 24$.

    An alternate solution would involve testing the answer choices on the calculator, which is feasible if you use an efficient method. For example, to test choice F, 25%, type $1.25 \times 1.10 \times 1.06$, which equals 1.4575, corresponding to an increase of 45.75%, a little too high. Choice A is eliminated as too small because $1.15 \times 1.1 \times 1.06 = 1.3409$, which corresponds to a 34.09% increase—less than the required 35%.

## Averages (Problems on page 160)

1. **(B)** The total in Quantity B is larger than the total in Quantity A. Since both have three numbers, the average will be larger in Quantity B. Alternatively, compute average $A = \frac{4+7+9}{3} = 6\frac{2}{3}$ and average $B = \frac{4+7+10}{3} = 7$.

2. **(C)** The mode is 3 (it appears four times). There are 12 numbers in the list and the sixth and seventh numbers (the middle numbers) are both 3. Thus the median is also 3.

3. **(A)** The average of A is $\frac{1+1+1+2+2+3+3+3+3+5+7+9}{12} = \frac{40}{12} = 3\frac{1}{3}$, which is bigger than 3.

4. **(D, E, F)** Let $x$ be her score on the fifth test, then $\frac{82+84+90+88+x}{5} \geq 85$. So $82 + 84 + 90 + 88 + x \geq 5 \times 85$. Solving, we find $x \geq 81$. Choose answers that are at least 81.

5. **(C)** First we list them in order: $57K, $85K, $90K, $99K, $104K, and $x$ and $y$. There are seven sale values so $90K being the median means three were priced above or equal to $90K and three were priced below or equal to $90K. C is the only answer that satisfies this. All other answers have both values below $90K. Also $x = $57K guarantees the unique mode is $57K.

6. **(15)** By our first tip, we know 21 is the middle integer, or fourth in the list of seven. Counting backwards three odd numbers, the first integer in the list is **15** (the full list must be 15, 17, 19, 21, 23, 25, and 27).

7. **(D)** 9.5 is the average of the two middle integers, which must be 9 and 10. So the full list is 7, 8, 9, 10, 11, and 12. The largest integer is 12.

8. **(66)** To earn an 85 average, Mary needs a total of $6 \times 85 = 510$ on her six tests. She already has $82 + 84 + 90 + 88 = 344$. If she gets 100 on her sixth test, she will have 444 points. That means the fifth test need only be $510 - 444 = 66$.

9. **(90)** Think of averaging as sharing. That extra 10 points will be shared among five tests raising the score of the first four by 2 points to get the average. That means her first four test scores were 80 and her fifth was 90. Alternatively, assume her first four test scores were each $x$. Then $\frac{x+x+x+x+(x+10)}{5} = 82$. Hence $5x + 10 = 410$, or $x = 80$. The fifth test score will be $x + 10 = 80 + 10 = 90$.

10. **(D)** Let the number of students be $n$. The total of the student scores will be $0 + 0 + 0 + 1 + 1 + 2 + (n - 6) \times 9$ at most. This total should equal $7n$. Solving for $n$, we find $4 + 9n - 54 = 7n$ or $2n = 50$. Hence $n = 25$. If any of the other students were to score less than $\frac{9}{10}$, it would take even more students in the class to achieve a $\frac{7}{10}$ average.

11. **(4)** The total of the student scores must be $8.5 \times 10 = 85$. The most anyone could earn was $\frac{9}{10}$. If nine of the ten students scored $\frac{9}{10}$ ($9 \times 9 = 81$), then the tenth could score $\frac{4}{10}$ ($85 - 81 = 4$). If the first nine scored less than $\frac{9}{10}$, it would force the tenth student to have a higher score.

12. **(C, F)** If $a = \frac{1}{2}$ and $b = 20.5$, then $a + b = 21$, which is not greater than 21, so choice A is incorrect. Using these same values, the average of $a$ and $b$ would be $\frac{a+b}{2} = \frac{21}{2} = 10.5$, so choice B is incorrect. For positive numbers $a$ and $b$, the maximum value of the product $ab$ would arise from multiplying the maximum value for each variable individually, so $ab < 10 \times 30 = 300$, making C correct. If $a$ equals $\frac{1}{2}$ and $b = 22$, then $ab = 11$, so D is incorrect. If $a = 9$ and $b = 29$, $a + b = 38$, so E is not correct. Finally, **F** is correct: $a$ is strictly less than 10 and $b$ is strictly greater than 20, so the difference between $a$ and $b$ is more than $20 - 10 = 10$.

## Charts and Graphs (Problems on page 165)

1. **(B)** It's easy to see that New South Wales has a larger piece of the pie and thus the greater population. You do not need to calculate the exact population of each state.

2. **(B)** Victoria has 24% of the population, which is $21,000,000 \times 0.24 = 5,040,000$. Certainly B, 7,000,000, is larger. An easier answer is to estimate Victoria's population at 25% of 20 million, which is 5 million. Clearly the actual figure cannot be so different from 5 million to exceed 7 million.

3. **(B)** The territories account for 3% of the population. Estimating, 3% of 20 million is 600,000. 3% of 21 million will be more than 600,000 and certainly more than A, 500,000.

4. **(C)** Once Queensland's population doubles, Australia's total population will be 120% of 21 million, and Queensland's will be 40% of 21 million. So Queensland will be $\frac{40}{120} = \frac{1}{3}$ of the new total population, or 33%.

5. **(D)** On the first chart, estimate the female-owned companies at 28% of 23 million = 23 million $\times 0.28 = 6.64$ million. This is closest to D.

6. **(C)** First, there are 23 million – 17.5 million = 5.5 million U.S. firms with employees. On the second chart, estimate female-owned companies at 18% of 5.5 million = 5.5 million $\times 0.18 = 0.99$ million or 990,000.

7. **(B)** Since you are not told the total receipts, it is impossible to calculate values here. We can still tell which is larger, though. For female-owned firms the ratio of percentage of total receipts over firms is less than $\frac{1}{3}$ as the bar in the left quantity is more than three times larger than the bar in the right quantity. For men it is close to $\frac{1}{2}$.

8. **(A)** We look at the second graph since we are concerned with salary and compare the total payroll to number of employees which would give the average salary. Again we cannot calculate exact figures but we can compare. For public firms, the ratio of

percentage of payroll to percentage of number of employees is greater than one, since the bar in the last quantity is larger than the bar in the second to last quantity. For private firms it is less than 1.

9. **(C)** Queensland still has 20% of 21 million while the total population is 110% of 21 million. Since $\dfrac{20\% \text{ of } 21 \text{ million}}{110\% \text{ of } 21 \text{ million}} = \dfrac{20}{110} = 0.18 = 18\%$, Queensland will now have 18% of the population of Australia.

10. **(C)** New South Wales will lose 25% or $\dfrac{1}{4}$ of *its* 34% of the population. That means it will lose $\dfrac{1}{4} \times 34\% = 8.5\%$ of the Australian population. Thus New South Wales now has 25.5% of the Australian population. New Victoria will have 7% + 25% = 32% of the Australian population. This will make it the new most populous state.

11. **(D)** Clear from examining the charts. D is the only place where the bars get larger (left to right).

12. **(B)** For each year we compare national male (second chart) to the indicated regional usage (first chart): 2007 Midwest 9.1 > 8.1, 2008 Northeast 8.6 < 8.7, 2009 South 8.1 > 6, 2010 West 7.5 > 6.8, and 2011 South 6.8 > 5.6.

13. **(D)** Here we have to calculate how many have tried marijuana in each region and then express that as a percentage of the total 12–17 population. In the Northeast, 7.8% of 7 million is 546,000. In the Midwest, 6.8% of 4 million is 272,000. In the South, 5.6% of 17 million is 952,000. In the West 7.3% of 13 million is 949,000. That is a total of 546,000 + 272,000 + 952,000 + 949,000 = 2,719,000 users out of a total of 7 + 4 + 17 + 13 = 41 million 12-to-17-year olds. So the percentage of users is $\dfrac{2.719 \text{ million}}{41 \text{ million}} = 0.066 = 6.6\%$. Clearly this answer should be somewhere between the percentage of female users (6.4%) and the percentage of male users (6.8%). Assuming the number of males and females to be equal, we would expect the answer to be the average of 6.4% and 6.8%, which it is. One should be careful, however; if the number of females was significantly larger than the number of males, the answer might have been (C) 6.5%.

14. **(B)** We calculated in the last answer that there were 949,000 users in the West and 952,000 users in the South. Even though the percentage in the South was lower, the number of users is higher because of a greater population base.

## Counting (Problems on page 175)

1. **(A)** The sum of the first 25 positive integers is $\dfrac{25(26)}{2} = 25 \times 13 = 325$.

2. **(A)** The sum of the first 25 odd positive integers is $25^2 = 625$.

3. **(C)** For combinations with no zeros there are nine choices (1–9) for each digit. By the counting principle, that makes $9 \times 9 \times 9 = 729$ combinations. For combinations with no ones, there are nine choices (0,2–9) for each digit. By the Basic Counting Principle that also makes $9 \times 9 \times 9 = 729$ combinations.

4. **(A, E, F, H)** You could test the answer choices, but because there are so many it is better to solve directly. Even though the question asks about the number of rice servings ordered, it is easier to consider the number of curry orders, because there are far fewer possibilities. For example, $8 \times \$5 = \$40$, which is greater than the \$39 total spent, so at most 7 curries were ordered. The cost of 7 curry servings is $7 \times 5 = \$35$, leaving \$4 to be spent on 2 orders of rice at \$2 each, making A correct. Six orders of curry is not possible because $6 \times 5 = 30$, and $39 - 30 = 9$, an odd number. The cost of 5 curries at \$5 each is \$25, which would leave $39 - 25 = \$14$ for rice, which would amount to $\frac{14}{2} = 7$ orders, so 7, choice E, is correct. Four curry orders is not possible, since $39 - 4 \times 5$ equals 19, which is not divisible by 2. The cost of 3 curries, \$15, leaves \$24 for rice, which is 12 orders, choice F. Finally, if only 1 curry is ordered, \$34 is spent on rice, which is $\frac{34}{2} = 17$ orders, choice H.

5. **(84)** By the counting principle she can make $7 \times 4 \times 3 = 84$ outfits.

6. **(E)** We'll make a Venn diagram to help. As 124 are in the band and 12 do both, $124 - 12 = 112$ who just play in the band. Since 78 play rugby and 12 do both, $78 - 12 = 66$ who just play rugby. Thus, there are $112 + 12 + 66 + 44 = 234$ students in the school.

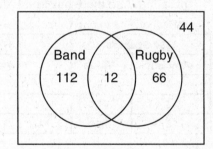

7. **(A)** The sum of the first 50 positive integers is $\frac{50(51)}{2} = 25 \times 51 = 1{,}275$. The sum of the first 35 odd numbers is $35^2 = 1{,}225$.

8. **(A)** Pages 1–9 use 9 digits in total. From page 10 to 99 there are 90 ($99 - 10 + 1$) pages that each use two digits. That's 180 digits. From page 100 to 999 there are 900 ($999 - 100 + 1$) pages that each use three digits. That's 2,700 digits. So in total $270 + 180 + 9 = 2{,}889$ digits are used.

9. **(B)** If a zero is in the units digit place we have pages 10, 20, 30, ..., 990, a total of 99 pages. We also count pages with a zero in the tens place, but not the ones we counted already, 101–109, 201–209, 901–909, a total of $9 \times 9 = 81$ pages. Zero is never in the hundreds place. Thus, there are at least 180 pages with a zero in the page number. A one, unlike a zero, can be in the hundreds place. In fact every page from 100 to 199 has a one in it, a total of 100 pages. When in the tens place we have pages 10–19, 210–219,... and 910–919, a total of $9 \times 10 = 90$ pages. That is already more pages with a one than a zero. But that is not all. If we add in 1, 201, 301,..., 901 (8 pages), we now have all pages that have a one on them. That totals 198 pages that have a one in the page number.

10. **(C)** Since ones and twos play identical roles in the numbers from 1 to 999, these values are equal (in fact both are 198).

11. **(A)** There are $37 - (-4) + 1 = 42$ integers from $-4$ to $37$ inclusive. There are 41 integers from 1 to 41 inclusive.

An alternate answer would be to say that $-4$ to 37 is comprised of 1 to 37 (37 integers), 0 (1 integer), and $-1$ to $-4$ (4 integers) for a total of $37 + 1 + 4 = 42$ integers.

12. **(A)** Since 85 is not a multiple of 10 or 3, there must be some 3¢ and some 10¢ stamps included. As no multiple of 10 ends in 5, the 3¢ stamps must produce the 5 ending. So, there are 5 stamps at 3¢, or 15 stamps at 3¢, or 25 stamps at 3¢. Hence the only possibilities are:

| 3¢ Stamps | | 10¢ Stamps | | |
|---|---|---|---|---|
| Amount | Value | Amount | Value | Total |
| 5 | 15¢ | 7 | 70¢ | 85¢ |
| 15 | 45¢ | 4 | 40¢ | 85¢ |
| 25 | 75¢ | 1 | 10¢ | 85¢ |

To make 85¢ from 4¢ and 15¢ stamps, for similar reasons we must have some of each type of stamp. And there must be 1, 3, or 5 of the 15¢ stamps to produce the 5 ending.

| 15¢ Stamps | | 4¢ Stamps | | |
|---|---|---|---|---|
| Amount | Value | Amount | Value | Total |
| 1 | 15¢ | Not possible to make 70¢ from 4¢ stamps. | | |
| 3 | 45¢ | 10 | 40¢ | 85¢ |
| 5 | 75¢ | Not possible to make 10¢ from 4¢ stamps. | | |

Hence there is only one way to make 85¢ from 4¢ and 15¢ stamps, while there are three ways to make 85¢ from 3¢ and 10¢ stamps.

13. **(A)** We see that $x$ has three possible values (5, 6, or 7), while $y$ has four possible values (2, 3, 4, 5) so we expect at most $3 \times 4 = 12$ values. Some of them might be duplicated so we make a table to check.

| + | 2 | 3 | 4 | 5 |
|---|---|---|---|---|
| 5 | 7 | 8 | 9 | 10 |
| 6 | 8 | 9 | 10 | 11 |
| 7 | 9 | 10 | 11 | 12 |

As you can see, there are exactly six different values: 7, 8, 9, 10, 11, and 12.

14. **(C)** A Venn diagram will help with this question. Let $x$ be the number of students who study in both places. Then $25 - x$ students study only in the library, and $15 - x$ students study only in the math lab. We don't know how many students study somewhere else entirely—call it $y$.

But the total number of students in the class is 34, so $(15 - x) + x + (25 - x) + y = 34$. We solve for $x$:

$$40 - x + y = 34 = 40 + y - 34 = x = x = 6 + y.$$

So $x$ will have a smallest value of 6, when $y = 0$.

15. **(2)** Counting Chris and Sara there are $27 - 12 + 1 = 16$ people in line between them. Not counting Chris and Sara, there are 14 people between them. If each of those 14 people buys eight tickets, there will be $114 - (8 \times 14) = 114 - 112 = 2$ tickets left when Sara gets to the booth.

## Probability (Problems on page 180)

1. **(C)** There are seven possible partners and Tom is one of them—so the probability of having Tom as a partner is $\frac{1}{7}$. Likewise Zoe is one of seven possible partners so the probability of having Zoe as a partner is also $\frac{1}{7}$.

2. **(A)** Three of her classmates (Fred, Sara, and Vera) have four-letter names. Only two of them have five-letter names (Alice and Jamal). So Quantity A is $\frac{3}{7}$, which is bigger than Quantity B, which is $\frac{2}{7}$.

3. **(B)** John is not in her class so the probability of John being her partner is zero. There are three boys in her class (Fred, Jamal, Tom) so zero is less than the probability of her having a male partner $\frac{3}{7}$.

4. **(B)** There are six equally likely outcomes (1 through 6). Three of them are even (2, 4, and 6) so $P(\text{even}) = \frac{3}{6} = \frac{1}{2}$. The probability of not rolling 6 is $P(\text{not } 6) = 1 - P(6) = 1 - \frac{1}{6} = \frac{5}{6}$.

5. **(A)** Four outcomes are greater than 2 (3, 4, 5, and 6). Three outcomes are prime numbers (2, 3, and 5). So $P(>2) = \frac{4}{6} = \frac{2}{3}$ while $P(\text{prime}) = \frac{3}{6} = \frac{1}{2}$.

6. $\left(\dfrac{3}{4}\right)$ There are 20 marbles in total and 15 of them are not white. $P(\text{not white}) = \dfrac{15}{20} = \dfrac{3}{4}$.

   Alternatively, $P(\text{not white}) = 1 - P(\text{white}) = 1 - \dfrac{5}{20} = 1 - \dfrac{1}{4} = \dfrac{3}{4}$ or an equivalent fraction.

7. **(B)** There are 100 equally likely outcomes for this experiment, ten choices for $x$ times ten choices for $y$: $\{(x, y)\ 1 \le x \le 10 \text{ and } 1 \le y \le 10\}$. The only outcomes that give a total of 18 or more are (8,10), (9,9), (9,10), (10, 8), (10,9), and (10,10). So the $P(\text{total} \ge 18) = \dfrac{6}{100} = \dfrac{3}{50} = 0.06$.

8. $\left(\dfrac{1}{2}\right)$ There are 8 equally likely outcomes for this experiment : {HHH, HHT, HTH, THH, TTH, THT, HTT, TTT}. The first four have more heads than tails. So the probability of flipping more heads than tails is $\dfrac{4}{8} = \dfrac{1}{2}$ or equivalent fraction.

9. $\left(\dfrac{7}{24}\right)$ There are two regions that have 1 in them. The top region is $\dfrac{1}{8}$ of the circle (it's half of a quarter circle), so the probability of spinning that 1 is $\dfrac{1}{8}$. The bottom region is $\dfrac{1}{6}$ of the circle (it's one third of a half circle) so the probability of spinning that 1 is $\dfrac{1}{6}$. Adding these together we get $\dfrac{1}{8} + \dfrac{1}{6} = \dfrac{3}{24} + \dfrac{4}{24} = \dfrac{7}{24}$. So the probability of spinning a 1 is $\dfrac{7}{24}$.

10. **(A)** Since there are more white marbles than green marbles, common sense tells us it is more likely to choose two white than two green. Calculating the actual probabilities here is complicated and not worth the time involved.

11. **(C)** Since there are four white and four "red or green" marbles, both probabilities are $\dfrac{4}{8} = \dfrac{1}{2}$.

12. **(C)** Each result in such an experiment is equally likely, $\dfrac{1}{2} \times \dfrac{1}{2} \times \dfrac{1}{2} = \dfrac{1}{8}$. As we saw in problem 8, there are eight equally likely outcomes.

13. **(E, F)** The probability of two independent events *both* happening is the product of the probabilities of each individual event occurring. Then $.6p \ge .5$. Divide both sides by 0.6 to obtain $p \ge .833$, or $p \ge \dfrac{5}{6}$. This is satisfied by choices E and F.

14. **(C, D, E, F)** Since green is at least twice as likely to be drawn as red, $x \ge 2 \times 8$, so $x \ge 16$. Since choosing green is less probable than choosing blue, there are fewer green chips than blue chips, and $x < 20$. Then $x$ may be 16, 17, 18, or 19. These values added to the known red plus blue chip total in the jar, 28, yields 44 through 47 as the range of possible values for total chips. Choose answers in this interval: C, D, E, and F.

# Geometry

6

Geometry questions occur frequently on the GRE. Perhaps this is because using just the basics of high school geometry you can ask a very large number of creative and interesting problems.

As you work through this chapter, remember that diagrams are not drawn to scale, nor are they accurate. What appears as a small angle in the diagram may be much larger. Reviewing strategy tips for diagrams in Chapter 2 can help in this regard.

In geometry it is convenient to use special notations. We give a brief explanation of the notation you are likely to encounter in this book. Some of this notation may not appear in the GRE, as they try very hard to minimize the use of special notation.

| Notation | Meaning | Figure |
|---|---|---|
| *A* | A point in space. Although it has no size, we may emphasize it with a black dot. | |
| *AB* | The line segment joining point *A* to point *B*. Also could mean the length of this segment. | 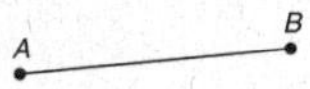 |
| $\widehat{AB}$ | The arc of the circle from point *A* to point *B*. Could also refer to the length of that arc. | 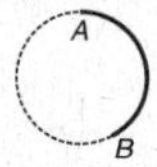 |
| ∠*A* or ∠*BAC* | The angle at vertex *A*, or the angle formed at vertex *A* between lines *BA* and *AC*. | 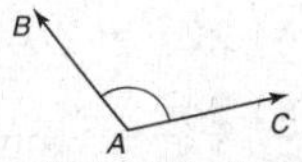 |
| △*ABC* | The triangle formed by the line segments *AB*, *BC*, and *CA*. | 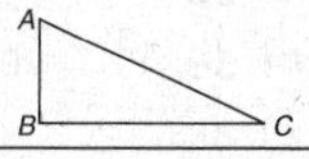 |
| *ABCD* | The quadrilateral formed from line segments *AB*, *BD*, *CD*, and *CA*. | 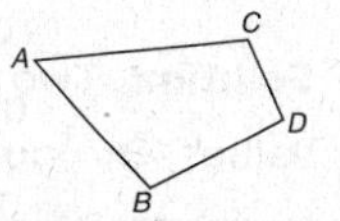 |
| | Equal angles can be indicated with matching arcs or symbols. In this example ∠*B* = ∠*C* as indicated by the matching double arcs. | 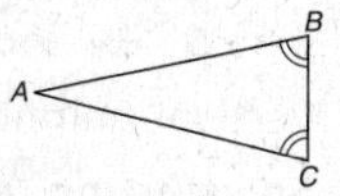 |
| | Equal lengths can be indicated by matching dashes. The top and bottom of the figure have equal lengths as indicated by the matching double hash lines (‖). The sides are also equal as indicated by the matching single lines (∣). | 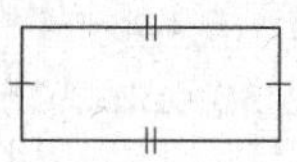 |

# PERIMETER

Perimeter is the distance around the outside of an object. For a square of side length $s$, the perimeter is just $s + s + s + s = 4s$. For a rectangle with side lengths $l$ and $w$, the perimeter is just $l + w + l + w = 2l + 2w$.

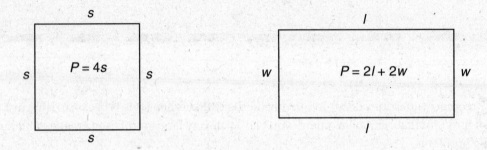

For other shapes with straight line segments on the boundary, simply add the lengths of all these segments.

---

**EXAMPLE 1**

All lines shown meet at right angles. Determine the perimeter of the object.

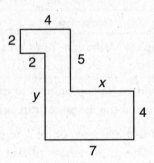

(A) 22
(B) 34
(C) 36
(D) 38
(E) 40

**Solution:** Two of the side lengths are not given, $x$ and $y$. We need to determine their values. By looking at the horizontal segments on the bottom we see that the total horizontal length of the object is $2 + 7 = 9$. That means that $4 + x = 9$, and thus $x = 5$. By looking at the vertical segments on the right, we see that the total vertical height of the object is $5 + 4 = 9$. That means that $2 + y = 9$, and thus $y = 7$. So, starting at the top and working clockwise, the perimeter of the object is $4 + 5 + x + 4 + 7 + y + 2 + 2 = 24 + x + y = 24 + 5 + 7 = 36$. Hence the total perimeter is 36 units. Choose **C**.

The perimeter of a circle is called the circumference, *C*. If the radius of the circle is *r*, its circumference is $2\pi r$; equivalently, if the diameter is *d*, the circumference is $\pi d$.

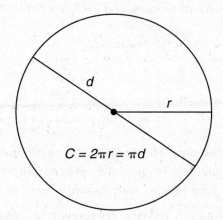

$$C = 2\pi r = \pi d$$

Once you know the circumference of a circle, you can find the length of any arc of a circle. For example, the arc length for $\frac{1}{3}$ of a circle (120° is $\frac{1}{3}$ of 360°) is $\frac{1}{3}$ of the circumference of a circle, or $\left(\frac{1}{3}\right)2\pi r = \frac{2\pi r}{3}$.

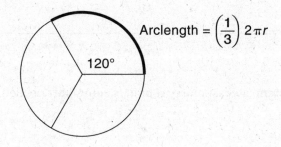

$$\text{Arclength} = \left(\frac{1}{3}\right)2\pi r$$

120°

**EXAMPLE 2**

Find the circumference of the figure below. Each circular arc has center and radius as shown. This figure is drawn to scale, and ∠*HJI* is a right angle.

- (A) 16 cm
- (B) (16 + 5π) cm
- (C) (16 + 9π) cm
- (D) (12 + 3π) cm
- (E) 12 cm

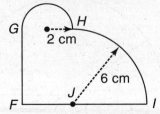

**Solution:** We can see the perimeter is given by the lengths of the line segments *FG*, *FJ*, and *JI* plus the arc lengths $\widehat{GH}$ and $\widehat{HI}$. $\widehat{HI}$ is a quarter circle, as the angle ∠*HJI* is a right angle, with radius 6 cm. So the length of $\widehat{HI}$ is $\left(\frac{1}{4}\right)2\pi r = \left(\frac{1}{4}\right)2\pi(6 \text{ cm}) = 3\pi$ cm. $\widehat{GH}$ is a semicircle with radius 2 cm so its length is $\left(\frac{1}{2}\right)2\pi r = \left(\frac{1}{2}\right)2\pi(2 \text{ cm}) = 2\pi$ cm. *JI* is a radius of the arc $\widehat{HI}$ so it is 6 cm. *JH* is also a radius of $\widehat{HI}$, and *JH* has the same length as *FG*. So *FG* is 6 cm in length. Finally, the line *GH* is a diameter of the semicircle $\widehat{GH}$, so line *GH* has length 4 cm, which is the same as the length of *FJ*. Thus *FJ* has length 4 cm. We conclude the perimeter is $FG + FJ + JI + \widehat{GH} + \widehat{HI}$ = 6 cm + 4 cm + 6 cm + 2π cm + 3π cm = (16 + 5π) cm. Choose **B**.

The Pythagorean theorem, at least one part of it, is commonly needed to find perimeters of triangles.

## PYTHAGOREAN THEOREM PART I

If *ABC* is a right triangle with right angle at *C* and side lengths *CA* = *b*, *AB* = *c*, *BC* = *a*, then $a^2 + b^2 = c^2$.

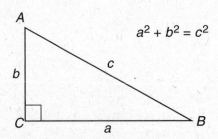

Note the largest side, *c*, called the *hypotenuse*, is always the side opposite the right angle. This theorem is particularly useful when you know two sides of a right triangle and wish to find the third. You can determine that $c = \sqrt{a^2 + b^2}$, $b = \sqrt{c^2 - a^2}$, and $a = \sqrt{c^2 - b^2}$.

EXAMPLE 3

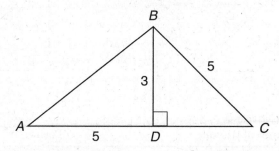

| Quantity A | Quantity B |
|---|---|
| Perimeter of △*ABD* | Perimeter of △*BCD* |

**Solution:** Let *AB* be *x* and *DC* be *y*. Since △*ABD* is a right triangle with right angle at *D*, $5^2 + 3^2 = x^2$. Thus $25 + 9 = x^2$ or $x^2 = 34$. So $x = \sqrt{34}$. Then the perimeter of △*ABD* is $5 + 3 + \sqrt{34}$, which is $8 + \sqrt{34}$. As $\sqrt{36} = 6$, $8 + \sqrt{34}$ is a little less than 14. Since △*BCD* is a right triangle with right angle at *D*, $3^2 + y^2 = 5^2$. So $y^2 = 5^2 - 3^2$, or $y^2 = 16$. Thus $y = 4$. So the perimeter of △*BCD* is $3 + 4 + 5 = 12$. Choose **A**.

---

**TIP**

- Some special right triangles appear frequently. Knowing their dimensions can save a lot of time. See the Appendix for suggested facts to memorize.
- There are a number of other formulas for the perimeter of certain shapes. They are not really necessary to memorize. Just remember to divide the perimeter of the object into pieces whose length is easy to calculate.

## PROBLEMS (Solutions on page 241)
### Basic Problems

1.

| Quantity A | Quantity B |
|---|---|
| Circumference of circle of radius 10 | Circumference of circle of diameter 20 |

2.

| Quantity A | Quantity B |
|---|---|
| Perimeter of square of side 4 | Circumference of circle of radius 4 |

**3.**

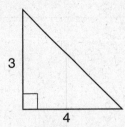 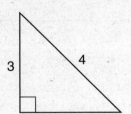

| Quantity A | Quantity B |
|---|---|
| Perimeter of triangle | Perimeter of triangle |

**4.**

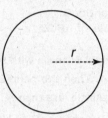 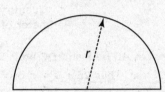

| Quantity A | Quantity B |
|---|---|
| Perimeter of circle | Perimeter of semicircle |

**5.**

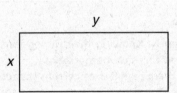 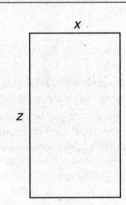

| Quantity A | Quantity B |
|---|---|
| Perimeter of rectangle | Perimeter of rectangle |

6. In the following diagram, grid points are separated vertically and horizontally by one unit. Find the perimeter of the given shape.

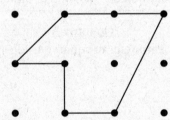

(A) $5 + 2\sqrt{2}$

(B) 5

(C) 6

(D) $5 + \sqrt{2} + \sqrt{5}$

(E) 8

## GRE Problems

7. Find the perimeter of the given shape. Each arc is half of a circle. This figure is drawn to scale.

Ⓐ 8 cm
Ⓑ 6 + π cm
Ⓒ 6 + 2π cm
Ⓓ 8 + π cm
Ⓔ 8 + 2π cm

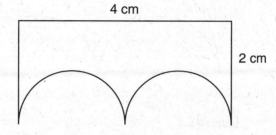

4 cm

2 cm

8. Assume all lines meet at right angles. Find the perimeter of the object.

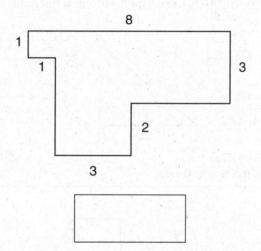

8

1

1

3

2

3

9. Find the perimeter of these stairs. All lines meet at right angles.

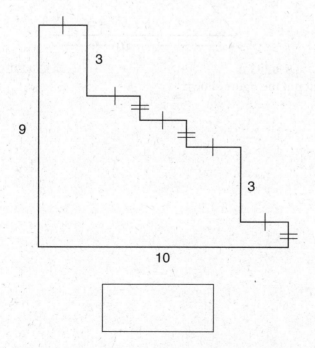

3

9

3

10

10. All arcs shown are semicircles. *B* is the midpoint of *AC*

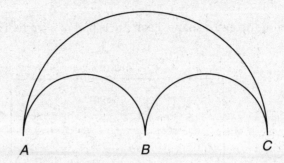

| Quantity A | Quantity B |
|---|---|
| Length of $\widehat{AC}$ | Length of $\widehat{AB} + \widehat{BC}$ |

11. *AB* is the diameter of the semicircle

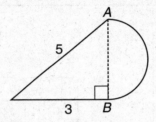

| Quantity A | Quantity B |
|---|---|
| Perimeter of the figure shown | $8 + 2\pi$ |

12.

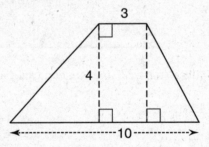

| Quantity A | Quantity B |
|---|---|
| Perimeter of the figure shown | $18 + 4\sqrt{2}$ |

13. The circles are centered at *A* and *B*, respectively, and both have radius 1. What is the perimeter of the object (solid line)?

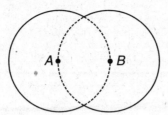

(A) $4\pi$

(B) $\dfrac{4\pi}{3}$

(C) $\dfrac{8\pi}{3}$

(D) $8\pi$

(E) $12\pi$

## ANGLES

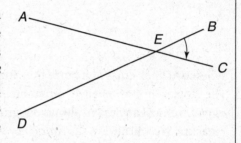

Whenever two lines (or line segments) meet at a point, angles are formed. An angle describes the rotation of a line around a point. The angle $\angle BEC$ is a measure of how much you would have to rotate $EB$ around the point $E$ to get to $EC$. In grade school terms it is a measure of "how wide the mouth is open." It does not depend on the length of the line segments. For instance $\angle AED = \angle BEC$ even though $AE$ and $DE$ are much larger than $BE$ and $CE$.

We usually measure angles in degrees. An angle of 360° is a full rotation, 180° is a half rotation, usually called a straight angle, and 90° is a quarter turn, called a right angle. We denote a right angle with a half a square ⌐ instead of an arc. Two lines, $EF$ and $EG$, that meet at right angles are called perpendicular, and we write $EF \perp EG$. Angles are classified as acute (between 0° and 90°), right (90°), and obtuse (more than 90°).

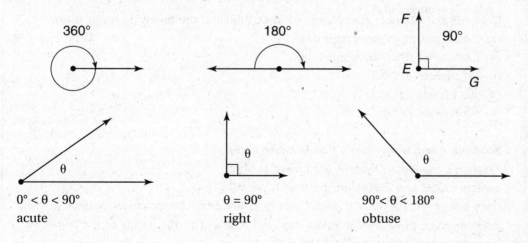

## EXAMPLE 1

Find *x*.

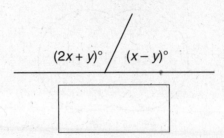

**Solution:** Since these two angles together form a straight angle, $(2x + y)° + (x - y)°$
$= 180° \Rightarrow 3x = 180 \Rightarrow x = \textbf{60}$.

Sometimes an angle ∠*ABC* is cut into two other angles by a line *BD*. If the new angles ∠*ABD* and ∠*DBC* are equal we say *BD bisects* ∠*ABC*, and call *BD* an angle *bisector*.

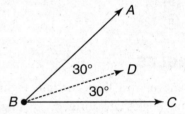

When two lines cross at a point they form four angles. The angles opposite each other are called *vertical angles*. Vertical angles are always congruent or equal in measure. We will always say *equal*. For example, ∠*AEB* and ∠*DEC* are vertical angles. Also ∠*AED* and ∠*BEC* are vertical angles.

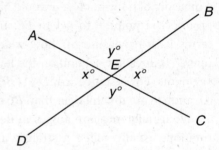

## EXAMPLE 2

Lines *AB* and *CD* meet at right angles at *O*. Which of the following is not true?

(A) ∠*AOD* and ∠*BOC* are congruent.
(B) ∠*AOC* and ∠*BOD* are congruent.
(C) $\overline{BO}$ bisects ∠*COD*.
(D) $\overline{AO}$ bisects ∠*DOC*.
(E) $\overline{BD}$ bisects ∠*AOD*.

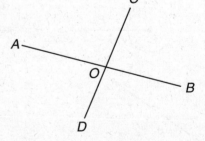

**Solution:** A and B are clearly true because vertical angles are equal. Since the lines meet at right angles, ∠*COB* and ∠*BOD* are both 90°. So *BO* does bisect ∠*COD*. Thus C and similarly D are true. *BD* does not appear in the diagram. Even if we draw it in, *BD* does not intersect *O*, the vertex of the angle. So it can't possibly bisect ∠*AOD*. Choose **E**.

**EXAMPLE 3**

If lines $L_1$ and $L_2$ cross at $O$, what is $y$?

**Solution:** Because of vertical angles, $80° = 2x°$. Divide by 2 to see that $x = 40$. We also see that $80°$ and $(x + y)°$ together form a straight angle. So $80° + (x + y)° = 180°$. Hence $80 + 40 + y = 180 \Rightarrow y = \textbf{60}$.

*(Diagram: Lines $L_1$ and $L_2$ crossing at $O$, with angles $(x+y)°$, $2x°$, and $80°$)*

Two lines in the plane that never meet are called *parallel lines*. We write $L_1 \parallel L_2$. In effect, parallel lines remain a fixed distance apart, like railroad tracks. Any two lines that are not parallel must meet. When a third line crosses a set of parallel lines, we call it a *transversal*. A transversal crosses each of the parallel lines at the same angles.

## PARALLEL LINES THEOREM

If line $L_1 \parallel L_2$ and are crossed by a transversal $L_3$, then the following angles are equal:
① = ④ = ⑤ = ⑧ and ② = ③ = ⑥ = ⑦.

Put another way, every time a transversal meets parallel lines there are only two numerical values for the angles created.

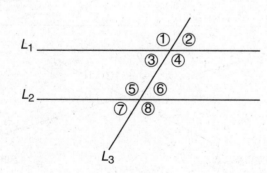

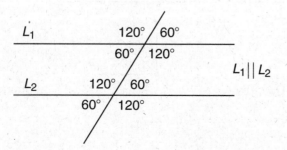

**TIP**

Although the word *transversal* may not appear on the GRE, this theorem appears very frequently.

EXAMPLE 4

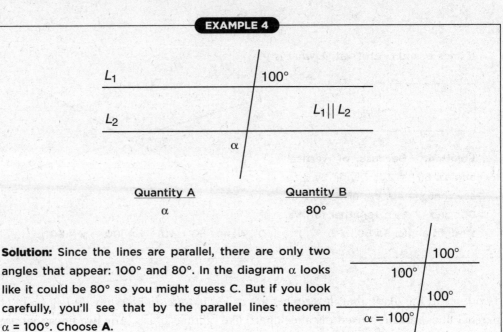

Quantity A
α

Quantity B
80°

**Solution:** Since the lines are parallel, there are only two angles that appear: 100° and 80°. In the diagram α looks like it could be 80° so you might guess C. But if you look carefully, you'll see that by the parallel lines theorem α = 100°. Choose **A.**

## PROBLEMS (Solutions on page 244)
## Basic Problems

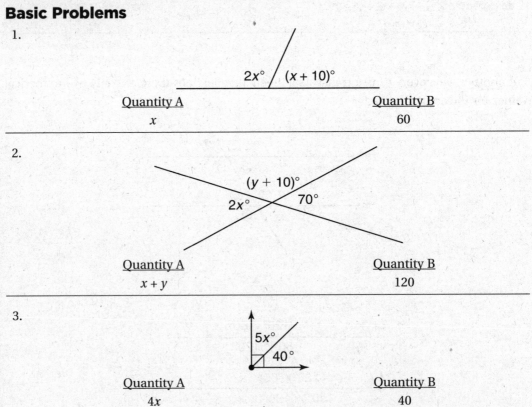

1.

2x°  (x + 10)°

Quantity A
x

Quantity B
60

2.

(y + 10)°
2x°  70°

Quantity A
x + y

Quantity B
120

3.

5x°
40°

Quantity A
4x

Quantity B
40

**4.**

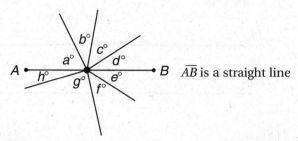

$\overline{AB}$ is a straight line

| Quantity A | Quantity B |
|---|---|
| $(a + b + c + d + e + f + g + h)/2$ | $a + b + c + d$ |

**5.**

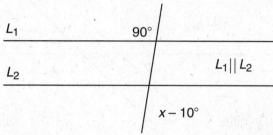

$L_1 \| L_2$

| Quantity A | Quantity B |
|---|---|
| $x + 10$ | 90 |

**6.** One angle is incorrect. Which one?

(A) ①
(B) ②
(C) ③
(D) ④
(E) ⑤

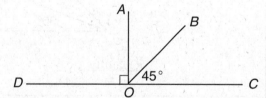

**7.** Which of the following are true?

Indicate *all* that apply.

[A] $\overline{OC}$ bisects $\angle AOB$

[B] $\overline{AO}$ bisects $\angle DOB$

[C] $\overline{OB}$ bisects $\angle AOC$

## GRE Problems

**8.**

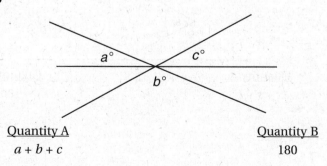

| Quantity A | Quantity B |
|---|---|
| $a + b + c$ | 180 |

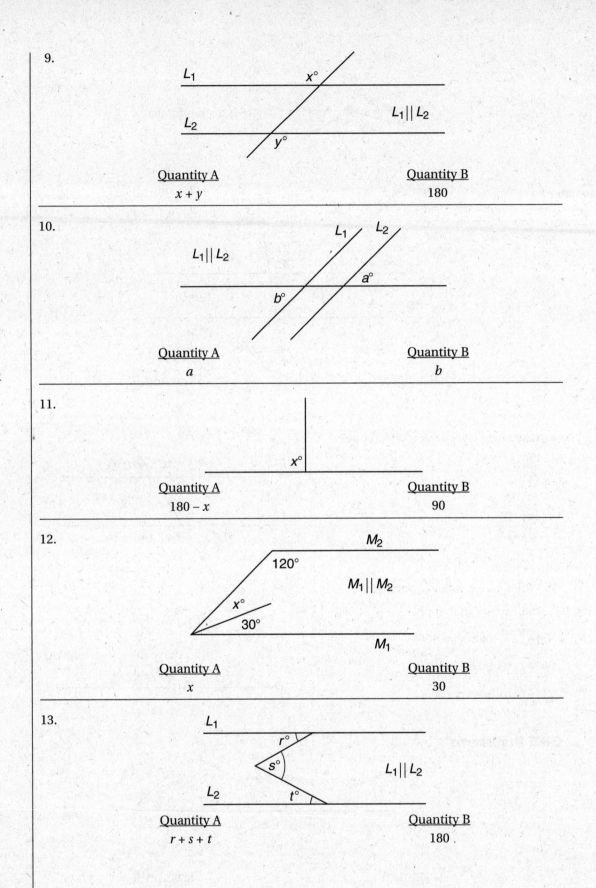

**9.**

$L_1$

$x°$

$L_2$

$y°$

$L_1 \| L_2$

| Quantity A | Quantity B |
|:---:|:---:|
| $x + y$ | 180 |

**10.**

$L_1 \| L_2$

$L_1$    $L_2$

$a°$

$b°$

| Quantity A | Quantity B |
|:---:|:---:|
| $a$ | $b$ |

**11.**

$x°$

| Quantity A | Quantity B |
|:---:|:---:|
| $180 - x$ | 90 |

**12.**

$M_2$

120°

$M_1 \| M_2$

$x°$

30°

$M_1$

| Quantity A | Quantity B |
|:---:|:---:|
| $x$ | 30 |

**13.**

$L_1$

$r°$

$s°$

$L_1 \| L_2$

$L_2$

$t°$

| Quantity A | Quantity B |
|:---:|:---:|
| $r + s + t$ | 180 |

14.

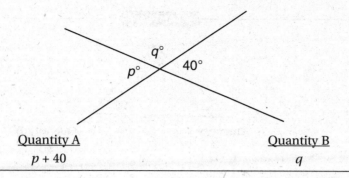

| Quantity A | Quantity B |
|:---:|:---:|
| $p + 40$ | $q$ |

15.

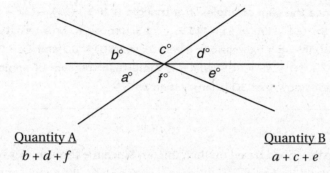

| Quantity A | Quantity B |
|:---:|:---:|
| $b + d + f$ | $a + c + e$ |

16. Given that *BO* bisects $\angle AOC$, *DO* bisects $\angle COE$, and $\angle AOE$ is a straight angle, find $x + y$.

(A) 45
(B) 60
(C) 90
(D) 100
(E) 180

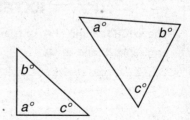

# TRIANGLES

A triangle is a closed curve with three straight sides. Triangles also have three interior angles and no matter how the triangle is shaped, the sum of those angles is always 180°.

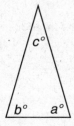

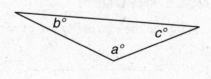

$a° + b° + c° = 180°$

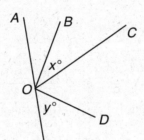

**EXAMPLE 1**

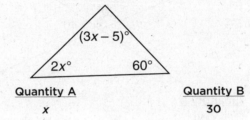

| Quantity A | Quantity B |
|---|---|
| x | 30 |

**Solution:** Since the sum of angles in a triangle is 180°, (2x) + (3x − 5) + 60 = 180. Simplifying 5x + 55 = 180 ⇒ 5x = 125 ⇒ x = 25. Choose **B**. An alternate answer would be to plug 30 into the expressions given: 2x = 2(30) = 60 and 3x − 5 = 3(30) − 5 = 85. Since 60 + 60 + 85 = 205, which is more than the sum of angles in a triangle should be, you know that 30 is larger than x.

Triangles can be described based on their angles. Since the three angles must add to 180°, at most one angle is 90° or more. A *right triangle* has a right (90°) angle and two acute angles. An *obtuse triangle* has one obtuse (>90°) angle and two acute angles. An *acute triangle* has three angles less than 90°.

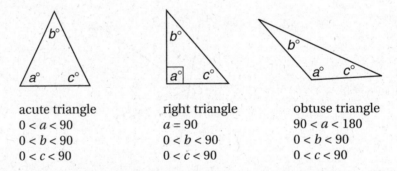

acute triangle
0 < a < 90
0 < b < 90
0 < c < 90

right triangle
a = 90
0 < b < 90
0 < c < 90

obtuse triangle
90 < a < 180
0 < b < 90
0 < c < 90

When one side of a triangle is extended it creates an exterior angle.

## EXTERIOR ANGLE THEOREM

The exterior angle at $A$, of triangle $\triangle ABC$, is equal to the sum of the two opposite interior angles (at $B$ and at $C$).

$$z° = x° + y°$$

It's not hard to see why this is true. $AB$ is a straight line so $z° + \angle CAB = 180°$. By the sum of angles in a triangle, $x° + y° + \angle CAB = 180°$. So $z° + \angle CAB = x° + y° + \angle CAB \Rightarrow z° = x° + y°$. Even if you don't remember this, you should be able to refigure it out on the test.

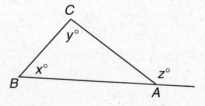

**EXAMPLE 2**

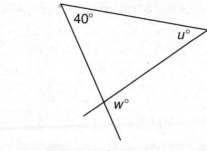

|   Quantity A   |   Quantity B   |
| :---: | :---: |
| $u$ | $w - 40$ |

**Solution:** By the exterior angle theorem, $w = 40 + u$. So solving for $u$ we find $u = w - 40$. Choose **C**. Alternatively, if you forget the external angle theorem you can still solve the problem. Label the third angle inside the triangle $x$. Then the sum of interior angles of the triangle is 180° so $x + u + 40 = 180$ (①). But $w$ and $x$ together form a straight angle so $w + x = 180$, and $x = 180 - w$. Substitute $x = 180 - w$ into ①, and we have $(180 - w) + u + 40 = 180$. This implies $-w + u + 40 = 0$, or $u = w - 40$.

Triangles can also be described based on the lengths of their sides. An *equilateral triangle* has three equal length sides and three equal angles. Since the sum of the angles is 180°, each angle must be 60°.

- If you know a triangle has three equal sides, then it has three equal angles.
- If you know a triangle has three equal angles, then it has three equal sides.

An *isosceles triangle* has at least two equal sides, and the angles opposite those sides are also equal.

- If you know a triangle has two equal angles, the sides opposite those angles are equal.
- If you know a triangle has two equal sides, the angles opposite those sides are equal.

**EXAMPLE 3**

If *ABDE* is a square find the perimeter of the given hexagon *ABCDEF*.

(A) 17 cm

(B) 20 cm

(C) 20 + √3 cm

(D) 23 cm

(E) 31 + √3 cm

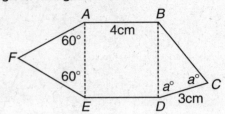

**Solution:** As *ABDE* is a square, all sides have the same length of 4 cm. Consider △*AFE*. It has two angles of 60° so the third angle is 180° − 60° − 60° = 60°. So △*AFE* is equilateral and *AF* = *FE* = *AE* = 4 cm. Now consider △*BCD*. As ∠*BCD* = ∠*BDC*, the triangle is isosceles, and *BC* = *BD*. As *BD* is a side of the square, *BC* = *BD* = 4 cm. Then the perimeter of *ABCDEF* is *AB* + *BC* + *CD* + *DE* + *EF* + *FA* = 4 + 4 + 3 + 4 + 4 + 4 = 23 cm. Choose **D**.

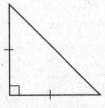

Isosceles right triangle

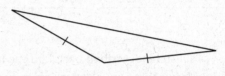

Obtuse isosceles triangle

## Triangle Inequality

Not just any three numbers can represent the side lengths of a triangle. For instance try to make a triangle with one side 10 cm and each of the other sides 3 cm. It's impossible! It won't close. This illustrates an obvious but important fact.

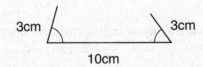

3cm     3cm

10cm

## TRIANGLE INEQUALITY

In any triangle, the length of any one side is less than the sum of the lengths of the other two sides.

Put another way, if the lengths of the triangle are $a$, $b$, and $c$, then $c < a + b$, $a < b + c$, and $b < a + c$. If even one of these three inequalities is not true, there cannot be a triangle with those side lengths.

## Pythagorean Theorem

As we saw earlier, right triangles have a special property called the Pythagorean Theorem.

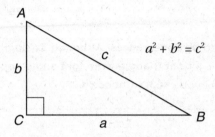

$$a^2 + b^2 = c^2$$

### PYTHAGOREAN THEOREM PART I

If $\triangle ABC$ is a right triangle with right angle at $C$ and side lengths $CA = b$, $AB = c$, and $BC = a$, then $a^2 + b^2 = c^2$.

---

**EXAMPLE 4**

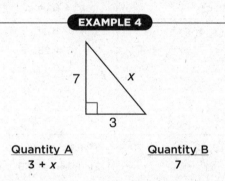

| Quantity A | Quantity B |
|:----------:|:----------:|
| $3 + x$ | 7 |

**Solution:** Most people will begin by using the Pythagorean theorem to solve for $x$. This is totally unnecessary. According to the triangle inequality, the length of any one side (7) is less than the sum of the other two sides ($3 + x$). Choose **A**.

---

The converse to this theorem is also true and very useful for finding right angles.

### PYTHAGOREAN THEOREM PART II

If $\triangle ABC$ has side lengths $a$, $b$, and $c$ (where $a = CB$, $b = AC$, $c = AB$) and $a^2 + b^2 = c^2$, then $\triangle ABC$ is a right triangle with right angle $\angle ACB$.

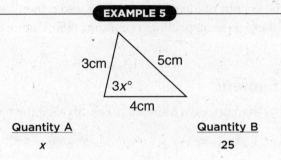

**EXAMPLE 5**

| Quantity A | Quantity B |
|:---:|:---:|
| $x$ | 25 |

**Solution:** Don't be fooled by appearances. Although $3x°$ looks like it's about 75°, it's not. As $3^2 + 4^2 = 5^2$ this is a right triangle with right angle opposite the side of length 5. That is, $3x = 90$ and hence $x = 30$. Choose **A**.

Because right triangles are so important in mathematics and appear so often on the GRE, it is worth memorizing the side lengths for the most common right triangles. Any multiple of the side lengths of a right triangle are also the side lengths of a right triangle. Since (3, 4, 5) forms a right triangle so does $(2 \times 3, 2 \times 4, 2 \times 5) = (6, 8, 10)$. Similarly as (5, 12, 13) forms a right triangle so does $(5/2, 12/2, 13/2) = (2.5, 6, 6.5)$.

## Common Right Triangles

| Side Lengths (*a, b, c*) | | $a^2 + b^2 = c^2$ | Common Multiples |
|:---:|:---:|:---:|:---:|
| (triangle: 3, 4, 5) | (3, 4, 5) | $3^2 + 4^2 = 5^2$ <br> $9 + 16 = 25$ | (6, 8, 10) <br> (9, 12, 15) <br> (12, 16, 20) <br> (1.5, 2, 2.5) <br> $\left(\dfrac{3}{10}, \dfrac{2}{5}, \dfrac{1}{2}\right)$ |
| (triangle: 12, 13, 5) | (5, 12, 13) | $5^2 + 12^2 = 13^2$ <br> $25 + 144 = 169$ | (10, 24, 26) <br> (1, 2.4, 2.6) |
| (triangle: 1, 1, $\sqrt{2}$) | $(1, 1, \sqrt{2})$ | $1^2 + 1^2 - (\sqrt{2})^2$ <br> $1 + 1 = 2$ | $(\sqrt{2}, \sqrt{2}, 2)$ <br> $\left(\dfrac{1}{\sqrt{2}}, \dfrac{1}{\sqrt{2}}, 1\right)$ |
| (triangle: 1, 2, $\sqrt{3}$) | $(1, \sqrt{3}, 2)$ | $1^2 + (\sqrt{3})^2 = 2^2$ <br> $1 + 3 = 4$ | $\left(\dfrac{1}{2}, \dfrac{\sqrt{3}}{2}, 1\right)$ |

**EXAMPLE 6**

Find *z*.

(A) 13
(B) 12√3
(C) 26
(D) 39
(E) 52

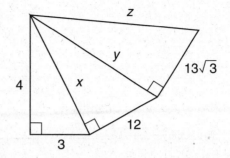

**Solution:** This question is surprisingly easy if you know your right triangles. First of all, *x* = 5, as (3, 4, 5) is a right triangle. Second, *y* = 13 as (5, 12, 13) is also a right triangle. Finally we have 13, 13√3, and *z* in a right triangle. We notice that this must be 13 times the (1, √3, 2) right triangle. So *z* = 2 × 13 = 26. Choose **C**.

# PROBLEMS (Solutions on page 246)
## Basic Problems

1.

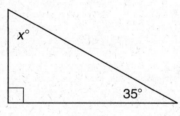

<u>Quantity A</u>          <u>Quantity B</u>
   65                      *x*

2.

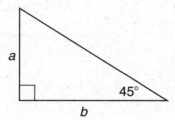

<u>Quantity A</u>          <u>Quantity B</u>
   *a*                      *b*

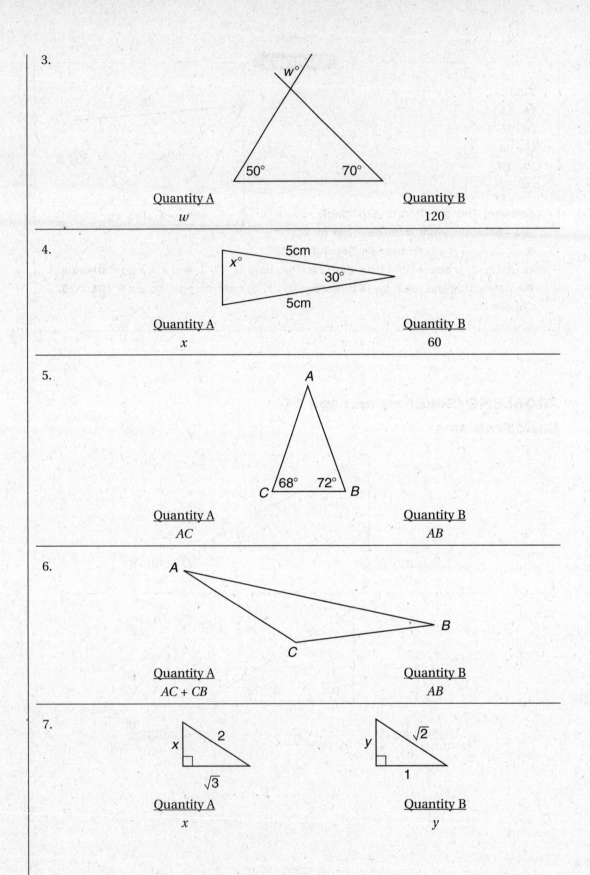

3.

| Quantity A | Quantity B |
|------------|------------|
| $w$ | 120 |

4.

| Quantity A | Quantity B |
|------------|------------|
| $x$ | 60 |

5.

| Quantity A | Quantity B |
|------------|------------|
| $AC$ | $AB$ |

6.

| Quantity A | Quantity B |
|------------|------------|
| $AC + CB$ | $AB$ |

7.

| Quantity A | Quantity B |
|------------|------------|
| $x$ | $y$ |

8. If $AB = AC$ in $\triangle ABC$, then find $(x + y + z)/2$.

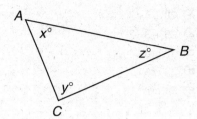

## GRE Problems

9. Find: $\dfrac{2}{3}x + \dfrac{1}{3}z$.

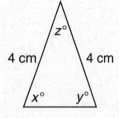

(A) 40

(B) 50

(C) 60

(D) 70

(E) Cannot be determined

10. $\triangle ABC$ is isosceles with $AB = AC$ and $\triangle BCD$ is equilateral. Find $y$ ($\angle ABD$).

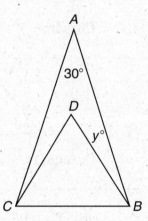

11. In $\triangle ACD$, $\angle ADC$ is bisected by $BD$. Determine $y$.

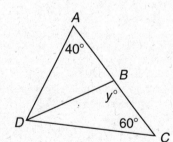

12. Find the perimeter of quadrilateral *ACDF*.

　Ⓐ $28 + 4\sqrt{2}$ cm
　Ⓑ $25 + 3\sqrt{2}$ cm
　Ⓒ 32 cm
　Ⓓ 33 cm
　Ⓔ 34 cm

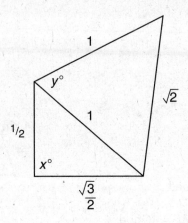

13.

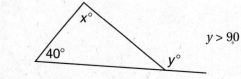

| Quantity A | Quantity B |
|------------|------------|
| *x* | *y* |

14.

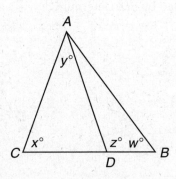

$y > 90$

| Quantity A | Quantity B |
|------------|------------|
| *x* | 50 |

PROBLEMS 15–17 CONCERN △*ABC*, WHERE *AD* = *AC*.

15.

| Quantity A | Quantity B |
|------------|------------|
| *x* | *z* |

16.

| Quantity A | Quantity B |
|------------|------------|
| w | x |

17.

| Quantity A | Quantity B |
|------------|------------|
| w | y |

For problems 18 and 19, a triangle has side lengths of 20 cm, 30 cm, and $k$ cm, where $k$ is a positive real number.

18. Which of the following could be the area of the triangle?

Indicate *all* that apply.

A  10 cm$^2$

B  20 cm$^2$

C  30 cm$^2$

D  300 cm$^2$

E  400 cm$^2$

19. If the triangle is a right triangle, which of the following could be the value of $k$?

Indicate *all* that apply.

A  $10\sqrt{3}$

B  $10\sqrt{5}$

C  $10\sqrt{7}$

D  $10\sqrt{11}$

E  $10\sqrt{13}$

## POLYGONS

A polygon is a closed figure with straight sides. These are usually classified by the number of sides they have. On the GRE we primarily see three-sided and four-sided polygons though with some regularity we see five-, six-, or eight-sided polygons. Others are rare.

| Number of Sides | Name | Examples |
|---|---|---|
| 3 | Triangle | |
| 4 | Quadrilateral | |
| 5 | Pentagon | |
| 6 | Hexagon | |
| 8 | Octagon | |

As long as the polygon is convex (has no indentation) the sum of its interior angles is determined by the number of sides it has. For a triangle its interior angles sum to 180°, for a quadrilateral 360°, and for a pentagon 540°. There is a formula to describe this:

The sum of the interior angles of a convex $n$-sided polygon is $(n - 2)$ 180°. It's not really necessary to memorize this. You can always figure it out by dividing the shape into triangles.

EXAMPLE 1

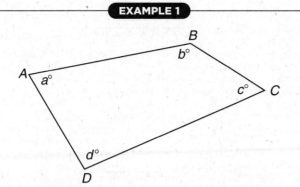

|  Quantity A  |  Quantity B  |
|---|---|
|  Average of *a*, *b*, *c*, and *d*  |  90°  |

**Solution:** The average of *a*, *b*, *c*, *d* is $\frac{(a+b+c+d)}{4}$. So we need to know the sum of the angles. If we don't recall the formula, we can still figure this out. If we draw a line from *A* to *C*, we have broken our quadrilateral into two triangles so that the interior angles of the triangles, together, comprise the interior angles of the quadrilateral. Since the interior angles in each triangle sum to 180°, the quadrilateral's interior angles add to 180° + 180° = 360°. So *a* + *b* + *c* + *d* = 360 and hence the average is $\frac{360}{4}$ = 90. Choose **C**.

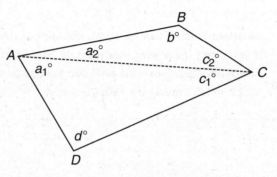

$$a + b + c + d = (a_2 + b + c_2) + (a_1 + d + c_1)$$
$$= 180 + 180 = 360$$

## Regular Polygons

*Regular polygons* have all sides equal and all interior angles equal. An equilateral triangle is a regular triangle. A square is a regular quadrilateral. In the previous table, the bold figures are regular polygons.

This makes it very easy to determine their interior angles. As the interior angles of a quadrilateral sum to 360°, in a regular quadrilateral (a square) each of those angles is $\frac{360°}{4} = 90°$. In a regular pentagon each interior angle is $\frac{540°}{5} = 108°$.

EXAMPLE 2

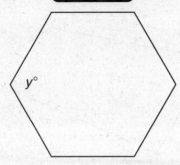

This is a regular hexagon.

| Quantity A | Quantity B |
|:---:|:---:|
| y | 120 |

**Solution:** Since it has six sides, the sum of the interior angles is (6 – 2)180° = 720°. If you don't remember that formula, just divide the hexagon into four triangles and 4(180°) = 720°. Since the hexagon is regular all the interior angles are equal. So 6*y* = 720 which implies *y* = 120. Choose **C**.

**TIP**

- Except for triangles, a polygon with all sides equal does not have to be regular.
- Except for triangles, a polygon with all angles equal does not have to be regular.

 This rhombus has four equal sides but is not regular—its angles are not all equal.

 This rectangle has four equal angles but is not regular—its sides are not equal.

**EXAMPLE 3**

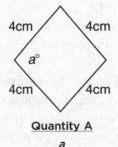

4cm  4cm
*a*°
4cm  4cm

4cm
4cm  4cm
*b*°
4cm

| Quantity A | Quantity B |
|:---:|:---:|
| a | b |

**Solution:** At first glance you might assume the figure at left is just a square rotated. It's not. As the tip above noted having four equal sides does not make it a square. It could be a tall skinny rhombus where *a* > 90 or a flat wide rhombus where *a* < 90 or even possibly a square where *a* = 90. In the figure at right, *b* must be 90 as the sum of the interior angles is 360° and the other three are 90°. Choose **D**.

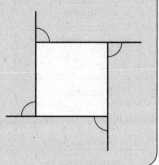
**EXAMPLE 4**

In the diagram, *ABCDE* is a regular pentagon, and *AB* and *DC* extend to meet at *F*. Find *w*.

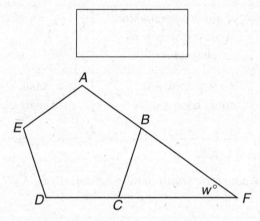

**Solution:** As *ABCDE* is a regular pentagon, each of its exterior angles is $\dfrac{360°}{5} = 72°$.

Note that ∠*BCF* and ∠*CBF* are exterior angles. Then the angles in △*BCF* sum to 180°, so 72° + 72° + *w*° = 180°. That means *w* = **36**.

## Quadrilaterals

There are many special four-sided polygons, and each of them has special properties. We cannot hope to inform you of all the properties of these figures (nor would you want to study that much material), but we will try to hit the highlights and the ideas most likely to appear on the GRE. In most cases, knowledge from this section will help you solve problems faster, though there may be other ways to solve the problem using basic geometric knowledge that you have.

We describe six types of quadrilaterals. There is significant overlap in these groups. For instance, a square belongs to all of them!

| Name | Definition | Properties to Note |
|------|-----------|--------------------|
| Square | A regular quadrilateral | Four equal sides<br>Four equal right interior angles<br>Diagonals are equal in length<br>Diagonals bisect each other |
| Rectangle | A quadrilateral with four interior right angles | Opposite sides parallel and equal<br>Diagonals are equal in length<br>Diagonals bisect each other |
| Parallelogram | A quadrilateral with two pairs of opposite parallel sides | Opposite sides equal<br>Diagonals bisect each other<br>Opposite interior angles equal |
| Rhombus | A quadrilateral with four equal sides | Opposite sides parallel and equal<br>Diagonals bisect each other<br>Diagonals are perpendicular |
| Trapezoid | A quadrilateral with at least one pair of parallel sides | |
| Isosceles trapezoid | A trapezoid with equal base angles | Diagonals are equal in length<br>Diagonals bisect each other |

Examples 5 and 6 are concerned with parallelogram *ABCD*.

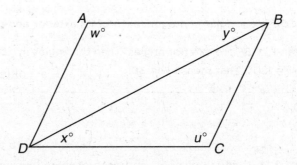

**EXAMPLE 5**

Quantity A
*w*

Quantity B
*u*

**Solution:** As ∠*A* and ∠*C* are opposite angles in a parallelogram, they are equal. Choose **C**.

**EXAMPLE 6**

| Quantity A | Quantity B |
|:---:|:---:|
| *x* | *y* |

**Solution:** As *ABCD* is a parallelogram, *AB* ∥ *CD*. Then *BD* is a transversal for parallel lines *AB* and *CD*. By the parallel lines theorem, *x* = *y*. Choose **C**.

## PROBLEMS (Solutions on page 248)
## Basic Problems

1.

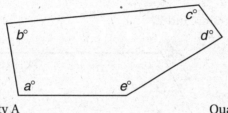

| Quantity A | Quantity B |
|:---:|:---:|
| *a* + *b* + *c* + *d* + *e* | 360° |

2. *ABCDE* is a regular pentagon

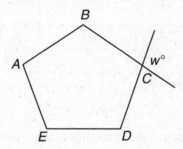

| Quantity A | Quantity B |
|:---:|:---:|
| *w* | 72° |

3. *ABCD* is a rectangle

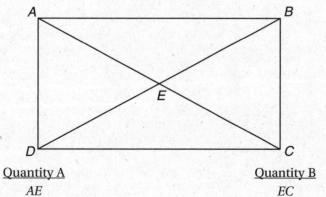

| Quantity A | Quantity B |
|:---:|:---:|
| *AE* | *EC* |

4.  A regular octagon has interior angle of $x°$ and exterior angle of $y°$

| Quantity A | Quantity B |
|---|---|
| $x$ | $180 - y$ |

5.  A regular hexagon has interior angle of $h°$ and an equilateral triangle has exterior angle of $t°$

| Quantity A | Quantity B |
|---|---|
| $h$ | $t$ |

6.  ABCDEF is a regular hexagon with perimeter 24 cm

| Quantity A | Quantity B |
|---|---|
| $AC$ | 8 cm |

7. ABCD is a parallelogram. Find $x$.

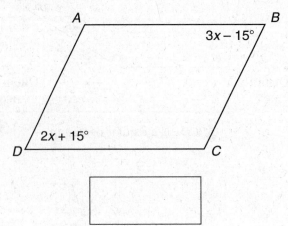

## GRE Problems

8.  Mary formed a new shape by gluing together four regular polygons. Find the perimeter of this figure.

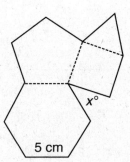

9. Find $x$ in Mary's figure.

   (A) 24°

   (B) 30°

   (C) 42°

   (D) 48°

   (E) 60°

10.            In quadrilateral $ABCD$, $AB = BC$ and $CD = DA$

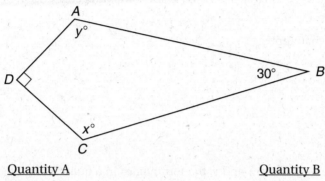

| Quantity A | Quantity B |
|:----------:|:----------:|
| $x$ | $y$ |

11.            This is a convex pentagon

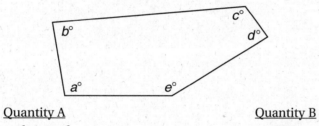

| Quantity A | Quantity B |
|:----------:|:----------:|
| $a + b + c + d$ | $360°$ |

12.            $ABCD$ is a rectangle

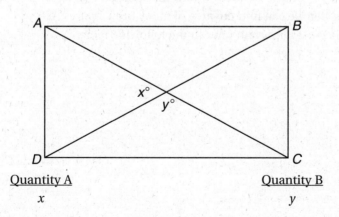

| Quantity A | Quantity B |
|:----------:|:----------:|
| $x$ | $y$ |

13. A regular polygon has exterior angles of $x°$ and interior angles of $3x°$. How many sides does the polygon have?

(A) 6

(B) 8

(C) 9

(D) 10

(E) 12

14. A triangle has side lengths 9, 19, and $x$, for some integer $x$. Which of the following could be $x$?

Indicate *all* that apply.

A 9

B 10

C 15

D 19

E 29

15. For some real numbers $x$ and $y$, the four angles in a quadrilateral have degree measures $2x°$, $3x°$, $4x°$, and $y°$. Which of the following could be the value of $x$?

Indicate *all* that apply.

A 35

B 37.5

C 40

D 42.5

E 45

## AREA

Area is a measure of the two-dimensional space an object occupies. The most basic definition of area is for the square. A square that is 1 unit by 1 unit is defined to have an area of 1 unit². By extending this idea we can find the area of many basic figures. We summarize the most important ones in the following table.

Area = 1 unit²    1 unit

1 unit

| Shape | Diagram | Area Formula |
|-------|---------|--------------|
| Square | $s$ (sides labeled $s$) | $A = s^2$ (side squared) |
| Rectangle | $w$, $l$ | $A = lw$ (length times width) |
| Circle | $r$ | $A = \pi r^2$ (pi times radius squared) |
| Triangle | $h$, $b$ | $A = \frac{1}{2}bh$ (one-half base times height) |
| Parallelogram | $h$, $b$ | $A = bh$ (base times height) |
| Trapezoid | $b_1$, $h$, $b_2$ | $A = \frac{1}{2}(b_1 + b_2)h$ (one-half the height times the sum of the bases) |

The height is always perpendicular to the base and is usually different from the slant height. Don't make the mistake of using the slant height (side length) when the height is needed.

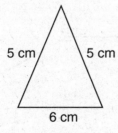

**Incorrect Area**

$A = \frac{1}{2}bh$

$= \frac{1}{2}(6)(5)$

$= 15$

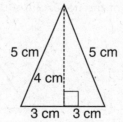

**Correct Area**

$A = \frac{1}{2}bh$

$= \frac{1}{2}(6)(4)$

$= 12$

It is essential to know the area formulas for a rectangle, circle, and triangle—often the others may be determined from them.

**EXAMPLE 1**

Find the area of parallelogram ABCD.

 cm²

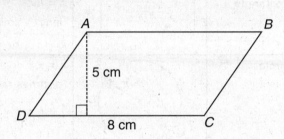

**Solution:** If you know the formula for area of a parallelogram this is very easy, $A = bh = (8 \text{ cm})(5 \text{ cm}) = 40 \text{ cm}^2$. If you don't, you can still solve the problem. Add a line from $A$ to $C$.

Now the area of $\triangle ACD$ is $\frac{1}{2} bh = $

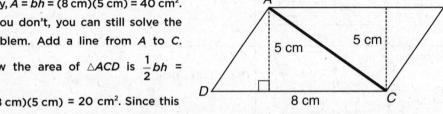

$\frac{1}{2}(8 \text{ cm})(5 \text{ cm}) = 20 \text{ cm}^2$. Since this is a parallelogram, the height from $C$ to $AB$ is also 5 cm and $AB$ is also 8 cm. So for $\triangle CAB$ with base $AB$, the area is $\frac{1}{2} bh = \frac{1}{2}(8 \text{ cm})(5 \text{ cm}) = 20 \text{ cm}^2$.

Adding the areas together, 20 cm² + 20 cm² = **40 cm²**.

**EXAMPLE 2**

Find the area of the trapezoid ABCD.

(A) 29
(B) 36
(C) 40
(D) 42
(E) 68

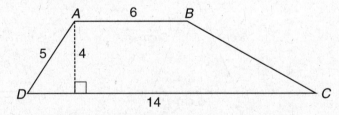

**Solution:** If you know the formula for area of a trapezoid, this is very easy: $A = \frac{1}{2}(b_1 + b_2)h = \frac{1}{2}(6 + 14)(4) = 40$. Choose C. If you don't, you can still solve the problem.

Drop a line at $B$ to intersect $CD$ at right angles. Call this new point $E$. Also use $F$ to denote the point where the original height meets $CD$. Now the area of the trapezoid is the area of the central rectangle, $ABEF$ plus the area of the two triangles $\triangle BEC$ and $\triangle AFD$. Since $\triangle AFD$ is a right angle triangle with hypotenuse 5 and side length 4, the other side length, *DF*, must be 3. So the area of △*ADF* is $\frac{1}{2}bh = \frac{1}{2}(3)(4) = 6$.

Now the area of *ABEF* is *lw* = 6 × 4 = 24. Finally, as *DF* = 3 and *FE* = 6, *EC* = 14 − 3

− 6 = 5. Then the area of △*BEC* = $\frac{1}{2}bh = \frac{1}{2}(5 \times 4) = 10$. So the total area of the

trapezoid is 6 + 24 + 10 = 40. Choose **C**.

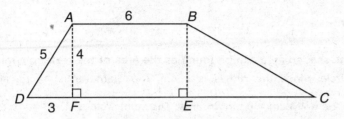

Of course, most often you need to find the area of a more complicated figure. In this case it is usually best to break the figure up into smaller pieces whose areas are easier to find. Some people call this the addition method.

---

**EXAMPLE 3**

If the grid has 1 inch between each dot horizontally and vertically, find the area of the given figure.

 in²

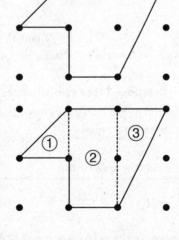

**Solution:** We divide the shape into regions whose area is easily recognized. Region ① is half, diagonally, of a 1 inch square so it has area $\frac{1}{2}$ in². If you prefer the formula its area is $\frac{1}{2}bh = \frac{1}{2}(1\,\text{in})(1\,\text{in}) = \frac{1}{2}$ in². Region ② is a 2 × 1 rectangle so it has area 2 in². Region ③ is half, diagonally, of a 2 × 1 rectangle so it has area $\frac{1}{2}(2\,\text{in}^2)$ = 1 in². If you prefer formulas, its area is $\frac{1}{2}bh = \frac{1}{2}(2\,\text{in})(1\,\text{in}) = 1$ in². In total we have

Area ① + Area ② + Area ③ = $\frac{1}{2}$ + 2 + 1 = **3.5 in².**

---

Sometimes it is easier to find areas with subtraction than with addition—that is, subtracting excess area from a larger region to leave the area of the region you want.

**EXAMPLE 4**

Find the area of the shaded region.

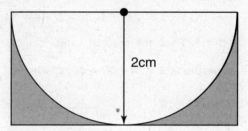

(A) $8 - 4\pi$ cm²

(B) $8 - 2\pi$ cm²

(C) $4$ cm²

(D) $\pi$ cm²

(E) $4 - \pi$ cm²

**Solution:** The shaded area can be found as the area of the rectangle minus the area of a semicircle. Since the radius is 2 cm, the diameter is 4 cm, and thus the rectangle is 2 cm × 4 cm = 8 cm² in area. The semicircle is $\frac{1}{2}\pi r^2 = \frac{1}{2}\pi(2 \text{ cm})^2 = 2\pi$ cm². So the shaded area is $8 - 2\pi$ cm². Choose **B**.

**EXAMPLE 5**

*ABCD* is a parallelogram

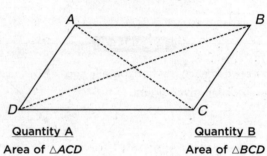

| Quantity A | Quantity B |
|---|---|
| Area of △ACD | Area of △BCD |

**Solution:** These two triangles share the same base *CD*. And as *AB* ∥ *DC*, they have the same height too. So their areas are equal.

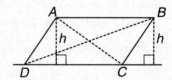

**TIP**

All triangles of the same height and base have the same area.

## Connecting Area and Perimeter

For some figures, like a square and circle, as the perimeter increases so does the area. For other shapes, like a rectangle, this may not be the case. Because this connection between perimeter and area is such an interesting relationship, it is the subject of many GRE problems.

EXAMPLE 6

A rectangle with area 28 has side lengths that are integers

| Quantity A | Quantity B |
|---|---|
| Perimeter of the rectangle | 22 |

**Solution:** We must find integer values for length and width so that $28 = lw$. We could have $l = 7$ and $w = 4$, and then the perimeter would be $4 + 7 + 4 + 7 = 22$. But we could also have $l = 14$ and $w = 2$ and then the perimeter would be $14 + 2 + 14 + 2 = 32$. Since we can't tell which, choose **D**.

This TIP is well worth memorizing. We can illustrate why it is true with an equilateral triangle of side length 1. Drop a perpendicular from $A$ to meet $BC$ at $D$. Then $D$ bisects $BC$, so $BD = CD = \frac{1}{2}$. Now, using the Pythagorean theorem in $\triangle ABD$, we have $\left(\frac{1}{2}\right)^2 + h^2 = 1^2$. So $h^2 = 1 - \frac{1}{4} = \frac{3}{4}$. Then $h = \frac{\sqrt{3}}{2}$. As the height of an equilateral triangle of side length 1 is $\frac{\sqrt{3}}{2}$, by scaling the height of an equilateral triangle of side length $x$ is $\frac{\sqrt{3}}{2}x$.

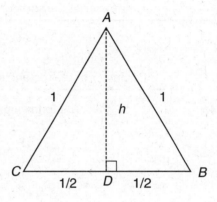

If an equilateral triangle has side length $x$, then it has height $\frac{\sqrt{3}}{2}x$.

EXAMPLE 7

A square with side $s$ and an equilateral triangle with side $x$ have the same area

| Quantity A | Quantity B |
|---|---|
| $x$ | $s$ |

**Solution:** The area of the square is $s^2$. To find the area of the triangle, we need to know the height—from above we know it will be $\frac{\sqrt{3}}{2}x$. So the area of the triangle is $\left(\frac{1}{2}\right)x\left(\frac{\sqrt{3}}{2}x\right) = \frac{\sqrt{3}}{4}x^2$. Setting them equal, $s^2 = \frac{\sqrt{3}}{4}x^2$, which implies $s = \sqrt{\frac{\sqrt{3}}{4}}x$. We know that $0 < \frac{\sqrt{3}}{4} < 1$ and so $0 < \sqrt{\frac{\sqrt{3}}{4}} < 1$. Thus $s$ is less than $x$. Choose **A**.

- **For a fixed area, the circle has the smallest perimeter.**

- **For a fixed perimeter, the circle encloses the most area.**

# PROBLEMS (Solutions on page 250)
## Basic Problems

1.

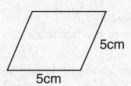

| Quantity A | Quantity B |
|---|---|
| Area of (nonsquare) parallelogram | 25 cm$^2$ |

2.

A given square has area 16 meters$^2$

| Quantity A | Quantity B |
|---|---|
| Perimeter of the square | 16 meters |

3.

A given rectangle has area 16 in$^2$

| Quantity A | Quantity B |
|---|---|
| Perimeter of the rectangle | 16 in |

4.

The following hexagon is drawn on a 1 cm grid

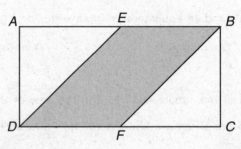

| Quantity A | Quantity B |
|---|---|
| Area inside the hexagon | 3.5 cm$^2$ |

5.

$ABCD$ is a rectangle, $EBFD$ is a parallelogram, and $EB = FC$

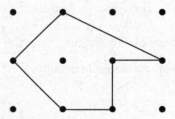

| Quantity A | Quantity B |
|---|---|
| The shaded area | The white area |

6. Find the area of the shaded figure. The semicircular regions have radius 3 cm.

(A) $60$ cm$^2$
(B) $60 - 2\pi$ cm$^2$
(C) $96 - 36\pi$ cm$^2$
(D) $96 - 9\pi$ cm$^2$
(E) $132 - 18\pi$ cm$^2$

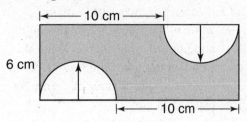

## GRE Problems

7. A regular hexagonal nut just fits into a circular hole, 2 inches in diameter. How much area, in square inches, surrounds the nut?

(A) $4\pi - \dfrac{3\sqrt{3}}{2}$

(B) $\pi - \dfrac{3\sqrt{3}}{2}$

(C) $4\pi - 3$

(D) $\pi - 3$

(E) $4\pi - 6\sqrt{2}$

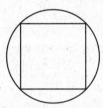

8. A square of area 4 m$^2$ fits snugly inside a circle. What is the circumference of the circle?

(A) $2\sqrt{2}\pi$ m
(B) $2\pi$ m
(C) $\pi$ m
(D) $2(\pi - 1)$ m
(E) $2\sqrt{2}$ m

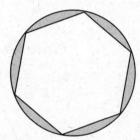

9. An ice hockey rink is formed from a rectangle with a semicircle attached at each end. If the width of the rink is 50 feet and the length is 200 feet, which of the following best approximates the area of the rink?

(A) $8{,}000$ ft$^2$
(B) $9{,}000$ ft$^2$
(C) $9{,}500$ ft$^2$
(D) $10{,}000$ ft$^2$
(E) $12{,}000$ ft$^2$

10. A rectangular 10-inch by 14-inch picture is framed with a uniform mat 2 inches wide. What is the area of the mat?

 in$^2$

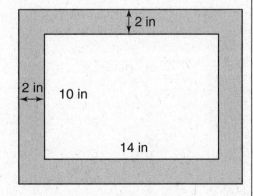

11. A rectangular framed picture measures $H$ inches by $W$ inches. If the width of the frame is 2 inches on top and bottom and 1 inch on each side, which of the following is *not* a correct expression for the area of the frame (shaded in grey)?

(A) $2H + 4(W - 2)$

(B) $2(H - 4) + 4W$

(C) $WH - (W - 2)(H - 4)$

(D) $2(H - 4) + 4(W - 2) + 4(2)$

(E) $(W + 1)(H + 2) - WH$

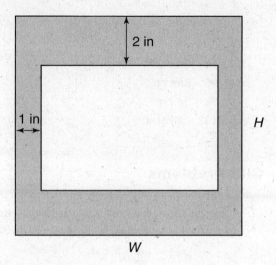

2 in

1 in

$H$

$W$

12.                                    In parallelogram $ABCD$, $4 < h < w$

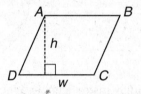

| Quantity A | Quantity B |
|---|---|
| Area of $ABCD$ | Perimeter of $ABCD$ |

13.            The circles are concentric. The smaller one has diameter 6 cm and the larger has radius 9 cm.

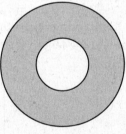

| Quantity A | Quantity B |
|---|---|
| Eight times the white area | The shaded area |

14.  A rectangle is inscribed in a circle of area 4π

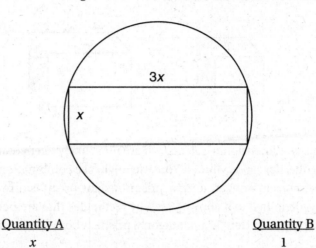

|  Quantity A  |  Quantity B  |
| :---: | :---: |
| x | 1 |

PROBLEMS 15 AND 16 CONCERN THE FOLLOWING BOOMERANG DESIGNS. ALL ARCS SHOWN ARE SEMICIRCLES. *AC* = *DG* = 12 CM. *B* IS THE MIDPOINT OF *AC* AND *DE* = *EF* = *FG*.

15.

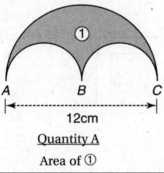

|  Quantity A  |  Quantity B  |
| :---: | :---: |
| Area of ① | Area of ② |

16.

|  Quantity A  |  Quantity B  |
| :---: | :---: |
| Perimeter of ① | Perimeter of ② |

17.  A rectangle has area 24 square inches. Its side lengths are whole numbers of inches. Which of the following could be the perimeter of the rectangle, in inches?

Indicate *all* that apply.

- **A** 18
- **B** 20
- **C** 22
- **D** 24
- **E** 26
- **F** 28
- **G** 40
- **H** 50

# SURFACE AREA AND VOLUME

  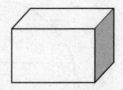 

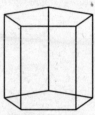

On the GRE the three-dimensional objects you are most likely to encounter are a sphere, cube, box, and cylinder. You also might see combinations or pieces of these objects or even a right prism. A right prism is a two dimensional polygon joined to a copy of itself by rectangles that are perpendicular to the polygons. Here is a pentagonal prism. A box is a rectangular prism.

The polygons on the surface of a solid are called *faces*. Two faces meet in a line that we call an *edge*. Three (or more) faces meet at a point we call a *vertex*. In the box below *ABCD* is the top face. *BC* is an edge where face *ABCD* meets face *BCEF*. *C* is a vertex where faces *ABCD*, *BCFE*, and *CDGF* all meet.

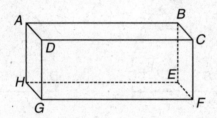

## Surface Area

Except for the sphere, each of these objects has a surface made of two-dimensional objects—polygons and circles. It seems reasonable to ask about the total area of these shapes—that is called surface area. In most cases, you can find surface area by looking at each part of the surface, finding its area, and adding up all those areas.

| Object | Surfaces | | | Surface Area |
|---|---|---|---|---|
| Cube | $s^2$ $s^2$ $s^2$ | | | $6s^2$ |
| | $s^2$ $s^2$ $s^2$ | | | |
| Box | $l \times h$ | $l \times w$ | $w \times h$ | $2lh + 2lw + 2wh$ |
| | $l \times h$ | $l \times w$ | $w \times h$ | |
| Cylinder | $\pi r^2$ | $2\pi r \times h$ | | $2\pi r^2 + 2\pi rh$ |
| | $\pi r^2$ | | | |
| Sphere | | | | $4\pi r^2$ |

In the case of a sphere, we use a formula derived from calculus. You should not need to memorize this formula—it is unlikely to appear on the test and if needed it should be given to you in the question.

## EXAMPLE 1

Find the surface area of the right triangular prism pictured here.

 cm²

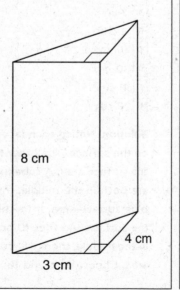

**Solution:** We recognize the bottom as a 3, 4, 5 right triangle. It has area $\frac{1}{2}(3)(4) = 6$ cm². The top has the same area of 6 cm². There are three rectangular faces. One is 3 × 8, one is 4 × 8, and the last is 5 × 8. Their areas are 24 cm², 32 cm², and 40 cm². So the total surface area is 6 + 6 + 24 + 32 + 40 = **108 cm²**.

**EXAMPLE 2**

| Quantity A | Quantity B |
|---|---|
| Surface area of cube of side length 1 | Surface area of sphere of diameter 1 |

**Solution:** A cube of side length 1 has surface area of $6s^2 = 6(1)^2 = 6$. A sphere of diameter 1 has radius $\frac{1}{2}$ so its surface area is $4\pi r^2 = 4\pi \left(\frac{1}{2}\right)^2 = \frac{4\pi}{4} = \pi$. As $6 > \pi$, choose **A**. You may not know the formula for surface area of a sphere and still be able to solve this problem. In this case, it is apparent the sphere would fit entirely inside the cube and thus have smaller surface area.

---

**EXAMPLE 3**

Two red cubes and two blue cubes are placed together to form a single rectangular prism. The order of their placement is not known. If each cube has side length 1 cm, which of the following could be the blue surface area?

Indicate *all* that apply.

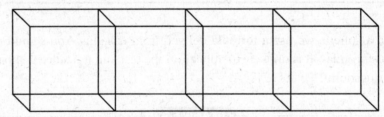

- [A] 7 cm²
- [B] 8 cm²
- [C] 9 cm²
- [D] 10 cm²
- [E] 11 cm²
- [F] 12 cm²

**Solution:** Notice each face of a cube has area 1 cm². A cube on the end has five faces on the surface. The other face is pressed against its neighbor and thus is not part of the surface area. A cube in the middle has four faces on the surface. If the blue cubes are both in the middle, there will be 8 blue faces on the surface and thus 8 cm² of blue surface area. If the blue cubes are on the ends, there will be 10 blue faces on the surface and thus 10 cm² of blue surface area. If one is on the end and the other in the middle, there will be 9 blue faces on the surface and thus 9 cm² of blue surface area. Choose 8, 9, and 10: **B**, **C**, and **D**.

**TIP**

For objects like a sphere, cube, box, or cylinder, if one fits inside another, the inner solid has lesser surface area. This is not true for all solid objects.

# Volume

Volume is the measure of the three-dimensional space inside an object. A basic unit of volume is the cubic centimeter defined as the space occupied by a cube with side length of 1 cm. This definition generalizes to give the formulas in the table on page 235.

| Object | Volume |
|---|---|
| Cube | $s^3$ |
| Box | $lwh$ |
| Cylinder | $\pi r^2 h$ |
| Sphere | $\dfrac{4\pi r^3}{3}$ |

You will not need to memorize the formula for volume of a sphere. In the unlikely case that you will need it, it should be given in the question. You should note that the volume formulas for a cube, box, and cylinder all follow the pattern: Volume = (Area of base) × (Height). This is a general rule for all prisms.

EXAMPLE 4

Two boxes of cereal have the same volume. One has dimensions 4 in × 9 in × x in, while the other has dimensions x in × x in × 6 in. What is x?

**Solution:** The volume of a box is length × width × height so the volume of the first box is $(4)(9)(x) = 36x$. The volume of the second box is $(x)(x)(6) = 6x^2$. As their volumes are equal $36x = 6x^2$. Divide both sides by $6x$, and we have **6 = x**.

EXAMPLE 5

A cube and a cylinder have the same volume

| Quantity A | Quantity B |
|---|---|
| Side length of the cube | Height of the cylinder |

**Solution:** As their volumes are equal, $s^3 = \pi r^2 h$. Solving for height, $h = \dfrac{s^3}{\pi r^2}$. The value

of $r$ will greatly affect the relationship between $h$ and $s$. If $r = s$, then $h = \dfrac{s}{\pi}$ and so

$h < s$. If $r = \dfrac{s}{\pi}$, then $h = \dfrac{s^3}{\pi r^2} = \dfrac{s^3}{\pi\left(\dfrac{s}{\pi}\right)^2} = \dfrac{s^3}{\dfrac{s^2}{\pi}} = \pi s$. So $h > s$. Choose **D**. In simpler terms,

a tall skinny cylinder could have the same volume as the cube, but the height will be greater than the cube's side length. A very flat wide cylinder could also have the same volume as the cube, but the height would be smaller than the side length.

EXAMPLE 6

What is the maximum length of a straw that could fit inside a can with radius 2 inches and height 10 inches?

Ⓐ $2\sqrt{39}$

Ⓑ $2\sqrt{21}$

Ⓒ $10.3$

Ⓓ $\sqrt{96}$

Ⓔ $11$

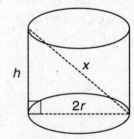

**Solution:** The key to solving this problem is noting the longest straw will be the hypotenuse of a right triangle formed by the diameter of the base and a perpendicular to the base on the side of the can. In this right triangle, $x^2 = (4)^2 + (10)^2$ and so $x^2 = 116$. Hence $x$ is $\sqrt{116} = \sqrt{4 \times 39} = 2\sqrt{39}$. Choose **A**.

## PROBLEMS (Solutions on page 253)

## Basic Problems

PROBLEMS 1 AND 2 CONCERN THE FOLLOWING BOX.

1.

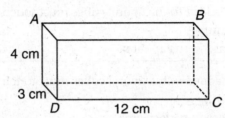

| Quantity A | Quantity B |
|---|---|
| Length of diagonal $AC$ | 15 cm |

---

2.

| Quantity A | Quantity B |
|---|---|
| 144 cm² | Surface area of the box |

---

3.                  A cube has side length $\sqrt{2}$

| Quantity A | Quantity B |
|---|---|
| Volume of the cube | 12 |

---

4.                  A cube has diagonal 4 cm

| Quantity A | Quantity B |
|---|---|
| 24 cm² | Surface area of the cube |

---

5.      A cube has surface area equal in magnitude to its volume

| Quantity A | Quantity B |
|---|---|
| Side length of the cube | 6 |

6. Which of the following have a volume equal in magnitude to its surface area?

   Indicate *all* that apply.

   A  Cube of side length 6
   B  Box with dimensions $4 \times 8 \times 8$
   C  Box with dimensions $1 \times 2 \times 3$

## GRE Problems

PROBLEMS 7–9 CONCERN THE L-SHAPED FIGURE BELOW, WHICH IS COMPOSED OF FOUR CUBES EACH WITH SIDE LENGTH 2 CM.

7.

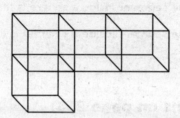

| Quantity A | Quantity B |
|---|---|
| Surface area of L shape | Surface area of $2 \times 4 \times 6$ box |

8. One cube is added to the figure; cubes must touch exactly face to face

| Quantity A | Quantity B |
|---|---|
| Minimum increase in surface area | Increase in volume |

9. One cube is added to the figure; cubes must touch exactly face to face

| Quantity A | Quantity B |
|---|---|
| Maximum increase in surface area | 16 |

10. A cube and a sphere have the same volume

| Quantity A | Quantity B |
|---|---|
| Surface area of cube | Surface area of sphere |

PROBLEMS 11 AND 12 CONCERN THE DIAGRAM BELOW. FOUR CUBES ARE STACKED AS SHOWN.

TWO ARE RED AND TWO ARE BLUE.

11.

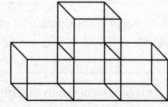

| Quantity A | Quantity B |
|---|---|
| Fraction of surface area that is blue | $\dfrac{1}{2}$ |

12.

| Quantity A | Quantity B |
|---|---|
| Maximum percentage of surface area that is red | 60% |

13. Marg wants to replace her cylindrical spaghetti can, of radius 2 in and height 8 in, with a tin box of dimensions 4 in × 4 in × 7 in

| Quantity A | Quantity B |
|---|---|
| Max. length that can fit into the cylindrical spaghetti can | Max. length that can fit into the tin box |

14. Find the volume of the triangular prism.

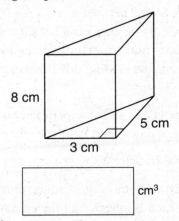

8 cm

5 cm

3 cm

cm³

15. How many 2 × 2 × 2 ice cubes can fit into an ice tray of dimensions 4 × 6 × 8?

16. A cube just fits inside a sphere. If the surface area of the cube is 36, what is the diameter of the sphere?

(A) $2\sqrt{3}$
(B) $3\sqrt{2}$
(C) $\sqrt{22}$
(D) 6
(E) 9

17. A certain box, or rectangular prism, has edges of length $x$ cm, $y$ cm, and $z$ cm, where $x$, $y$, and $z$ are positive integers. If the length of each side is greater than 1, and the area of one face (side) of the box is 35 cm², which of the following could be the volume of the box?

Indicate *all* that apply.

A   35 cm³
B   60 cm³
C   70 cm³
D   100 cm³
E   105 cm³
F   120 cm³
G   140 cm³

## SOLUTIONS TO PRACTICE PROBLEMS
## Perimeter (Problems on page 195)

1. **(C)** A circle of diameter 20 has radius 10, as diameter is twice the radius. Thus these circles are identical and hence their circumference is equal.

2. **(B)** The square has perimeter $P = 4s = 4(4) = 16$. The circle has circumference $C = 2\pi r = 2\pi(4) = 8\pi$. As $\pi > 3$, $8\pi > 24$.

3. **(A)** In A, the third side can be found from the Pythagorean theorem. As $3^2 + 4^2 = x^2$, we find $x^2 = 25$ and thus $x = 5$. So the perimeter is $3 + 4 + 5 = 12$. In B, $3^2 + y^2 = 4^2$ implies $y^2 = 16 - 9 = 7$ and thus $y = \sqrt{7}$. So the perimeter is $3 + 4 + \sqrt{7} = 7 + \sqrt{7} < 7 + 3 = 10$. Choose A. An easier answer would be to notice that the hypotenuse is always larger than the other sides in a right triangle. Hence the missing side is larger than 4 in A and less than 4 in B. Hence the perimeter in A is larger.

4. **(A)** In A the circumference is $2\pi r$. In B the perimeter of the shape is composed of the circular part and the diameter; hence, it is $\frac{1}{2}(2\pi r) + 2r = \pi r + 2r$. Since $2 < \pi$, $\pi r + 2r < \pi r + \pi r = 2\pi r$. If you notice they both have the same radius, then the question boils down to "Which is longer, half the circumference of the circle, or the length of $XY$?" The shortest path between two points is a straight line so the length of $XY$ is less than the arc from $X$ to $Y$. The answer follows.

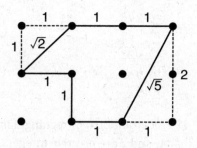

5. **(D)** Although the rectangle in B looks larger, you can't trust appearances. In A the perimeter is $x + y + x + y = 2x + 2y$. In B the perimeter is $x + z + x + z = 2x + 2z$. Since we don't know what $z$ and $y$ are, there is no way to know which is larger.

6. **(D)** There are two diagonals in this diagram. The smaller one, call it $x$, is the diagonal of a $1 \times 1$ square, and thus we should recall it has length $\sqrt{2}$ (you can find this using the Pythagorean theorem $1^2 + 1^2 = x^2$). The larger diagonal, call it $y$, is part of a right triangle with other sides 1 and 2. Thus $y^2 = 1^2 + 2^2$, which implies $y^2 = 5$ and hence $y = \sqrt{5}$. Hence the perimeter is $\sqrt{2} + 1 + 1 + \sqrt{5} + 1 + 1 + 1 = 5 + \sqrt{2} + \sqrt{5}$.

7. **(E)** We can see that the diameter of the semicircles is half of 4 cm or 2 cm. Thus the radius of each semicircle is 1 cm. The circumference of two semicircles is the same as the circumference of one circle, $2\pi r = 2\pi(1) = 2\pi$. To complete the perimeter, we add the three other sides $2\pi + 2 + 4 + 2 = 8 + 2\pi$ cm.

8. **(26)** Call the missing side lengths $x$ and $y$. We can find $y$ by equating the horizontal sides: $8 = 1 + 3 + y$, and hence $y = 4$. We can find $x$ by equating the vertical sides: $1 + x = 2 + 3$ and hence $x = 4$. Finally the perimeter is $8 + 3 + y + 2 + 3 + x + 1 + 1 = 8 + 3 + (4) + 2 + 3 + (4) + 1 + 1 = 26$.

There is also a quick and tricky answer for this question. By moving the dotted lines to the solid lines, we can change the shape into a rectangle with the same perimeter. And the perimeter of the rectangle is $2(8 + 5) = 26$.

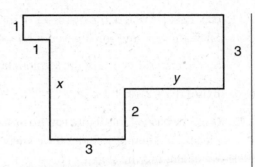

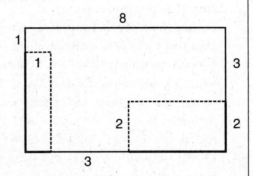

9. **(38)** We could do a lot of reasoning to determine the lengths of all the sides shown. It is much easier to look at horizontal and vertical pieces separately. The five small horizontal pieces must add up to the width of the figure, which is 10. The five smaller vertical pieces must add to the height of the figure which is 9. Hence the perimeter of the object is $9 + 10 + 9 + 10 = 38$. In general, such a figure always has the same perimeter as the corresponding rectangle.

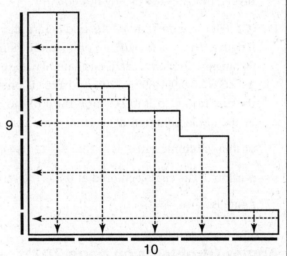

10. **(C)** No measurements are given in the question. So let's assume that $AC = 8$. Then $AB = 4$ and $BC = 4$. So the radius for the semicircle $AC$ is 4 and for $AB$ (or $BC$) is 2. Hence the length of arc $\overarc{AC} = \frac{1}{2}(2\pi 4) = 4\pi$. Meanwhile the length of $\overarc{AB} + \overarc{BC}$ is $\frac{1}{2}(2\pi 2) + \frac{1}{2}(2\pi 2) = 4\pi$.

Hence the path from $A$ to $C$ has the same length as the path from $A$ to $B$ to $C$.

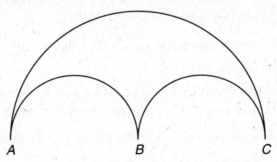

11. **(C)** First we find $d$, the diameter of the circle, which is also the third side of the triangle. So $3^2 + d^2 = 5^2$ and solving we find $d = 4$ (you might have recognized the 3, 4, 5 triangle). So the circumference of the semicircle is $\frac{1}{2}(\pi d) = \frac{1}{2}(\pi 4) = 2\pi$. Finally the perimeter of the figure is $3 + 5 + \pi = 8 + 2\pi$.

12. **(D)** The base of this figure can be broken into three pieces, call them $x$, $y$, and $z$. If we knew these values, we could find the sloped sides and thus the perimeter. It is immediately clear that $y = 3$ since the central piece of the figure is a rectangle. It is not clear that $x$ and $z$ can be determined—but does that affect the perimeter? It should. In the triangle on the left, $x^2 + 4^2 = d^2$ and hence $d = \sqrt{x^2 + 4^2}$. In the triangle on the right, $z^2 + 4^2 = e^2$ and hence $e = \sqrt{z^2 + 4^2}$. So the perimeter is $P = 3 + e + 10 + d = 13 + \sqrt{x^2 + 4^2} + \sqrt{z^2 + 4^2}$. When $x = 3$ and $z = 4$, this is $13 + \sqrt{3^2 + 4^2} + \sqrt{4^2 + 4^2} = 13 + 5 + 4\sqrt{2} = 18 + 4\sqrt{2}$. When $x = 1$ and $z = 6$, this is $13 + \sqrt{1^2 + 4^2} + \sqrt{6^2 + 4^2} = 13 + \sqrt{17} + \sqrt{52} = 13 + \sqrt{17} + 2\sqrt{13}$. We can't easily tell which is bigger, but they are clearly not equal!

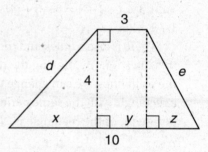

13. **(C)** First we note that $AC$, $AB$, and $BC$ are all radii and hence length 1. That makes $ABC$ an equilateral triangle with three $60°$ angles. Similarly $ABD$ is equilateral with three $60°$ angles. As $\angle CAD = 60° + 60° = 120°$, and $120°$ is one-third of $360°$, the arc from $C$ to $B$ to $D$ is one-third of the circumference of the circle centered at $A$. Hence the remaining portion of the circumference is $\frac{2}{3}(2\pi r) - \frac{2}{3}(2\pi 1) = 4\frac{\pi}{3}$. The dark portion of the circle centered at B has the same length. So the total circumference of the figure is $\frac{4\pi}{3} + \frac{4\pi}{3} = \frac{8\pi}{3}$.

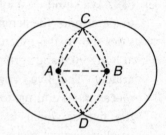

# Angles (Problems on page 202)

1. **(B)** Since a straight angle is $180°$, $2x + (x + 10) = 180$. Solving we find $3x + 10 = 180 \Rightarrow 3x = 170 \Rightarrow x = 56\frac{2}{3}$.

2. **(A)** By vertical angles $2x = 70$, and so $x = 35$. Also $2x° + (y + 10)°$ forms a straight angle or $180°$. Then $2x + y + 10 = 180$ or $x + x + y + 10 = 180$. Substitute 35 for one of the $x$'s, $35 + x + y + 10 = 180$ and hence $x + y = 180 - 10 - 35 = 135$.

3. **(C)** The two angles form a right angle so $5x + 40 = 90$. This implies $5x = 50$ and hence $x = 10$. So $4x = 40$.

4. **(C)** Since there are $360°$ in a circle $(a + b + c + d + e + f + g + h) = 360$. So $(a + b + c + d + e + f + g + h)/2 = 180$. Also $a + b + c + d = 180$ since those four angles form a straight angle.

5. **(A)** Since the lines are parallel $90° = (x - 10)°$. Hence $x = 100$. Certainly $x + 10 > 90$.

6. **(D)** When a transversal crosses parallel lines only two angles appear. If the 70° or 110° angles were incorrect, then more than one angle would be incorrect. The 120° ④ angle is incorrect. You would also note that 120° + 70° = 190°, not 180° as it should be for a straight angle.

7. **(C)** Since $\angle AOD = 90°$ and $\angle AOD + \angle AOC = 180°$, then $\angle AOC = 90°$. As $\angle AOC = \angle AOB + \angle BOC$, $90° = \angle AOB + 45°$ and hence $\angle AOB = 45°$. Now $OC$ is not in $\angle AOB$ so it cannot bisect it. A is false. $AO$ is in $\angle DOB$ but does not divide it into two equal angles as $\angle AOB = 45°$ and $\angle DOA = 90°$. B is false. $OB$ is in $\angle AOC$ and divides it into two equal angles as $\angle AOB = 45°$ and $\angle BOC = 45°$. C is true.

8. **(C)** Label the angle vertical to $b°$ as $y°$. Then $a°$, $y°$, and $c°$ together form a straight angle, so $a + y + c = 180$. But $y = b$ by vertical angles so $a + b + c = 180$.

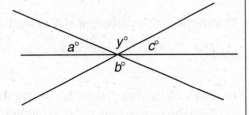

9. **(D)** By parallel lines we know that $x = y$. But what about their sum? Although the angle $x°$ appears large, we cannot trust the diagram. The angle could be small, like 80°, where $x + y = 80 + 80 = 160 < 180$. It could also be large like 135°, where $x + y = 135 + 135 = 270 > 180$.

10. **(C)** Although the diagram has been turned sideways compared to what we are used to, this is still just an application of the parallel lines theorem. Here $a = b$, so choose C.

11. **(D)** Although it appears like a right angle, we cannot trust the diagram to be accurate. So $x°$ could be more or less than 90°. Hence $180 - x$ could be more or less than 90.

12. **(C)** We extended the transversal to form an angle of $y°$. Since a straight angle is 180°, $y + 120 = 180$ and hence $y = 60$. Now by parallel lines $60° = x° + 30°$, so $x = 30°$.

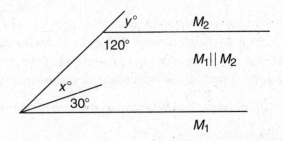

13. **(D)** A good way to solve this problem is to exaggerate the diagram. If the vertex at $s$ is moved far to the left, then it is clear that $r$, $s$, and $t$ are all very small angles and hence their sum is less than 180. If the vertex at $s$ is moved to the right, we can have $s$ nearly 180°, while $r$ and $s$ are clearly not small. So their sum is more than 180°.

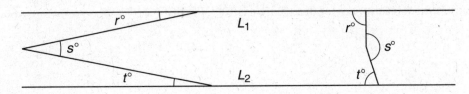

14. **(B)** Because of vertical angles, we know that $p = 40$. Because they form a straight angle $p + q = 180$. So $40 + q = 180$, or $q = 140$. Then $p + 40 = 40 + 40 = 80$. Hence A < B.

15. **(C)** By vertical angles, $a = d$, $c = f$, and $e = b$. So $a + c + e = d + f + b$ and rearranging $a + c + e = b + d + f$. Alternatively, by the argument in problem 8, each is 180° and thus equal.

16. **(C)** Since $BO$ bisects $\angle AOC$, $\angle AOB = \angle BOC = x°$. As $DO$ bisects $\angle COE$, $\angle COD = \angle DOE = y°$. As a straight angle $180° = \angle AOE = \angle AOB + \angle BOC + \angle COD + \angle DOE = x° + x° + y° + y° = 2x° + 2y°$. Then divide both sides by 2 to see that $90° = x° + y°$.

## Triangles (Problems on page 211)

1. **(A)** The sum of angles in a triangle is 180°, so $x + 35 + 90 = 180$. Hence $x = 180 - 35 - 90 = 55$.

2. **(C)** Call the missing angle $x$. Since the sum of angles in a triangle is 180°, $x + 45 + 90 = 180$. Solving we find $x = 45$. That means that the triangle is isosceles and the two sides opposite the 45° angles are equal. That is $a = b$.

3. **(B)** Assume the unnamed angle inside the triangle is $x°$. As the sum of interior angles of a triangle is 180°, we have $50 + 70 + x = 180$. Hence $x = 60$. Finally, by vertical angles $w = x$. So $w = 60$.

4. **(A)** As two sides are equal, this is an isosceles triangle. So the angles opposite those sides must also be equal. Hence they are both $x°$. Finally the sum of interior angles of a triangle is 180° so $x + x + 30 = 180$. This simplifies to $2x = 150$, which implies $x = 75$.

5. **(A)** Sides opposite larger angles are larger. As $72 > 68$, $AC > AB$.

6. **(A)** By the triangle inequality theorem, the sum of any two sides must be larger than the third.

7. **(C)** In A we use the Pythagorean theorem to solve for $x$: $2^2 = x^2 + (\sqrt{3})^2$. Then $4 = x^2 + 3$ or $x^2 = 1$. Hence $x = 1$. In B we again use the Pythagorean theorem: $(\sqrt{2})^2 = y^2 + 1^2$. Then $2 = y^2 + 1$ or $y^2 = 1$. Hence $y = 1$, also. If you have memorized your common right triangles, you could have recognized both of these and saved considerable time.

8. **(90)** Knowing $AB = AC$ proves to be irrelevant. As the sum of interior angles of a triangle is 180°, $x + y + z = 180$. Hence $\dfrac{(x + y + z)}{2} = 90$.

9. **(C)** First note that the triangle is isosceles and hence $x = y$. Then $\dfrac{2}{3}x + \dfrac{1}{3}z = \dfrac{2x + z}{3} = \dfrac{x + x + z}{3}$.

   As $x = y$, we can replace one of the $x$'s with a $y$. So $\dfrac{2}{3}x + \dfrac{1}{3}z = \dfrac{x + y + z}{3}$. And $x + y + z = 180$

   as the sum of interior angles in a triangle is 180°. Finally $\dfrac{2}{3}x + \dfrac{1}{3}z = \dfrac{x + y + z}{3} = \dfrac{180}{3} = 60$.

10. **(15)** As $AB = AC$, we know that $\angle ABC = \angle ACB$. Then summing angles in $\triangle ABC$ we have $180° = \angle ABC + \angle ACB + 30° = 2\angle ABC + 30°$. Solving we find $\angle ABC = 75°$. Now $\triangle BDC$ is equilateral so each angle is 60°. In particular $\angle DBC = 60°$. Then $\angle DBC + y° = \angle ABC$. So $60° + y° = 75°$, and thus $y = 15$.

11. **(80°)** Summing angles in $\triangle ACD$, we find that $180° = 40° + 60° + \angle ADC$. Hence $\angle ADC = 80°$. As $BD$ bisects $\angle ADC$, which is 80°, $\angle ADB = \angle CDB = 40°$. Then, summing angles in $\triangle BDC$, we find that $40° + 60° + y° = 180°$ and hence $y° = 80°$.

12. **(A)** We recognize $\triangle CBD$ as a 3, 4, 5 triangle so $CD = 5$ cm. $ABDE$ is a rectangle (because of the right angles) and hence $DE = AB = 8$ cm. Also $AE = BD = 4$ cm. Then $AEF$ is a (4 cm, 4 cm, $AF$) right triangle, which is a multiple of the $(1, 1, \sqrt{2})$ triangle. Hence $AF = 4\sqrt{2}$ cm. Then the perimeter of $ACDF$ is $AB + BC + CD + DE + EF + FA = 8$ cm $+ 3$ cm $+ 5$ cm $+ 8$ cm $+ 4$ cm $+ 4\sqrt{2}$ cm $= 28 + 4\sqrt{2}$ cm.

13. **(C)** We recognize $(1, 1, \sqrt{2})$ as a right triangle, so $y = 90°$. Also $\left(\dfrac{1}{2}, \dfrac{\sqrt{3}}{2}, 1\right)$ is a multiple (one-half) of the $(1, \sqrt{3}, 2)$ right triangle. Hence $x° = 90°$.

14. **(A)** By the exterior angle theorem $y = x + 40$. As $y > 90$, this implies $x + 40 > 90$ or $x > 50$.

15. **(B)** By the exterior angle theorem, $z = x + y$, hence $z > x$.

16. **(B)** As $AC = AD$, $\angle ADC = x°$. By the exterior angle theorem in $\triangle ADB$, $\angle ADC = \angle DAB + w°$, so $x° = \angle DAB + w°$. As $\angle DAB > 0$, this implies that $w < x$.

17. **(D)** This is a really interesting question. The answer depends on what $y$ is. First notice that summing angles in $\triangle ABC$, $180° = x° + y° + \angle DAB + w°$. If $y$ is larger than 90°, $w$ must be smaller than $y$ or the sum of angles in $\triangle ABC$ would be greater than 180°. If $y$ is small, say 20°, then $x° = 80°$. Taking $B$ very close to $D$ would make $w°$ close in value to $x°$, certainly more than 20°.

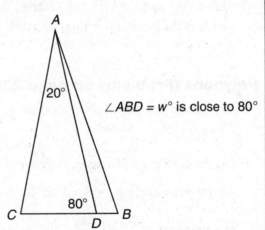

$\angle ABD = w°$ is close to 80°

18. **(A, B, C, D)** Choice A may seem too small as the area, but a diagram illustrates how a very small area may be obtained.

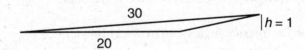

A narrow angle between the sides of length 20 and 30 makes the height equal to only 1, so that area, given by $\dfrac{1}{2}b \times h$, equals $\dfrac{1}{2} \times 20 \times 1 = 10$. Similarly, the area could equal 20 cm² or 30 cm², by creating triangles of height 2 or 3, relative to the base of 20, by varying the angle between the given sides. This makes A, B, and C correct. The maximum area occurs when the two known sides are perpendicular to each other, creating the maximum height of 30:

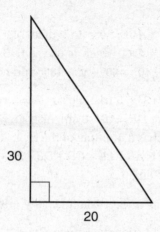

In this case, area $= \dfrac{1}{2} \times 20 \times 30 = 300$. Then D is correct and E is eliminated; the triangle's area must be less than or equal to 300.

19. **(B, E)** If the triangle is right, the Pythagorean theorem applies and $a^2 + b^2 = c^2$. One possibility is for $k$ to be the hypotenuse, and $20^2 + 30^2 = k^2$, or $400 + 900 = 1,300 = k^2$. This would mean $k = \sqrt{1,300} = \sqrt{100 \cdot 13} = 10\sqrt{13}$, choice E. But if $k$ is one of the legs and 30 is the hypotenuse, then $20^2 + k^2 = 30^2$. In this case, $400 + k^2 = 900$, so $k^2 = 500$, and $k = \sqrt{500} = \sqrt{100 \cdot 5} = 10\sqrt{5}$, choice B.

## Polygons (Problems on page 221)

1. **(A)** This is a pentagon (five sides) so the sum of its interior angles is $(5 - 2)\,180° = 540°$. So $a + b + c + d + e = 540$.

2. **(A)** As $ABCDE$ is a pentagon, the interior angles sum to $(5 - 2)180° = 540°$. As it is regular, each interior angle is $\dfrac{540°}{5} = 108°$. By vertical angles at $C$, $w = 108$. Each exterior angle of a pentagon is $72° = \left(\dfrac{360°}{5}\right)$, but $w$ is not an exterior angle. The other two angles at $C$ are exterior angles—they are formed by extending a side of the polygon.

3. **(C)** In a rectangle, diagonals bisect each other. So $AE = EC$.

4. **(C)** In an octagon the interior angles sum to $(8 - 2)\,180° = 1,080°$.

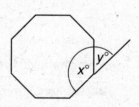

As it is regular, each of the interior angles is $\dfrac{1,080°}{8} = 135°$. So $x = 135$. The exterior angles sum to 360°, and as it is regular, each exterior angle is $\dfrac{360°}{8} = 45°$. So $y = 45$ and $180 - y = 135$.

The short answer to this question is that an interior and the corresponding exterior angle always form a straight angle so $x + y = 180$, and hence $x = 180 - y$.

5. **(C)** A regular hexagon has six sides so its interior angles sum to $(6-2)\,180° = 720°$ and each interior angle is $\dfrac{720°}{6} = 120°$. Each exterior angle of the equilateral triangle is $\dfrac{360°}{3} = 120°$.

6. **(B)** A hexagon has six sides and since it is regular each side has the same length. So each side is $\dfrac{24\,\text{cm}}{6} = 4$ cm. But $AC$ is not a side! It is the line joining vertices $A$ and $C$. Of course, $\triangle ABC$ is a triangle and obeys the Triangle Law. So $AC < AB + BC = 4$ cm $+$ 4 cm $= 8$ cm.

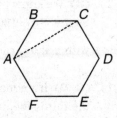

7. **(30)** Opposite interior angles in a parallelogram are equal. So $2x + 15 = 3x - 15$. Add 15 to both sides to get $2x + 30 = 3x$, then subtract $2x$ from both sides, and we have $30 = x$.

8. **(60)** As the hexagon is regular, each of its sides is 5 cm. But it shares one side with the pentagon, so each of its sides is also 5 cm. But the pentagon shares a side with the square so each side of the square is also 5 cm. Finally the equilateral triangle shares a side with the square so each of its sides is also 5 cm. Counting sides, Mary's figure has 12 sides each 5 cm long, so its perimeter is $12 \times 5$ cm $= 60$ cm.

9. **(C)** At the vertex along with $x°$ we have the interior angle of a regular hexagon, a regular pentagon, and a square. A regular hexagon has interior angles sum $(6-2)180° = 720°$; hence, each interior angle is $\dfrac{720°}{6} = 120°$. A regular pentagon has interior angles that sum $(5-2)180° = 540°$; hence, each interior angle is $\dfrac{540°}{5} = 108°$. Each interior angle in a square is 90°. These four angles form a full rotation so $120° + 108° + 90° + x° = 360°$. Then $x = 360 - 120 - 108 - 90 = 42$.

10. **(C)** First draw line segment $AC$. As $AB = BC$, $\triangle ABC$ is isosceles and $\angle BAC = \angle BCA = z°$. As $CD = DA$, $\triangle DAC$ is isosceles and $\angle DAC = \angle DCA = w°$. Then $y° = z° + w° = x°$. Notice we could have found the values of $z$ and $w$, but it was not necessary to solve the problem.

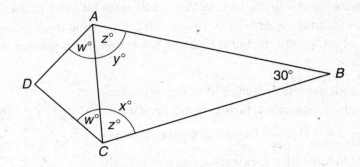

11. **(A)** As this is a convex pentagon, we know the interior angles sum to $(5-2)180° = 540°$. So $a + b + c + d + e = 540$, and $a + b + c + d = 540 - e$. How big could $e$ be? Since it is convex, $e°$ must be less than 180° and hence $540 - x > 360$.

12. **(D)** First note that $x° + y° = 180°$ since together they form a straight angle. In the given diagram, it appears that $x$ is much less than $y$. But this may not always be the case. If *ABCD* is a square, $x$ will equal $y$, and if *ABCD* is a tall skinny rectangle, $x$ will be greater than $y$.

13. **(B)** We know that in any polygon at a vertex the exterior and interior angles add to 180°. So $x + 3x = 180$, which implies that $4x = 180$ and thus $x = 45°$. In a regular polygon with $n$ sides, each exterior angle is $\frac{360°}{n}$. If $\frac{360°}{n} = 45°$, then $n = \frac{360°}{45} = 8$.

14. **(C, D)** If $x$ equaled only 9 or 10, then the sum of the two smaller sides would not exceed the third side, in violation of the triangle inequality, so choices A and B may be eliminated. In other words, the triangle inequality implies that $9 + x > 19$; A and B are too small to satisfy this strict inequality. On the other hand, choice E, 29, is too large because $9 + 19 = 28 < 29$. This would again violate the triangle inequality because the length of one side would exceed the sum of the other two. Choose the remaining choices, C and D, or 15 and 19, which are neither too small nor too large.

15. **(A, B)** This question is about recognizing that the sum of the measures of the interior angles of a quadrilateral is 360°. If you are not sure why, recall that drawing the diagonal of a quadrilateral creates two triangles, each with 180° as the angle sum. Then $2x + 3x + 4x + y = 360$, or $9x + y = 360$. We conclude that $x$ must be less than 40, because if $x ≥ 40$, then $9x ≥ 360$, which would mean $y ≤ 0$. Note: $9 × 40 = 360$. Since $y$ represents an angle measure it cannot have a zero or a negative value. This eliminates choices C, D, and E. Choose answers such that $x < 40$, A and B.

## Area (Problems on page 230)

1. **(B)** The height of a parallelogram (or triangle) must be measured along a perpendicular to the base. Unless this parallelogram is a square, the height must be less than 5 cm. As the area of a parallelogram is base times height, $A = bh = (5)h < (5)5 = 25$.

2. **(C)** For a square, $A = s^2$. So $16 = s^2$, and solving we find $s = 4$. The perimeter of a square is given by $P = 4s$ and thus $P = 4(4) = 16$.

3. **(D)** For a rectangle $A = lw$, so $16 = lw$. We cannot solve for $l$ and $w$, they could be $l = 4$ and $w = 4$, $l = 2$ and $w = 8$, or even $l = 16$ and $w = 1$. If $l = 4$ and $w = 4$, then the perimeter is $P = 2(l + w) = 2(4 + 4) = 16$, but if $l = 2$ and $w = 8$, then the perimeter is $P = 2(l + w) = 2(2 + 8) = 20$.

4. **(B)** We find the area by dividing the region into simple shapes. Region ① has area 1. Region ② is half of a $2 \times 1$ rectangle, so it has area $\frac{1}{2}(2 \times 1) = 1$. Region ③ and ④ together would form a $1 \times 1$ square—an area of 1. So the total area is $1 + 1 + 1 = 3$.

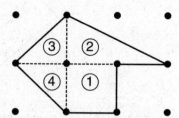

5. **(C)** If we draw in a line from $E$ to $F$, it should be apparent that $\triangle ADE$, $\triangle DFE$, $\triangle EBF$, and $\triangle CFB$ all have the same area, call it $x$. So the shaded area is $2x$ and the white area is also $2x$. Alternatively, let the height of the rectangle be $h$ and the width $w$. Then $EB = DF$ (opposite sides of a parallelogram are equal) and $EB = FC$ (given) so $DF = FC = \frac{w}{2}$.

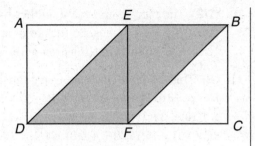

It follows that $AE = EB = \frac{w}{2}$ as well. Then the area of $\triangle AED$ is $\frac{1}{2}bh = \frac{1}{2}\left(\frac{w}{2}\right)h$. The area of $\triangle FCB$ is also $\frac{1}{2}\left(\frac{w}{2}\right)h$. So the white area is $\frac{1}{2}\left(\frac{w}{2}\right)h + \frac{1}{2}\left(\frac{w}{2}\right)h = \frac{wh}{2}$. The area of the shaded parallelogram is $bh = \left(\frac{w}{2}\right)h = \frac{wh}{2}$. So the shaded and white areas are equal.

6. **(D)** The shaded area equals the area of the rectangle minus the area of the semicircles. Since the semicircles have radius 3, they have diameter 6 and thus the width of the rectangle is $10 + 6 = 16$ cm. The area of the rectangle is $6 \times 16 = 96$ cm$^2$. Two semicircles make one full circle so the white area is $\pi r^2 = \pi(3)^2 = 9\pi$ cm$^2$. So the shaded area is $96 - 9\pi$ cm$^2$.

7. **(B)** The radius of the circle is 1 inch since the diameter of the circle is 2 inches. The area inside the circle is $\pi r^2 = \pi(1)^2 = \pi$ in$^2$. By connecting opposite vertices of the hexagon, you can see the hexagon is made of six equilateral triangles. (Why are they equilateral? The six angles at the center of the circle are equal and together add to 360°. As two sides of each triangle are radii, and the angle between them is 60°, the other two angles are equal and add to $180 - 60 = 120°$ and thus are also 60°.) The height of an equilateral triangle is $\frac{\sqrt{3}}{2}$ times the side length. In this case, the side length is 1 in. So each of those equilateral triangles has area $\frac{1}{2}(1)\left(\frac{\sqrt{3}}{2}\right) = \frac{\sqrt{3}}{4}$ in$^2$. Finally the shaded area is $\pi - 6\left(\frac{\sqrt{3}}{4}\right) = \pi - \frac{3\sqrt{3}}{2}$ in$^2$.

8. **(A)** The key to this question is to notice that the diagonal of the square must be the diameter of the circle. As the area of the square is 4 m$^2$, each side is 2 m. The diameter of any square is $\sqrt{2}$ times its side length. That means the diagonal of the square (and the diameter of the circle) is $2\sqrt{2}$ m. Hence the circumference of the circle is $\pi d = \pi(2\sqrt{2}) = 2\sqrt{2}\pi$ m.

9. **(C)** As the width of the rink is 50, the diameter of the circles is 50 and thus the radius is 25. The two circular ends together make a circle of area $\pi r^2 = \pi(25)^2 = 625\pi$ ft$^2$. Roughly approximating $\pi$ as 3, this is $625 \times 3 = 1{,}875$ ft$^2$. Since $\pi$ is greater than 3, maybe the area is closer to 2,000 ft$^2$. The remaining rectangle has height 50 ft and length 150 ft (because it is 200 – two radii). So its area is $50 \times 150 = 7{,}500$ ft$^2$. Added together the area of the rink is at least $7{,}500 + 1{,}875 = 9{,}375$ and maybe about $7{,}500 + 2{,}000 = 9{,}500$ ft$^2$. 9,500 seems to be the best approximation.

10. **(112)** The picture and mat together has a width of $14 + 2 + 2 = 18$ inches and height of $10 + 2 + 2 = 14$ inches. So that total area is $14 \times 18 = 252 \text{ in}^2$. The area of the picture is $10 \times 14 = 140 \text{ in}^2$. Thus the area of the mat is $252 - 140 = 112 \text{ in}^2$.

11. **(E)** This is a good problem to try substituting numbers into the given answers. Let's use $H = W = 10$. Then A is $2H + 4(W - 2) = 2(10) + 4(8) = 20 + 32 = 52$, B is $2(H - 4) + 4W = 2(6) + 4(10) = 52$, C is $WH - (W - 2)(H - 4) = (10)(10) - (8)(6) = 100 - 48 = 52$, D is $2(H - 4) + 4(W - 2) + 4(2) = 2(6) + 4(8) + 4(2) = 12 + 32 + 8 = 52$, and E is $(W + 1)(H + 2) - WH = (11)(12) - 10^2 = 132 - 100 = 32$. Since only E has a different value, it must be the case that it is the incorrect formula.

    Alternate approach: Although it would seem strange to use $H = W = 0$ (since the width has to be greater than 2 and the height greater than 4), it would be a valid and much simpler way to find which formula is not equal to the others.

12. **(D)** No matter what $\angle ADC$ is, the area of the parallelogram is $hw$. When $\angle ADC$ is a very small angle (like 1°), the sides $AD$ and $BC$ become very large, and thus the perimeter can be incredibly large, certainly more than the area. When $\angle ADC$ is 90°, the perimeter of $ABCD$ is smallest with a value of $2(h + w)$. Is that smaller than the area? As $h < w$, $2(h + w) < 2(w + w) = 4w$. But $4 < h$ so $4w < hw$. Yes, the perimeter can be smaller than the area.

13. **(C)** The small white circle has diameter 6 cm and thus radius 3 cm. So eight times its area is $8\pi r^2 = 8\pi(3)^2 = 72\pi$. The large circle has radius 9 cm so its area is $\pi(9)^2 = 81\pi$. We subtract the area of the white circle to find the shaded area $81\pi - \pi(3)^2 = 81\pi - 9\pi = 72\pi$.

14. **(A)** The area of the circle is $\pi r^2$, which equals $4\pi$. So $4 = r^2$ and hence $r = 2$ and the diameter of the circle is 4. The key to this question is to note that a diagonal of the rectangle is a diameter of the circle. Now using Pythagoras's Theorem $x^2 + (3x)^2 = 4^2$. We simplify to see $x^2 + 9x^2 = 16 \Rightarrow 10x^2 = 16 \Rightarrow x^2 = 1.6$. Then as $1 < x^2$ and $x$ is positive, we can conclude that $1 < x$. Alternatively, if $x < 1$, it is clear that $x^2$ would be less than 1, but it's not. So $x > 1$.

15. **(B)** In ① the large semicircle has radius 6, which is the diameter of the small semicircle. So the small semicircle has radius 3. To find the area of ①, we find the area of the large semicircle and subtract the area of a small circle (the two semi-circles = 1 small circle). So the area of ① is $\frac{1}{2}\pi(6)^2 - \pi(3)^2 = \frac{1}{2}(36\pi) - 9\pi = 18\pi - 9\pi = 9\pi$. In ② the three small semicircles share the diameter of the large semicircle. So the diameter of each small semicircle is $\frac{12}{3} = 4$. Then the radius of a small semicircle is 2. To find the area of ② we find the area of the large semicircle minus the area of three small semicircles. The area of ② is $\frac{1}{2}\pi(6)^2 - 3\left(\frac{1}{2}\pi(2^2)\right) = 18\pi - \frac{3}{2}(4\pi) = 18\pi - 6\pi = 12\pi$.

16. **(C)** The perimeter of the large semicircle (in ① and ②) is $\frac{1}{2}\pi d = \frac{1}{2}\pi(12) = 6\pi$. The perimeter of the two semicircles is like the perimeter of one small circle, $\pi d = \pi(6) = 6\pi$. The total perimeter of ① is $12\pi$. In ② each small semicircle has perimeter $\frac{1}{2}(2\pi r) = \frac{1}{2}(2\pi(2)) = 2\pi$. So the total perimeter of ② is $6\pi + 2\pi + 2\pi + 2\pi = 12\pi$. Remarkably, both figures have the same perimeter.

17. **(B, C, F, H)** The area of a rectangle equals length × width, so try to find pairs of whole numbers whose product is 24. These are (6, 4), (8, 3), (12, 2), and (24, 1). Then find the perimeter associated with a rectangle having these pairs of values as $l$ and $w$, length and width, respectively. Perimeter equals $2(l + w)$, so we have four possibilities for perimeter:

$2(6 + 4) = 2 \times 10 = 20$

$2(8 + 3) = 2 \times 11 = 22$

$2(12 + 2) = 2 \times 14 = 28$

$2(24 + 1) = 2 \times 25 = 50$

Choose 20, 22, 28, and 50.

## Surface Area and Volume (Problems on page 239)

1. **(B)** To find the diagonal, we first find the length of $AD$. We can see that it is the hypotenuse of a (3, 4, 5) triangle so $AD$ is 5. Now $\triangle ADC$ is also a right triangle. So $AD^2 + DC^2 = AC^2$. But $AD = 5$ and $DC = 12$, so $5^2 + 12^2 = AC^2$, and thus $169 = AC^2$ or $AC = 13$. A quicker answer is to notice that $\triangle ADC$ is a (5, 12, 13) triangle. As 13 < 15 choose B. If you noted the tips, you would know the shortest way to find the diagonal of the box is $\sqrt{3^2 + 4^2 + 12^2} = 13$.

2. **(B)** The surface area of the box is given by $SA = 2lw + 2wh + 2lh = 2(12)(3) + 2(3)(4) + 2(12)(4) = 72 + 24 + 96 = 192 \text{ cm}^2$.

3. **(B)** The volume is given by $V = s^3 = (\sqrt{2})^3 = 2\sqrt{2}$.

4. **(B)** The diagonal of a cube is always $\sqrt{3}s$. If $4 = \sqrt{3}s$ then $s = \dfrac{4}{\sqrt{3}}$. The surface area is $SA = 6s^2 = 6\left(\dfrac{4}{\sqrt{3}}\right)^2 = \dfrac{6 \times 16}{3} = 32$.

5. **(C)** Since surface area equals volume in magnitude, we have $6s^2 = s^3$. Divide both sides by $s^2$, and we see that $s = 6$.

6. **(A, B)** For a cube of side length 6, $V = s^3 = (6)^3 = 216$ while $SA = 6s^2 = 6(6)^2 = 216$. A is true. For a box with dimensions $4 \times 8 \times 8$, $V = lwh = (4)(8)(8) = 256$, while $SA = 2lw + 2hw + 2lh = 2(4)(8) + 2(8)(8) + 2(4)(8) = 64 + 128 + 64 = 256$. So B is true. For a box with dimensions $1 \times 2 \times 3$, $V = lwh = (1)(2)(3) = 6$, while $SA = 2lw + 2hw + 2lh = 2(1)(2) + 2(3)(2) + 2(1)(3) = 4 + 12 + 6 = 22$. C is not true.

7. **(B)** We label the cubes to aid our discussion. The surface area of this shape includes five faces from ①, four faces from ②, four faces from ③, and five faces from ④. Each face is $2 \times 2$ so it has area 4. That makes a total of $18 \times 4 = 72$ square units of surface area. The box with dimensions $2 \times 4 \times 6$ has surface area $2lw + 2wh + 2lh = 2(2)(4) + 2(4)(6) + 2(2)(6) = 16 + 48 + 24 = 88$. As 88 > 72.

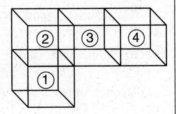

8. **(C)** The least (or minimum) increase in surface area occurs when the new cube covers as many existing faces as possible. In this case that would be two when the new cube is placed under ③. Then it covers two faces and adds four more in surface area. That's a net change of 2 faces or $2(2)(2) = 8$ square units increase in surface area. Adding one cube, the increase in volume is the volume of the new cube or $V = s^3 = (2)^3 = 8$. Ignoring units, the values are equal.

9. **(C)** To have a maximum increase in surface area, we want to cover as little as possible of the existing surface area. If the new cube touches the existing figure in just one face, say if it was placed on top of ②, then it covers one face and adds five more in surface area. That's a net change of 4 faces or $4(2)(2) = 16$ square units increase in surface area.

10. **(A)** The volume of the cube is $V = s^3$ while the sphere has volume $V = \dfrac{4\pi r^3}{3}$. If they are equal, then $s^3 = \dfrac{4\pi r^3}{3}$ so $s = \sqrt[3]{\dfrac{4\pi r^3}{3}} = \left(\sqrt[3]{\dfrac{4\pi}{3}}\right) r$. Notice some estimation shows us that $\sqrt[3]{\dfrac{4\pi}{3}} \cong \sqrt[3]{4} = \sqrt[3]{2}\sqrt[3]{2} \cong (1.7)$. $(1.7)^2 = 2.89$. Then the surface area of the sphere is $4\pi r^2$ while the surface area of the cube is $6s^2 = 6\left(\sqrt[3]{\dfrac{4\pi}{3}}\right)^2 r^2$, which is approximately $6(2.89)^2 r^2$, which is certainly more than $4\pi r^2$. This is a terribly tricky estimation even with the calculator—perhaps too much to expect on the GRE. But if you remember the tip that for a fixed volume the sphere has the smallest surface area, this and any related problems become very simple.

11. **(D)** Boxes ①, ②, and ④ each contribute five faces of surface area. Box ② only contributes three faces of surface area (the other three are hidden). In total the object has $3 \times 5 + 3 = 18$ faces of equal size for surface area. If the blue boxes are two of ①, ②, and ④, then there will be 10 blue faces and thus $\dfrac{10}{18} = \dfrac{5}{9}$ of the surface area will be blue.

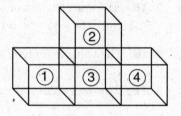

If the blue boxes are ③ and one of the other boxes, then there will be 8 blue faces, and thus $\dfrac{8}{18} = \dfrac{4}{9}$ of the surface area will be blue. As one possible answer is greater than $\dfrac{1}{2}$ and the other is less than $\dfrac{1}{2}$, choose D.

12. **(B)** Red surface area is maximized when the red cubes are some two of boxes ①, ②, and ④, in which case they have $\dfrac{10}{18}$ faces of surface area. As a percentage $\dfrac{10}{18} \times 100\% = \dfrac{5}{9} \times 100\% = \dfrac{500}{9}\%$, which is approximately 55.6%.

13. **(B)** From our tips, the largest distance inside the cylindrical can is $\sqrt{(2r)^2 + h^2} = \sqrt{(2 \times 2)^2 + (8)^2} = \sqrt{16 + 64} = \sqrt{80}$. The largest distance inside the box is the diagonal, which is $\sqrt{l^2 + w^2 + h^2} = \sqrt{4^2 + 4^2 + 7^2} = \sqrt{81} = 9$.

14. **(60)** Volume can be found by area of the base times height. In this case that is $\frac{1}{2}(3)(5)(8)$ = 60 cm$^3$. If you don't remember that formula, you could think of it as one-half of a $3 \times 5 \times 8$ box.

15. **(24)** The tray has volume $V = lwh = (4)(6)(8) = 192$. Each cube has volume $V = s^3 = (2)^3 = 8$. Based strictly on volume, there could be $192 \div 8 = 24$ cubes in the tray. Do they actually fit? Since all the dimensions are multiples of 2, the side length of the cube, they will indeed fit.

16. **(B)** As the cube just fits, the longest length in the cube, the diagonal, must be the diameter of the sphere. The surface area of the cube is given by $6s^2$. Since that must equal 36, we conclude that $s^2 = 6$ and thus $s = \sqrt{6}$. The diagonal of the cube will be $\sqrt{3}s = \sqrt{3}\sqrt{6} = \sqrt{18} = 3\sqrt{2}$. Thus the diameter of the sphere is $3\sqrt{2}$.

17. **(C, E, G)** A common formula for the volume of a box is $l \times w \times h$. Since the area of one side of the box—say the base—is $l \times w$, we can also think of volume as base area $\times$ height. The area of the base is given as 35, so

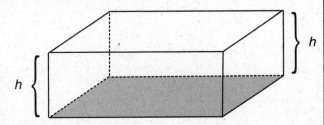

possible volumes are those of the form $35n$ for integers $n$, or in other words, integer multiples of 35. We are given that each side length is an integer *greater than 1*, so choice A, 35, is eliminated. The correct multiples of 35 listed in the choices are 70, 105, and 140. If you can't compute these in your head, the calculator shows that $35 \times 2 = 70$, while $35 \times 3 = 105$, and $35 \times 4 = 140$. In these cases the height would be 2, 3, or 4; for all remaining choices, the height would not be an integer.

# Sample Exams and Solutions | 7

When trying these two sample sections, which would make up the quantitative reasoning part of a GRE exam, try to simulate the actual circumstances of the test as best as possible.

- Take this test in a quiet room.
- Turn off all cell phones, pagers, music players, and other possible disturbances.
- Keep a clock handy and give yourself exactly 35 minutes to complete each section.
- Your only aids should be a pencil, basic calculator, and several sheets of blank paper.

As you take the sample test, take it seriously.

- Focus on the test and each problem, but try to stay calm and relaxed.
- Keep a careful watch of the time left.
- Try to average 90 seconds per question.
- Guess if you cannot complete all questions in the time allotted.

Good luck!

# ANSWER SHEET 1
# SAMPLE TEST 1

1. (A) (B) (C) (D)
2. (A) (B) (C) (D)
3. (A) (B) (C) (D)
4. (A) (B) (C) (D)
5. (A) (B) (C) (D)
6. (A) (B) (C) (D)

7. (A) (B) (C) (D)
8. (A) (B) (C) (D)
9. (A) (B) (C) (D)
10. (A) (B) (C) (D) (E)
11. (A) (B) (C) (D) (E)
12. (A) (B) (C) (D) (E)

13. (A) (B) (C)
14. (A) (B) (C) (D) (E)
15. (A) (B) (C) (D) (E)
16. _____
17. _____
18. (A) (B) (C) (D) (E)

19. _____
20. (A) (B) (C) (D) (E) (F)
21. (A) (B) (C) (D) (E) (F)

In this section use scrap paper to solve each problem. Then decide which is the best of the choices given and fill in the corresponding circle on the Answer Sheet.

**Time—45 Minutes, 21 Questions**

1.

| Quantity A | Quantity B |
|---|---|
| $\left(\dfrac{1}{3}\right)^8$ | $\left(\dfrac{1}{8}\right)^3$ |

2.

| Quantity A | Quantity B |
|---|---|
| $\dfrac{4}{5}$ of $\dfrac{6}{7}$ | $\dfrac{7}{8}$ of $\dfrac{9}{10}$ |

3.

$p$ is a prime

| Quantity A | Quantity B |
|---|---|
| The number of factors of $p + 1$ | The number of factors of $p$ |

4.

63% of $a$ is 72

| Quantity A | Quantity B |
|---|---|
| $2a$ | 250 |

5.

| Quantity A | Quantity B |
|---|---|
| $5 \times 5^2 \times 5^3$ | $\dfrac{1}{\left(\dfrac{1}{5}\right)^3}$ |

6.

| Quantity A | Quantity B |
|---|---|
| Remainder when 1,003 is divided by 4 | Remainder when 1,004 is divided by 3 |

7.

$$x + 2y = 4$$
$$2x + y = 5$$

| Quantity A | Quantity B |
|---|---|
| Average (arithmetic mean) of $x$ and $y$ | 4.5 |

8.

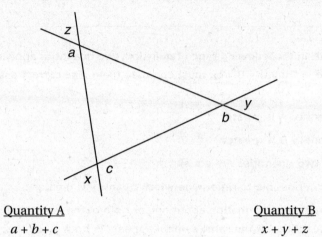

| Quantity A | Quantity B |
|---|---|
| $a + b + c$ | $x + y + z$ |

9.     The midpoints of a square are joined to form another square

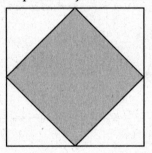

| Quantity A | Quantity B |
|---|---|
| Shaded area | Unshaded area |

**DIRECTIONS:** In the following questions, choose the best answer from the five choices listed.

QUESTIONS 10 AND 11 ARE CONCERNED WITH THE TABLES BELOW.*

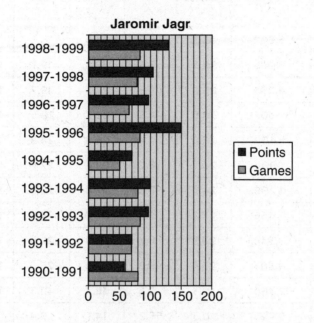

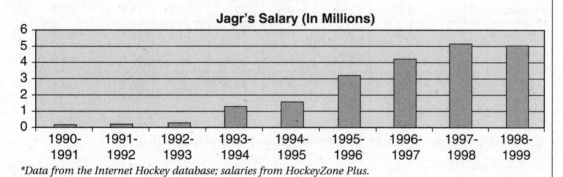

*Data from the Internet Hockey database; salaries from HockeyZone Plus.*

10. In which season did Jagr earn the most money per game?

   (A) 1994–1995

   (B) 1995–1996

   (C) 1996–1997

   (D) 1997–1998

   (E) 1998–1999

11. In which season did Jagr average the most points per game?

   (A) 1990–1991

   (B) 1995–1996

   (C) 1996–1997

   (D) 1997–1998

   (E) 1998–1999

## U.S. Census 2000 for St. Lawrence County, New York

| Place | Population | Under 18 (%) | 18–24 (%) | 25–44 (%) | 45–64 (%) | 65+ (%) | Males per 100 females |
|---|---|---|---|---|---|---|---|
| Brasher Falls-Winthrop | 1,140 | 23.4 | 7.7 | 24.9 | 23.9 | 20.1 | 89.4 |
| Canton | 5,882 | 12.3 | 45.8 | 16.7 | 13.6 | 11.7 | 101.2 |
| Edwards | 465 | 29.5 | 7.3 | 27.5 | 19.1 | 16.6 | 90.6 |
| Gouverneur | 4,263 | 29.8 | 9.5 | 27.3 | 19.7 | 13.7 | 90.6 |
| Hammond | 302 | 30.5 | 4.3 | 26.2 | 20.5 | 18.5 | 85.3 |
| Hermon | 402 | 26.4 | 7.2 | 26.6 | 24.8 | 15.2 | 103.0 |
| Heuvelton | 804 | 24.3 | 6.0 | 28.7 | 27.0 | 14.1 | 86.1 |
| Massena | 11,209 | 24.1 | 7.0 | 27.4 | 22.6 | 18.9 | 88.4 |
| Morristown | 456 | 27.9 | 5.7 | 27.0 | 25.9 | 13.6 | 92.4 |
| Norfolk | 1,334 | 23.9 | 8.2 | 26.5 | 22.5 | 18.9 | 94.2 |
| Norwood | 1,685 | 23.4 | 8.8 | 28.4 | 25.6 | 13.7 | 97.5 |
| Ogdensburg | 12,364 | 21.3 | 9.5 | 35.3 | 21.3 | 12.4 | 127.6 |
| Potsdam | 9,425 | 11.3 | 56.2 | 14.1 | 9.4 | 9.1 | 110.1 |
| Rensselaer | 337 | 28.5 | 8.6 | 29.4 | 20.2 | 13.4 | 93.7 |
| Richville | 274 | 23.7 | 9.5 | 32.8 | 21.5 | 12.4 | 101.5 |
| Star Lake | 860 | 23.6 | 6.7 | 26.3 | 26.6 | 16.7 | 95.9 |
| Waddington | 923 | 18.2 | 7.2 | 23.4 | 30.8 | 20.5 | 93.1 |

*Data from the U.S. Census Bureau.*

12. Which place has the largest number of minors (those younger than 18)?

   Ⓐ Massena
   Ⓑ Ogdensburg
   Ⓒ Potsdam
   Ⓓ Hammond
   Ⓔ Gouverneur

13. Which of the following statements can be inferred from the data given?

Indicate *all* that apply.

   [A] There are more teenage girls than teenage boys in Star Lake.
   [B] The only places with at least 1,000 minors are Potsdam, Massena, Ogdensburg, and Gouverneur.
   [C] There are 45 more men than women in Hammond.

14. All three circles shown have radius 1 and are tangent to each other. Find the perimeter of the shaded region.

    (A) 3

    (B) $\pi$

    (C) $\dfrac{3}{2}\pi$

    (D) $2\pi$

    (E) $3\pi$

15. The USS *Mathematica* sailed 6 knots north, then 5 knots east, then 2 knots south. How far, in knots, was the ship from her starting point?

    (A) 3

    (B) $\sqrt{41}$

    (C) $\sqrt{61}$

    (D) 41

    (E) 61

16. If $2x + 35 = 9x$, then what is the value of $\dfrac{3}{5}x$?

17. The advertised rate for roaming charges is 0.002 cents per second. What is that in dollars per hour?

    $\dfrac{\$}{hr}$

18. What is the average of four consecutive odd numbers starting with $2n + 1$?

    (A) 4

    (B) $2n + 3$

    (C) $2n + 4$

    (D) $2n + 5$

    (E) $n + 4$

19. In the year 2007 Paul was twice as old as his brother Biko. In the year 2015 Paul was only four years older than his brother. In what year was Biko born?

20. The functions $f$ and $g$ are defined as follows: $f(x) = 4x + 3$ and $g(x) = x^2 - 10$. Which of the following is greater than $f(9)$?

Indicate *all* that apply.

A   $g(5)$
B   $g(7)$
C   $g(9)$
D   $g(-6)$
E   $g(-8)$
F   $g(-10)$

21. A box contains various lettered tiles. When a tile is drawn at random, the probability of selecting the letter D is $\frac{1}{8}$, the probability of selecting the letter N is $\frac{1}{12}$, and the probability of selecting the letter F is $\frac{1}{9}$. Which of the following could be the total number of tiles in the jar?

Indicate *all* that apply.

A   60
B   72
C   96
D   144
E   256
F   288

## ANSWERS

| | | | |
|---|---|---|---|
| **1.** B | **7.** B | **13.** B | **19.** 2003 |
| **2.** B | **8.** A | **14.** B | **20.** C, E, F |
| **3.** D | **9.** C | **15.** B | **21.** B, D, F |
| **4.** B | **10.** D | **16.** 3 | |
| **5.** A | **11.** B | **17.** .072 | |
| **6.** A | **12.** A | **18.** C | |

## Detailed Solutions

1. **(B)** This question really asks which is bigger, $\dfrac{1}{3^8}$ or $\dfrac{1}{8^3}$. A feasible but time-consuming strategy is to multiply out the denominators. Alternatively you can notice that $3^8 = 3^{2 \times 4} = (3^2)^4 = 9^4$, and since $9 > 8$, we conclude that $9^3 > 8^3$. Then clearly $9^4 = 9 \times 9^3 > 8^3$; hence $3^8 > 8^3$ and $\dfrac{1}{3^8} < \dfrac{1}{8^3}$.

2. **(B)** A computational approach would be to multiply out and then do equal operations to each quantity until it is clear which is bigger. For instance,

$$\frac{4}{5} \times \frac{6}{7} \qquad \frac{7}{8} \times \frac{9}{10}$$

Clear the denominators by multiplying each quantity by $7 \times 8 \times 10$, cancelling where you can.

$$2 \times 8 \times 4 \times 6 \qquad 7 \times 7 \times 9$$

$$64 \times 6 \qquad 49 \times 9$$

Clearly Quantity B is larger so choose B.

   Alternatively, we can type these values on the calculator. Quantity A is $24 \div 35 \approx 0.69$, while B is $63 \div 80 \approx 0.79$.

3. **(D)** If $p$ is prime, $p$ has precisely two factors—one and itself. If $p$ is an odd prime, then $p + 1$ is even and always has at least three factors (1, 2, and itself). But when $p = 2$, the only even prime, then $p + 1 = 3$, and it also has two factors. Hence sometimes they have an equal number of factors and sometimes $p + 1$ has more.

4. **(B)** We solve for $a$. $\dfrac{63}{100} \times a = 72$; hence, $a = 72 \times \dfrac{100}{63}$ and $2a = 144 \times \dfrac{100}{63}$. We don't know exactly what $100 \div 63$ is, but it is a little more than $1.5 \left( \dfrac{100}{63} = 1 + \dfrac{37}{63} \right)$. 1.5 times 144 is 216, nowhere near 250, so 250 must be larger than $2a$. Alternatively, set up the equation $.63a = 72$. Divide both sides by $.63$ to get $a = 72 \div 63 \approx 114$. Twice this is less than 250.

5. **(A)** We use rules of exponents to see that Quantity A is $5 \times 5^2 \times 5^3 = 5^6$. Quantity B is equal to $\dfrac{1}{\frac{1}{5^3}} = 1 \times \dfrac{5^3}{1} = 5^3$.

6. **(A)** Since 1,000 is divisible by 4, $1{,}003 \div 4 = 250$ R 3. The remainder when dividing by 3 is always less than 3. Alternatively just use long division—it shouldn't take too long and leads to the same conclusion.

7. **(B)** One can solve for $x$ and $y$ and then compute their average, but it's not necessary to do so. Adding both equations together we get $3x + 3y = 9$. Divide both sides by 3 to see that $x + y = 3$. Hence the average of $x$ and $y$ is $\frac{3}{2}$ or 1.5.

8. **(A)** Label the internal angles of the triangles as $A$, $B$, and $C$. Then by vertical angles, $x = A$, $y = B$, and $z = C$. As the sum of interior angles of a triangle is 180°, $A + B + C = 180°$ and hence $x + y + z = 180°$. If you recall that the sum of the exterior angles of a triangle are 360° and notice that $a$, $b$, $c$ are exterior angles, then you will know that $a + b + c = 360°$.

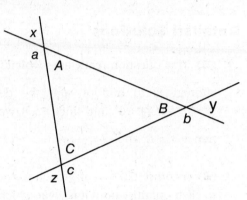

Alternatively, since $a$ and $x$ are supplementary angles, $a + x = 180°$. Similarly $c + z = 180°$ and $b + y = 180°$. Adding all three equations, we see that $a + z + c + x + b + y = 540°$. Rearranging the left-hand side $(a + b + c) + (x + y + z) = 540°$. But $x + y + z = 180°$, so $(a + b + c) + 180° = 540°$. Hence $a + b + c = 360°$.

9. **(C)** If you add a vertical and horizontal line to the diagram at the midpoints of the square, you should be able to see that the shaded and unshaded areas are each composed of four congruent triangles. Hence their areas are equal.

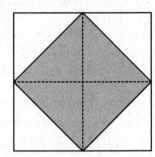

10. **(D)** We need to compare the ratios salary/games. The first graph tells us how many games he played each season, and the second graph tells us his salary. Estimating carefully we see that the ratios are approximately A: $\frac{1.5}{50}$, B: $\frac{3.2}{80}$, C: $\frac{4.1}{64}$, D: $\frac{5.1}{75}$, and E: $\frac{5}{80}$.

Each ratio is in millions of dollars per game. Which of those fractions is largest? Clearly E > B and C > A so A and B are out. Also E has a smaller numerator and a larger denominator than D, so D > E. E is out. That just leaves C and D to consider. If we approximate $\frac{4.1}{64} \approx \frac{4}{64} = \frac{1}{16}$, while $\frac{5.1}{75} \approx \frac{5}{75} = \frac{1}{15}$. As $\frac{1}{15} > \frac{1}{16}$.

If you are uncomfortable with that approximation (yes, they are very close in value), let's check this precisely. Finding common denominators we see that $\frac{4.1}{64} \times \frac{75}{75} = \frac{307.5}{64 \times 75}$, while $\frac{5.1}{75} \times \frac{64}{64} = \frac{326.4}{64 \times 75}$. Again D is larger.

11. **(B)** We can read both points and games from the first graph and simply compare the length of the dark rectangle (points) to the light rectangle (games) for each season. In 1995–1996, the dark rectangle is much larger than the light rectangle; in fact, it is almost twice as large (150 points/81 games). No other ratio comes close.

12. **(A)** To find the number of minors we must multiply the percentage of the population younger than 18 by the population. It would be too time consuming to do this for all the places so start with the one with the largest population. Consider Massena and roughly estimate a population of 10,000 with 25% minors or 2,500 minors. Only places with more population than 2,500 could have more minors. This immediately rules out all places except Canton, Gouverneur, Ogdensburg, and Potsdam. Rough estimates show that Canton has approximately 10% of 5,000 or 500 minors, Gouverneur has 30% of 4,000 or 1,200 minors, Ogdensburg has 20% of 12,000 or 2,400 minors, and Potsdam has 10% of 9,000 or 900 minors. Massena and Ogdensburg are close so we will estimate more precisely.

| Massena | 11,209 people | Ogdensburg | 12,364 people |
|---|---|---|---|
| 10% | 1,121 | 10% | 1,236 |
| 20% | 2,242 | 20% | 2,472 |
| 1% | 112 | 1% | 124 |
| 2% | 224 | 21% = 20% + 1% | 2,596 |
| 4% | 448 | | |
| 24% = 20% + 4% | 2,690 | | |

Choose Massena, A.

13. **(B)** In Star Lake there are 95.9 males for each 100 females so there are more females than males. But there is no way to infer how that affects a segment of the population like teenagers. In fact we don't know how many teenagers there are—just minors. It cannot be inferred from the data.

We have already seen in question 12 that Massena, Ogdensburg, and Gouverneur have at least 1,000 minors. For Potsdam our rough estimate of 900 suggests we try a more precise estimate.

| Potsdam | 9,425 people |
|---|---|
| 10% | 942 |
| 1% | 94 |
| 11% = 10% + 1% | 1,036 |

Potsdam, with 11.3% minors, will have more than 1,036 minors. Yes, B can be inferred from the data

Hammond has 85.3 men for each 100 women. That means Hammond has more women than men. C cannot be inferred from the data because it is false!

14. **(B)** If you connect the centers of the three circles you will form an equilateral triangle. The shaded region is formed from the triangle by removing the pie-shaped pieces, each with angle 60° as an equilateral triangle has 60° angles. If we reassemble the arcs forming the perimeter of the shaded area we can form a semicircle ($3 \times 60° = 180°$). So the perimeter of the shaded area equals the circumference of the semicircle $P = \dfrac{1}{2} \times 2\pi r = \pi(1) = \pi$.

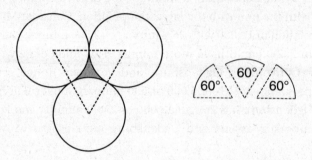

15. **(B)** Draw a diagram.

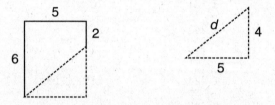

You can see that the ship is 5 knots east of its starting point and by subtraction we know it is $6 - 2 = 4$ knots north of its starting point. We simply use the Pythagorean theorem to find $d$. So $4^2 + 5^2 = d^2$ and thus $d = \sqrt{4^2 + 5^2} = \sqrt{41}$.

A common error here would be to assume that this is a 3, 4, 5 triangle. It's not. The hypotenuse must be 5 in a (3, 4, 5) triangle.

16. **(3)** First we solve for $x$. If $2x + 35 = 9x$, subtract $2x$ from both sides to get $35 = 7x$. Then divide by 7 to see that $x = 5$. Finally $\dfrac{3}{5}x = \dfrac{3}{5} \times 5 = 3$. $\dfrac{3}{5}x = \mathbf{3}$.

17. **(.072)** We use simple conversion factors.

$$\frac{0.002¢}{s} \times \frac{1\$}{100¢} \times \frac{60\,s}{1\,min} \times \frac{60\,min}{1\,hr} = \frac{0.002 \times 3600}{100} \frac{\$}{hr} = \frac{7.2}{100} \frac{\$}{hr} = 0.072 \frac{\$}{hr}.$$

When multiplying, think $2 \times 3{,}600$, and then move the decimals to find the final answer.

18. **(C)** Remembering to add 2 to get to the next odd number, the four numbers in question are $2n + 1$, $2n + 3$, $2n + 5$, and $2n + 7$. The average of consecutive (odd) numbers is the middle number (odd amount of numbers) or the average of the two middle numbers (even amount of numbers). In this case (4 is even) the middle numbers $2n + 3$ and $2n + 5$ have an average of $2n + 4$.

Alternatively, add and divide by 4.

$$[(2n + 1) + (2n + 3) + (2n + 5) + (2n + 7)] \div 4 =$$

$$[8n + 16] \div 4 = 2n + 4$$

19. **(2003)** A table can help here.

|      | Paul      | Biko  |
|------|-----------|-------|
| 2007 | 2*x*      | *x*   |
| 2015 | *x* + 8 + 4 | *x* + 8 |

Let Biko's age in 2007 be *x*. Since Paul is twice Biko's age, Paul is 2*x*. In 2015, 8 years have passed so Biko is now *x* + 8. Paul is only four years older so Paul is *x* + 8 + 4. But Paul is also 2*x* + 8 since 8 years have passed for him as well. So 2*x* + 8 = *x* + 8 + 4, and solving we find *x* = 4. That means Biko was 4 in 2007 and hence he was born in 2003.

20. **(C, E, F)** Find $f(9)$ by putting 9 in as *x*: $f(9) = 4(9) + 3 = 36 + 3 = 39$. Now evaluate each answer choice by the given rule $g(x) = x^2 - 10$. Choice A is $g(5) = 5^2 - 10 = 25 - 10 = 15$. Choice B is $g(7) = 7^2 - 10 = 49 - 10 = 39$. Choice C is $g(9) = 9^2 - 10 = 81 - 10 = 71$. Of these, only C is correct, since 71 > 39. For the negative values of *x*, E and F are correct, because $(-8)^2 - 10 = 64 - 10 = 54$ and $(-10)^2 - 10 = 100 - 10 = 90$. Both 54 and 90 are greater than 39.

21. **(B, D, F)** If the probability of selecting letter D is $\frac{1}{8}$, then letter D tiles must comprise $\frac{1}{8}$ of the total number of tiles in the box. Then the number of D's equals the total number of tiles divided by 8, so this total must be divisible by 8. Similarly, the total number of tiles is divisible by both 9 and 12 because of the given proportions of the letters N and F. Then the correct answers are exactly those that are multiples of all three of these numbers. The least common multiple of 8, 9, and 12 is 72, which can be obtained by finding the prime factorization of the three numbers, or by simply noting 8 × 9 = 72 and 12 × 6 = 72. This means B, 72, is correct. Any other multiple of 8, 9, and 12 will also be a multiple 72, the least common multiple. Note that 144 = 72 × 2, and that 288 = 144 × 2, or 72 × 4. So 72, 144, and 288 are correct, or B, D, and F.

# ANSWER SHEET 2
# SAMPLE TEST 2

1. Ⓐ Ⓑ Ⓒ Ⓓ    7. Ⓐ Ⓑ Ⓒ Ⓓ Ⓔ    13. Ⓐ Ⓑ Ⓒ Ⓓ Ⓔ    18. Ⓐ Ⓑ Ⓒ Ⓓ

2. Ⓐ Ⓑ Ⓒ Ⓓ    8. Ⓐ Ⓑ Ⓒ Ⓓ Ⓔ    14. ⬚    19. Ⓐ Ⓑ Ⓒ Ⓓ Ⓔ Ⓕ

3. Ⓐ Ⓑ Ⓒ Ⓓ    9. Ⓐ Ⓑ Ⓒ Ⓓ Ⓔ    ⬚    20. Ⓐ Ⓑ Ⓒ Ⓓ

4. Ⓐ Ⓑ Ⓒ Ⓓ    10. Ⓐ Ⓑ Ⓒ Ⓓ Ⓔ    15. Ⓐ Ⓑ Ⓒ Ⓓ Ⓔ

5. Ⓐ Ⓑ Ⓒ Ⓓ    11. ⬚    16. Ⓐ Ⓑ Ⓒ Ⓓ Ⓔ

6. Ⓐ Ⓑ Ⓒ Ⓓ    12. Ⓐ Ⓑ Ⓒ Ⓓ Ⓔ    17. Ⓐ Ⓑ Ⓒ Ⓓ Ⓔ

# SAMPLE TEST 2

In this section use scrap paper to solve each problem. Then decide which is the best of the choices given and fill in the corresponding circle on the Answer Sheet.

---

**DIRECTIONS:** In the following type of question, two quantities appear, one in Quantity A and one in Quantity B. You must compare them. The correct answer to the question is

Ⓐ if Quantity A is greater

Ⓑ if Quantity B is greater

Ⓒ if the two quantities are equal

Ⓓ if it is impossible to determine which quantity is greater

**NOTE:** Sometimes information about one or both of the amounts is centered above the two quantities. If the same symbol appears in both quantities, it represents the same thing each time.

---

**Time—45 Minutes, 20 Questions**

1.
| Quantity A | Quantity B |
|---|---|
| $\dfrac{-1}{2} \times \dfrac{-2}{3} \times \dfrac{-3}{4} \times \dfrac{-4}{5}$ | $\dfrac{-5}{4} \times \dfrac{-4}{3} \times \dfrac{-3}{2}$ |

2.
| Quantity A | Quantity B |
|---|---|
| $64^3$ | $2^{16}$ |

3. For all real numbers $f$ and $g$ let the operation be defined by

$$f \blacklozenge g = f g^2 + g f^2$$

| Quantity A | Quantity B |
|---|---|
| $4 \blacklozenge 8$ | $\dfrac{1}{4} \blacklozenge 16$ |

4.
$$0 < a < b < c$$

| Quantity A | Quantity B |
|---|---|
| $(abc)^0$ | $\dfrac{b^3}{abc}$ |

5. A jar contains $n$ red and $n$ green marbles where $n \geq 2$. You pick two marbles from the jar.

| Quantity A | Quantity B |
|---|---|
| Number of ways to pick one of each color | $n^2$ |

6.     The circle below has center *O* and radius 1.

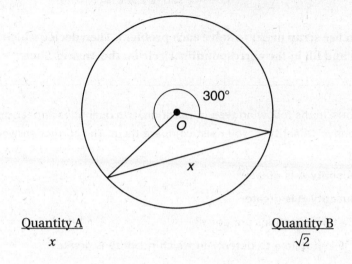

Quantity A          Quantity B
     *x*                 $\sqrt{2}$

**DIRECTIONS:** In the following questions, choose the best answer from the five choices listed.

QUESTIONS 7 AND 8 ARE BASED ON THE FOLLOWING DATA ON VOLUNTEERISM.*

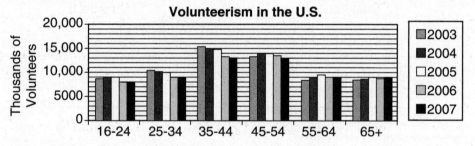

*Based on data released by the U.S. Department of Labor 1/23/2008.*

7.  Which age group, between which two years, had the greatest decrease in the number of volunteers?

Ⓐ  16–24 from 2004 to 2005
Ⓑ  25–34 from 2005 to 2006
Ⓒ  35–44 from 2005 to 2006
Ⓓ  45–54 from 2005 to 2006
Ⓔ  65+   from 2006 to 2007

8. The number of seniors (age 65+) volunteering has remained fairly constant even when the total number of volunteers fluctuates. In which year, 2003–2007, do the seniors have their best proportion of all volunteers?

Ⓐ 2003
Ⓑ 2004
Ⓒ 2005
Ⓓ 2006
Ⓔ 2007

QUESTIONS 9 AND 10 ARE BASED ON THE FOLLOWING DATA.*

| Average U.S. apple prices by consumption | 2001 | 2002 | 2003 | 2004 |
|---|---|---|---|---|
| All sales (cents per pound) | 15.80 | 18.90 | 20.90 | 15.80 |
| Fresh consumption (cents per pound) | 22.90 | 25.80 | 29.40 | 21.70 |
| All processing (dollars per ton) | 108.00 | 130.00 | 131.00 | 107.00 |
| Canned (dollars per ton) | 139.00 | 161.00 | 154.00 | 149.00 |
| Juice and cider (dollars per ton) | 83.40 | 104.00 | 103.00 | 73.00 |
| Frozen (dollars per ton) | 139.00 | 175.00 | 173.00 | 172.00 |
| Dried (dollars per ton) | 84.70 | 108.00 | 107.00 | 77.30 |

*Data from U.S. Apple Association www.usapple.org.

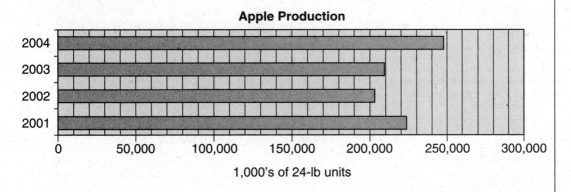

**Apple Production**

1,000's of 24-lb units

9. Comparing 2001 to 2003 what is the approximate percentage change in *value* of the apple crop?

Ⓐ increase of 18%
Ⓑ decrease of 18%
Ⓒ increase of 6%
Ⓓ decrease of 6%
Ⓔ increase of 12%

10. Which is worth the most?

(A) 25% of the 2001 crop sold for juice

(B) 10% of the 2002 crop sold for canning

(C) 5% of the 2003 crop sold for freezing

(D) 15% of the 2004 crop sold dried

(E) 1% of the 2001 crop sold fresh

11. Find the perimeter of the figure at right, assuming all segments meet at right angles.

 m

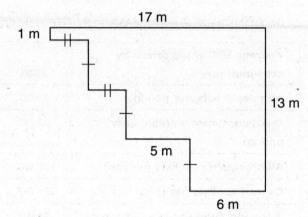

12. What is the area of a regular six-sided polygon where each side has length 2?

(A) 6

(B) $3\sqrt{3}$

(C) $6\sqrt{2}$

(D) $6\sqrt{3}$

(E) 12

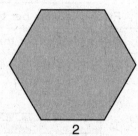

2

13. What is the surface area of a cube with side length $\sqrt{2}$?

(A) $\sqrt{2}$

(B) $2\sqrt{2}$

(C) 6

(D) $6\sqrt{2}$

(E) 12

14. Martina needs 35 gallons of fuel in each winter month to heat her home. Each spring and fall month she uses 15 gallons of fuel. She uses no fuel during the summer. What part of her annual heating bill is spent during the winter?

Give your answer as a fraction:

15. A right triangle has sides 12, 15, and $x$. How many possible values are there for $x$?

(A) 0

(B) 1

(C) 2

(D) 3

(E) Infinite

16. If $n$ and $m$ are integers so that $nm = 30$ and $\dfrac{1}{n} - \dfrac{1}{m} = \dfrac{1}{30}$, then what is $n - m$?

(A) −1

(B) 1

(C) −2

(D) 2

(E) 5

17. Which of the following can be expressed as the sum of three consecutive integers?

(A) 278

(B) 49

(C) 11

(D) −1

(E) −6

18. A nurse dilutes a solution that has an 8% concentration of medicine by adding water, so that the concentration of medicine in the new solution is no greater than 2%. If the nurse had 200 ml of the 8% solution, which of the following could be the volume of water that is added? (Assume that the water added contains 0% medicine.)

Indicate *all* that apply.

A  200 ml

B  400 ml

C  600 ml

D  800 ml

19. A number squared plus 12 times the number is equal to 45. Which of the following could be the number?

Indicate *all* that apply.

A  −18

B  −15

C  −12

D  −9

E  2.5

F  3

20. At a certain college, the ratio of first-year to second-year to third-year to fourth-year students is $6:5:4:3$, in order. If there are 900 total students at the school, which of the following must be true?

Indicate *all* that apply.

[A] The number of first-year students plus the number of fourth-year students is equal to the number of second-year students plus the number of third-year students.

[B] There are twice as many first-year students as fourth-year students.

[C] There are at least 320 first-year students at the college.

[D] There are 200 third-year students at the college.

# ANSWERS

| | | | |
|---|---|---|---|
| **1.** A | **7.** C | **13.** E | **18.** C, D |
| **2.** A | **8.** E | **14.** $\dfrac{7}{13}$ | **19.** B, F |
| **3.** A | **9.** A | | **20.** A, B, D |
| **4.** D | **10.** A | **15.** C | |
| **5.** C | **11.** 60 | **16.** A | |
| **6.** B | **12.** D | **17.** E | |

## Detailed Solutions

1. **(A)** Most people will use cancellation.

$$\frac{-1}{\cancel{2}}\times\frac{-\cancel{2}}{\cancel{3}}\times\frac{-\cancel{3}}{\cancel{4}}\times\frac{-\cancel{4}}{5}=\frac{(-1)^4}{5}=\frac{1}{5}\qquad \frac{-5}{\cancel{4}}\times\frac{-\cancel{4}}{\cancel{3}}\times\frac{-\cancel{3}}{2}=\frac{(-1)^3 5}{2}=\frac{-5}{2}$$

Clearly $\dfrac{1}{5}>-\dfrac{5}{2}$.

A quicker answer would be to note that Quantity A is the product of four negative numbers and hence positive. Quantity B is the product of three negative numbers and hence negative. Positive is always larger than negative.

2. **(A)** We express 64 as a power of two and use our laws for exponents to simplify: $64^3 = (2^6)^3 = 2^{18}$. Certainly $2^{18}$ is larger than $2^{16}$.

3. **(A)** A straightforward calculation is best here.

$$\frac{1}{4}\blacklozenge 16=\frac{1}{4}\times16^2+16\times\left(\frac{1}{4}\right)^2=4\times16+1=64+1=65$$

$$4\blacklozenge 8 = 4 \times 8^2 + 8 \times 4^2 = 4 \times 64 + 8 \times 16 = 256 + 128 = 384$$

If you calculate Quantity B first, you may not have to complete your calculation of Quantity A, since part way through it becomes clear that Quantity A is larger than Quantity B.

4. **(D)** Quantity A is 1 as a nonnegative to the exponent zero is 1. And if we simplify Quantity B, we get $\dfrac{b^2}{ac}=\dfrac{b}{a}\cdot\dfrac{b}{c}$. Notice that, since $b > a$, $\dfrac{b}{a}$ is always greater than 1. Similarly $\dfrac{b}{c}$ is always less than 1. Let's try $a = 1$, $b = 2$, and $c = 3$. Then we get $\dfrac{2}{1}\cdot\dfrac{2}{3}=\dfrac{4}{3}$, which is greater than 1. This will change if we make $c$ much larger. Try $a = 1$, $b = 2$, and $c = 8$. Then $\dfrac{2}{1}\cdot\dfrac{2}{8}=\dfrac{4}{8}$, which is less than 1. Hence Quantity B is sometimes larger and sometimes smaller.

5. **(C)** There are $n$ choices for which green marble to take and $n$ choices for which red marble to take. That makes $n \times n = n^2$ ways to pick one of each color.

6. **(B)** A full circle has 360° so the triangle has an angle at $O$ of 60°. Also, the two sides that extend from $O$ to the circle are both radii, so the triangle is actually isosceles. Furthermore, each base angle must be $\frac{(180° - 60°)}{2} = 60°$. So the triangle is actually equilateral. Since this is a unit circle the two radii have length 1. That means $x$ is also 1.

7. **(C)** This question asks for the greatest decrease in *numbers*—not percentage decrease. You cannot just compare the size of the bars. You must look at the scale—but luckily all the bars use the same scale. By inspection you can see the largest drop comes between 2005 and 2006 for age 35–44.

8. **(E)** We must look at seniors as a portion (or percentage) of all volunteers, that is (65 + volunteers) ÷ (sum all volunteers). We could calculate these values for each year but that is tedious and time consuming. Since the numerator is roughly constant, we just need to find the year where the sum of all volunteers was lowest. Year 2007 is lowest for all groups except 55–64. Even so, the difference there (1,000 volunteers) is much less than the differences in other age groups. 2007 will be the lowest total of volunteers. Hence seniors had their best proportion of all volunteers in 2007.

9. **(A)** For 2001, 225,000 thousand units × 24 lb/unit is 5,400 million pounds. At a value of 15.8 cents/lb, we have a total crop value of 15.8 × 5,400 million cents, or 85,320 million cents. That is about 850 million dollars. For 2003, 210,000 thousand units × 24 lb/unit is 5,040 million pounds. At a value of 20.9 cents/lb, we have a total crop value of 20.9 × 5,040 million cents, or 105,336 million cents. That is about 1,000 million dollars. Thus, the increase is about 150 million dollars compared with the 850 million dollar value of 2001s crop. We find that $\frac{150}{850} \times 100\%$ is approximately 18%.

10. **(A)** Using the price of each product and the percentage assigned, we get the following table. It would be hard to find the actual tons produced, so we will try to find the answer by comparison (estimates).

| | Answer | Value | Approximation |
|---|---|---|---|
| A | 25% of 2001 crop for juice | .25 × $83.40/ton × (2001 tons produced) | $20 × (2001 tons) |
| B | 10% of 2002 crop for canning | .10 × $161/ton × (2002 tons produced) | $16 × (2002 tons) |
| C | 5% of 2003 crop for freezing | .05 × $173/ton × (2003 tons produced) | $9 × (2003 tons) |
| D | 15% of 2004 crop dried | .15 × $77.30 × (2004 tons produced) | $11 × (2004 tons) |
| E | 1% of 2001 crop fresh | .01 × 15.80¢ × (2001 tons produced) × 1,000 lbs/ton | $1.58 × (2001 tons) |

Clearly A > E. Since the production in 2002 and 2003 is similar, B > C. Since 2001 production was more than 2002 production and $20 > $16, then A > B. Now, compare A and D. 2004 production is more than 2001 production, but it would have to be close to twice the 2001 production for D to be greater than A. It's not. So A > D.

**Alternate solution:** If we had used the figures in the production table as if they were tons produced (even though they are not) and multiplied with our calculators, we would still be able to see which is largest, since the proportions are correct. Again, we see A is largest.

| | Answer | Value |
|---|---|---|
| A | 25% of 2001 crop for juice | .25 × $83.40 × 245 = 5,108.25 |
| B | 10% of 2002 crop for canning | .10 × $161 × 205 = 3,300.5 |
| C | 5% of 2003 crop for freezing | .05 × $173 × 210 = 1,816.5 |
| D | 15% of 2004 crop dried | .15 × $77.30 × 248 = 2,875.56 |
| E | 1% of 2001 crop fresh | .01 × 15.80¢ × 245 × 1,000 = $38.71 |

11. **(60)** It is best to recall the perimeter of such a shape is the same as a rectangle with side lengths 13 m and 17 m. Hence $P = 2(l + w) = 2(13 \text{ m} + 17 \text{ m}) = 60$ m.

Alternatively, label the missing vertical length $x$ and the missing horizontal length $y$. Equating the vertical sides we have $3x + 1 = 13$; hence, $x = 4$. Equating the horizontal sides we have $2y + 5 + 6 = 17$, hence, $y = 3$. Adding clockwise from 1, the perimeter of the figure is $1 + 17 + 13 + 6 + 4 + 5 + 4 + 3 + 4 + 3 = 60$.

12. **(D)** If you connect each vertex to the center of the hexagon you obtain six congruent equilateral triangles. Convince yourself of why the triangles are equilateral and congruent.

We recall that the height of an equilateral triangle is $\frac{\sqrt{3}}{2}$ times its side length. Hence the area of one of the triangles is $A = \frac{1}{2}bh = \frac{1}{2}(2)\left(\frac{\sqrt{3}}{2}2\right) = \sqrt{3}$. So the area of the hexagon is $6\sqrt{3}$.

13. **(E)** The surface area of a cube of six times the area of one face $SA = 6s^2$. In this case that is $SA = 6\left(\sqrt{2}\right)^2 = 12$.

14. $\left(\frac{7}{13}\right)$ There are three months in each season. She uses $3 \times 35 = 105$ gallons of fuel in winter. She uses $3 \times 15 = 45$ gallons of fuel each spring and fall. Hence the portion used in winter is $\frac{105}{105 + 45 + 45 + 0} = \frac{105}{195} = \frac{21}{39} = \frac{7}{13}$. Give your answer as a fraction: $\frac{7}{13}$

15. **(C)** By the Pythagorean theorem and depending on which side is the hypotenuse, either $12^2 + 15^2 = x^2$ or $12^2 + x^2 = 15^2$ or $15^2 + x^2 = 12^2$. The last case is impossible since the hypotenuse must be the largest side. Each of the other two cases will lead to one answer for $x$.

16. **(A)** Start with the equation $\frac{1}{n} - \frac{1}{m} = \frac{1}{30}$ and multiply both sides by $nm$:

$nm\left(\frac{1}{n} - \frac{1}{m}\right) = nm\frac{1}{30}$, to clear the denominators. Distribute and cancel, remembering that

$nm = 30$, $\frac{nm}{n} - \frac{nm}{m} = nm\frac{1}{30}$ to get $m - n = 1$. Multiply both sides by negative one and you get $n - m = -1$. Alternatively, try to find values that make both equations work. Use $n = 5$ and $m = 6$ because $5 \times 6 = 30$ and $\frac{1}{5} - \frac{1}{6} = \frac{6}{30} - \frac{5}{30} = \frac{1}{30}$. Then $n - m = 5 - 6 = -1$.

17. **(E)** We try a few examples: $1 + 2 + 3 = 6$, $2 + 3 + 4 = 9$, $3 + 4 + 5 = 12$, and $11 + 12 + 13 = 36$. The sum of three consecutive numbers is always a multiple of three. The only answer that is a multiple of three is $-6$. In fact, $-6 = -3 + -2 + -1$.

18. **(C, D)** One approach is to find the initial amount of medicine in the solution, which is 8% of 200 ml = $.08 \times 200 = 16$ ml. Since the nurse adds water only, 16 ml remains the volume of medicine in the diluted solution. After dilution, the volume of medicine, 16 ml, becomes less than or equal to 2% of the total volume, so $16 \leq .02T$. Divide both sides by .02 to obtain $16 \div .02 = 800 \leq T$. This means that the total volume of the combined solution is at least 800 ml, so the nurse must have added at least 800 ml – 200 ml (initial volume) = 600 ml. Choose answers that are at least 600, C and D.

An alternate approach is to treat this as a weighted average problem. The desired concentration, 2%, is 6 units from 8%, the initial concentration, and 2 units from 0%, the concentration of the water added. Since 6 units = $3 \times 2$ units, the combined average of 2% is 3 times farther from 8% than from 0%. The combined average may be thought of as a balancing point, and we can create a balance by using 3 times as much of the 0% solution as the 8% solution. This implies that at least $3 \times 200$ ml = 600 ml were added. Again, choose C and D because both are $\geq 600$.

19. **(B, F)** Translate the given word problem into an algebraic equation. Let $n$ represent the number, so $n^2 + 12n = 45$. Solve this type of equation by first getting one side equal to zero, so subtract 45 from each side. Then $n^2 + 12n - 45 = 0$. The left side may be factored as by noting that $(n + 15)(n - 3) = n^2 - 3n + 15n - 45 = n^2 + 12n - 45$. Since the product $(n + 15)(n - 3) = 0$, one of the factors must equal zero. That is, $n + 15 = 0$, making $n = -15$, or $n - 3 = 0$, making $n = 3$. Choose $-15$ and $3$, or B and F.

20. **(A, B, D)** There are 6 first-year students for every 5 second-year students for every 4 third-year students for every 3 fourth-year students, for every $6 + 5 + 4 + 3 = 18$ total students. A is correct, because $6 + 3 = 5 + 4$. B is correct, because 6 is twice 3.

First-year students make up 6 out of every 18 total students, so they comprise $\dfrac{6}{18} = \dfrac{1}{3}$ of the student body. Therefore, there are one third of $900 = 900 \div 3 = 300$ first-year students. Because 300 is not at least 320, C is incorrect. Third-year students are 4 out of every 18 total students, so there are $\dfrac{4}{18} \times 900 = 200$ third-year students, making D correct.

# Appendix

## SUGGESTED FACTS TO MEMORIZE

Common fractions and their decimal equivalents

$$\frac{1}{8}=0.125 \quad \frac{1}{6}\approx0.16 \quad \frac{1}{5}=0.2 \quad \frac{1}{4}=0.25 \quad \frac{1}{3}\approx0.33$$

Common irrational numbers square roots and their decimal equivalents

$$\sqrt{2}\approx1.4 \quad \sqrt{3}\approx1.7 \quad e\approx2.7 \quad \pi\approx3.14$$

Perfect squares

$$11^2 = 121, \; 12^2 = 144, \; 13^2 = 169, \; 14^2 = 196, \; 15^2 = 225,$$
$$16^2 = 256, \; 17^2 = 289, \; 18^2 = 324, \; 19^2 = 361$$

Inequalities

$$\text{If } 0 < a < 1, \text{ then } 0 < a^2 < a < 1$$

$$\text{If } 1 < a, \text{ then } 1 < a < a^2$$

Algebra

$$(x + y)^2 = x^2 + 2xy + y^2 \quad (x - y)^2 = x^2 - 2xy + y^2 \quad x^2 - y^2 = (x - y)(x + y)$$

**Special right triangles**

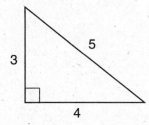

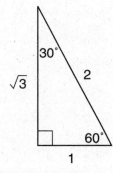

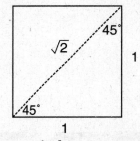

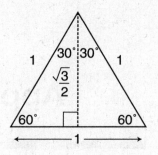

**Geometrical measurement**

Area = $\pi r^2$
Circumference = $\pi d$

**Areas and perimeter**